Goldachhof

A Piece of Me

MY CHILDHOOD IN WARTIME BAVARIA

Beatrix Ost

Translated from the German
by Jonathan McVity with the author

**INTRODUCTION BY
ANDREW SOLOMON**

TURTLE POINT PRESS
BROOKLYN, NEW YORK

First Turtle Point Press edition, 2017

First published in 2004 by Verlagsgruppe Weltbild GmbH
as *Als wärs ein Teil von mir*

Published in 2007 by Helen Marx Books/Books & Co.
as *My Father's House*

Turtle Point Press
208 Java Street, 5th Floor
Brooklyn, NY 11222
www.turtlepointpress.com

Library of Congress Cataloging-in-Publication Data is available from the publisher
upon request

Design by Phil Kovacevich
Printed in Canada

ISBN: 978-1-933527-91-8

For Adi and Fritz

For my grandchildren
Ronnie. Viva. Luna.
Christoph. Ava. Stella.
Julian. Liam. Sophie. Anna.

We have to go see our cousins—
it creates childhood memories,

says Viva, and off they run to play.

Contents

PART THREE

Introduction

THE FIRST TIME I MET BEATRIX OST was in my living room, where a friend had brought her to tea, and I was overwhelmed by what she looked like: this beautiful woman with her piercing sapphire eyes, and her gray hair streaked with bright blue as though she had come from the atelier of Yves Klein, and her bright red lips, and the elegant jewelry, and a perfectly tailored suit, and that amazing Bavarian accent that resonated from some more civilized time and world but also seemed to know the underside of the avant-garde. Here was a refined mix of extravagance and severity, as though she had allowed herself everything and then, with rigorous self-discipline, had removed half from the mix. I was so struck by her almost forbidding glamour that I didn't notice, for the moment, that she also has a smile in which all the world's openness and generosity are expressed. After she left, the friend who had introduced us asked whether I didn't think she was the warmest person I'd ever met, and only then did I retrospectively notice the thrill of her enthusiasm, which I later learned to know as love.

Six months later, Beatrix and I went to Nepal together, along with other friends. There are not so many people with whom one would be bound for Nepal on such brief acquaintance, but once you enter Beatrix's world, you are in it deep, and we had both wanted to visit the monasteries of the highlands and the palaces of Kathmandu and Patan. Halfway through our wonderful trip, we ended up waiting for several hours at an airstrip near the foot of Mt. Everest, and it was there that Beatrix began telling me stories of her past. It is not always the case that a great storyteller has great stories to tell, but Beatrix's life in Germany was as fascinating as her recitation was eloquent, and on that windy mountain, a history and a sensibility were revealed to me. Some of the anecdotes were diffi-cult ones, but she recounted them with joy.

Her book is a lot like her. It's impressionistic; it scuttles along from one thing to another in a way that can be confusing; it's very stylized and yet also dis-armingly frank, with its gentle humor and its embracing of collective humanity. So often in literature, style obscures content, but here the content feels transpar-ently exposed even though the style is highly visible, much as in real life Beatrix's naturalness of emotion coexists with her chic self-presentation. The book expresses a child's naive pleasures, and so its evocation of childhood is utterly convincing; but it also reflects the astuteness of someone in the later part of her life, who can compare her own youth to that of her grandchildren. What one most senses here is an underlying kindness. In an age when fashionable memoirs recount the lurid foibles of dysfunctional families, this one is written with authentic affection and great respect. But it is no gauzy fantasy. These are real people, with their many imperfections: the pretentious Aunt Julia, the nightmar-ish Marie-Louise, the nervous General Brün, the resigned Grandfather Theodor. Through it all runs the melancholy of Beatrix's father, Fritz, the stern and capable master of Goldachhof, aristocratic and repressed, loved but feared and never quite known. The only person who seems unequivocally rosy is Adi, the mother who holds the center with her infinite gentleness and mercy and wisdom: some-times stern, as when she takes the chambermaid to get an abortion; sometimes heroic, as when one of the farmworkers murders another and she has to restore order; but always empathetic, knowing, as mothers should, the feelings of her children before the children do themselves. She is sympathetic magic incarnate.

The process of this book is the accrual of anecdote. There is no grand underlying narrative trajectory except the passage of time and a child's slow mat-uration. Still, these are not just discrete sketches; they accumulate to form rich characters and evoke a vanished life so palpably that one tastes it. The author rekindles the sensuality of things long gone: the flavor of the black-market coffee to which Grandmother was addicted as though it were opium, selling off family treasures to get it; the smell of the cigar Beatrix stole from her father's drawer for the neighborhood boys; the sweet taste of berries gathered at a secret spot deep in the woods. In the way of children, Beatrix makes little social distinction between her relatives and the foreign servants who kept the household running: passionate, homesick Olga, the Russian cook; flighty, irrepressible Justa, the Yugoslavian chambermaid; and elegant Umer, the Hungarian coachman, with his intuitive control over the horses and his deep connection to Fritz. These staff members worked hard, and in turn were cared for and educated by the family. The local farmworkers and their bewildering kin also figure large: the sinister Sepp with his dead moles, the sprawling König family with their cheerful violence. Even the animals have vivid personalities: the terrifying, tumescent bull seeking his cow; the high-strung horses who could turn wild at any time; and, most wonderfully, the doe who came to stay for a winter and slept under the kitchen stove until springtime tempted her back to the wild.

A Piece of Me is imbued with a profound sense of place. Every aspect of Goldachhof's hallway and kitchen and living room is evoked, and the shapes of the royal-crested furniture, the textures of the woods and the moor, the very dirt of the fields. The farm is a character in the lives of the people whom it has embraced, and the landscape of Bavaria is a necessary condition to these stories. Beatrix Ost has lived most of her life in the United States, and that particular yearning that is the harsh fate of expatriates comes through in the sharpness of her recollections. Her regional pride is rendered more vivid because so many of the domestics and farmworkers who lived beside her dreamt of homelands to the east. Little Beatrix could not fathom how or why they would want to be anyplace but right where she was happiest, but that very happiness throws their sadness and longing into poignant relief.

The good manners that Fritz and Adi taught to the children and servants are somehow borne out in the way Beatrix tells the stories, apt and precise but always a little deferential to those who were older and wiser than she. Despite this reserve, she acknowledges how the sinister quality of the outside world impinged on Goldachhof, and the book has a richly specific flavor of its time. Adi had to buy and sell food illegally, and Beatrix was afraid of these clandestine acts committed in the half-light of dusk. From time to time, the impoverished gleaners would come to pick whatever the farmworkers had left behind, and she did not miss the hungry rumble of their despair. When the air raid sirens sounded, and they sounded often, the children hid under the bridge, barely protected. And yet for Beatrix, it was possible to love the Americans when they came, not as liberators and not as conquerors, but as an interesting new variety of people among whom she would spend her adult life.

America's perspective on wartime Germany remains famously tortured. We see it through the eyes of victims: the Poles, and the Jews, and the brave men who plotted against Hitler, and the Allied soldiers. We hear almost nothing of what happened to ordinary Germans. The idea of "two Germanys" is often used in relation to the subsequent division of the country into East and West, but there is another Teutonic dichotomy, and it is between the Germany of brutalism and expansionism and concentration camps, and the Germany that is all gingerbread and music and apple-cheeked women in dirndls, and this book is a resounding affirmation that this good Germany existed even in the period when the evil Germany was ascendant. Fritz managed to resign from the Nazi party after serving in North Africa; he detested Hitler and the war, but he kept a policy of "don't ask, don't tell" in his own ever-expanding household, which was constantly absorbing displaced relatives and friends. Beatrix's troublesome brother, Uli, on the other hand, happily signed up for Hitler Youth and was kept out of the S.S. only by his authoritarian father. The dinnertime debates about the Nazis took much the form of political debate in any family in any place; these could be arguments about George W. Bush, and do not participate in the absolutism with which history has treated National Socialism. One of the refinements of this narrative is not to sentimentalize the characters into false acts of political courage. Mostly, these people were engaged not with politics but with immutable rural concerns, cycles and struggles more fundamental than those of policy. Their idyll was not about formulating a better social system, but about escaping systems they could not hope to change. Of course, for the child through whose eyes we see, these matters were all incomprehensibly abstract anyway. The fact that the book is neither an indictment nor a rationalization makes more touching the scene in which a group of Serbs and Gypsies appear on the horizon and walk toward the farm, refugees from Dachau. The kindness that Beatrix's mother shows them, nursing one through his final hours, is universal, an embodiment of character rather than of politics. The most evil things imaginable happened in wartime Germany, but all of humanity was not corrupted. Beside unspeakable horror and great moral courage, simple benevolence also persisted.

At the end of this book, the reader is nostalgic for someone else's childhood. That is no mean accomplishment. It is particularly impressive given that the tale is set in a malevolent larger context. These stories are not saccharine, but their message is that wartime is not antithetical to love or to beauty. Those dark days formed the person who is our narrator, whom one cannot help but like and admire, in part for the way she likes and admires her own past self. Between the young Beatrix who is described and the Beatrix who is describing, there is unbroken continuity, and that is as reassuring to the reader as recollection of the farm's cozy solace is to the author.

Andrew Solomon

Part One

Where is it written what one gets in life, or what one really needs? The body remembers everything, remembers what happened, too: blows, shoves, drowning, tender gestures, rhythms, screams, whispers. Stench. French kisses. The scent of the hand that pressed itself across your face to stifle a scream remains in your memory forever.

Letters

I HAD NOT MEANT TO START MY CLEANING THERE, not wanted to open the wardrobe I had inherited after Mother's death, to turn the great key embedded in the embossed door and peer into the dim chaos my eyes would have to adjust to; nor to draw the ribboned packet from the jumble of papers and photo albums; nor be curious; nor even put on the eyeglasses dangling around my neck. What awakened my curiosity was not a chain of events linking one thing with another, but a deeper connection wearing the face of coincidence.

I am in my house in Virginia, holding the sixty-year-old bundle, green heat pressing in from outdoors. A ceiling fan groans above me. For twenty years people have worried it could come crashing down. I take a seat, loosening the knotted rose and yellow ribbon holding the letters together, and pick up the first envelope. Scribbled across it: *From the front.*

I know this hand from signed documents, and from the end of letters typed with his two middle fingers, closing with the zigzag signature: *Your Fritz* or *Your obedient servant, Fritz Ost.* Precipices, nothing round.

Once my father wrote me a letter, the only one ever. I was at boarding school and had just made it through my second year of Latin. I opened the envelope and read: *Beata Filia.* He had written the letter in Latin, and I was to answer him in Latin, too. I knew the length of the letter was laid down in advance: one whole page. My father had never asked me for anything. It would have been unthinkable not to play along, unthinkable not to comply with his wish. A lot depended on it, though exactly what was not clear. I just had to write this letter.

Pater Carus, I began. Then, *agricola cum equi appropinquat*, inquiring whether the farmer is approaching with his horse. My large ornamented letters were designed to fill the page. So different from the letters I wrote to my mother from boarding school, where I could just drivel on and she would find it all "exquisite." Including the letter I wrote when the dress, the one she had promised me, the one with cornflowers printed on rayon, was stolen or lost in the mail. It was my postwar dream dress, cut for me, not just a smaller version of something I had inherited from my sister, Anita, no, tailored solely for me from its very own piece of fabric. I dreamt of this dress and mourned its loss in my lonely dayroom bed, oh so far away from Mother.

I have to think of my mother. Everyone who came in contact with her loved and admired her. Twelve years earlier, when she was ninety, I had made the journey from New York to Munich and found her lying in her bed for hours each day, dreaming. I washed her face, her back, her arms, her legs. It did her good. I oiled the tender skin. We scarcely spoke.

My mother swam on a foggy river of memories, playing tennis with her brother, who had fallen seventy years earlier in the First World War. Holding her father's hand, she stepped into the Royal Porcelain Works, where one could buy his china designs. If the Queen was out and about on foot, the child made a deep curtsey; her father bowed, lifting his hat: Your Royal Highness. The Jugendstil house where they lived. In its garden, the goldfish pond. The palazzo on the island of Giudecca where they wintered. The Venetian mirror.

I can still remember the steep staircase, she whispered.

On a wave she rocked back into her childhood, back into the room, back to me. I was her mother now.

Between breathing and silence, we strolled through her life. Now she could talk about everything. There were no more secrets. No barriers between mother and child.

My Fritz was a difficult man, made it hard on himself. A textbook pessimist. I would never have left him, she said in a hushed tone.

You, Mama, by contrast, were that much more cheerful.

Oh, one has to be. Yes, you get that way; otherwise, you're done for. After the war he lost interest, my Fritz. The collapse of Germany suited him. Then he finally could have his breakdown, too. You were our straggler. The Fritz I knew...

Her voice lost itself in the garden of thought. A strip of lace from her slip was visible at the bodice of her blouse.

You still wear your beautiful slips, I said.

Yes, yes.

And the perfumed cotton ball in your bosom.

My Fritzl gave me the lingerie. Always salmon-colored—he loved that. This is the last of it.

For a long week her spirit fluttered from the bed to the window, until one night the glass broke: the draft made off with her soul. When I stepped into her room she was no longer there, only the cool skin, the bones, the profile on the white pillow. She lay between sheet and coverlet like a flower between the pages of a book. A legend, an earthly goddess.

After her death Anita and I organized an auction between the two of us at her house. We took turns picking out objects. The little packet of letters lay on a table next to photo albums and other bric-a-brac. I cried, hazy from exhaustion, from the loss. It hit me like a slap in the face as I smelled the odors, saw everything that had nothing more to do, yet had everything to do with my mother. These objects would never again feel her touch, nor her gaze. Split between me and Anita, they would metamorphose into our possessions.

Anita, too, had cried her share. Yesterday, at the crematorium, she had still been sobbing. She was the last to arrive. Her children and her husband had already taken their seats. She had on a new fur, which impressed itself on my memory, although it had nothing really to do with mourning the death of our mother.

Anita took a picture from the wall and piled it onto her stack. That was when the ribboned packet caught my eye: coincidence, non-coincidental. I recognized the handwriting and reached for it.

Those have to be burned, said Anita sternly. Too intimate.

I'll think it over, I replied. Perhaps I will want to read them.

I thrust the packet into my purse, took it with me to America, and forgot it for twelve years in the shadow of the wardrobe.

Now I am as old as Father was when he took his life, and I have found these letters.

•

A Minotaur guards the place and time whence they came: Bavaria, 1939–40. My mother was in her last month of pregnancy with me; my father had already been called up to the front.

> *Ninety-five days already. The physical and mental waste the military mentality forces upon a man in professional life. My good heart, my very dearest, measured against me you are so incomparably grand and brave in your steady grasp of life, while I have tormented myself like a hobgoblin throughout these days of war, and have found no redemption so far. Sometimes my sense of humor helps me through, and my ability to get along with people. But you must be grander, and be able to forgive me many a weakness, so that I can make it through all these alterations of my spiritual equilibrium and manage to bridge this period of madness. Make yourself beautiful when I come around on Tuesday. I like it so very much.*

My father's handwriting no longer strikes me as jagged and steep like the Alps. It got that way later on, perhaps, or seemed to, because I only knew him from another angle. But the man sitting next to me, writing these letters, is a stranger. Him I do not know. There are gentle meadows between the cursive mountains, rounded valleys polished by glaciers. The soft gray pencil woos the page, shadows cast by the intimate thoughts of a father I never knew, actually never thought possible.

I unfold the letters, smooth them on the table with my hand, and order them by date. At the time I was born, my parents had already been married for eighteen years, and still they wrote one another love letters. My heart is pounding. I've been letting the telephone ring. It's like…Like what? Like the reel of my parents' life running backward before my eyes. By the time I reach the last letter, I will have accompanied them on a long walk, as if I had been there with them back then.

In the next letter I have just been born.

> *Dearest Adi,*
>
> *I trust you will have withstood the strains endured by body and soul. I would like to wait a bit before my vacation, until the household has adjusted smoothly to the improvement in your health, so that we, too, get something for ourselves. We both should just wish and hope that little Beatrix will flourish. It would all be so lovely, if this war did not bring fresh sorrows for us and everyone else. Which makes me glad you are always so full of optimism and really never despondent.*
>
> *The imperfect management of the estates put under my command weighs heavily upon me, but what should I do? What can I do? Otherwise, forced to be conscious of the inalterable, I have accustomed myself quite well to the soldier's life in general*

and my area of service in particular. But you have no idea how hard this sometimes is for me. There is just one comfort: that things are just as bad for thousands of others who must also take upon themselves this situation that has been forced upon us. But it must come to an end sometime, and I do not believe in any way that there will be too long a war. And this simply from the realization that after the experience of 1914–19, mankind can no longer be as moronic as it was. So I am hoping our final decades will generally prove rather more leisurely than the difficult past. Then our children too will have a future, and we will know what we have lived and suffered for.

Keep a closer eye on Uli so he does not lose his trust in you and in me. He is at a nasty age: intensely independent, grown up too early, coarse and yet sensitive, a child and a man at the same time. He is, in short, a difficult case. You, my darling, have difficult tasks and duties before you. Meanwhile, Anita, my Butz— this willful little person must not be allowed to drift into the shadows. Plenty to accomplish and to answer for.

The most grating thing for me is this current powerlessness, all these questions of the present and the future that move us both. I feel the lack of your closeness so badly. You have always given me so much, with your great love and clever appraisals of my personality. When you are present I need no "accent." You alone are enough! Is that not delightful for you, to have a confession like that from me in writing for once? You know, when one is alone one realizes for the first time what one has left behind. So what I wish for you is that you recover thoroughly, regain your strength, and become a pretty, slender Adelheid again.

•

The Minotaur keeping my parents' secret opens the door to the labyrinth. I step inside.

A tanned, powerful hand rests on my mother's belly, caresses the length of her thighs, touches her breast, kisses her eyelids. I gaze through the wall with the bird wallpaper I remember so well, into my parents' bedroom.

Adi sits at the vanity with the oval porcelain Nymphenburg mirror. It still existed then, had not yet slipped off the nail and gone crashing down upon the dresser and the flacons, bursting into a thousand slivers. She weaves her hair into a long braid for the night. The sleeve of her lace nightgown glides from her shoulder.

Fritz lies in bed and reads by the light of the bedside lamp. Now he sets his book aside.

Come to beddy-bye. We have already been standing at attention here for five minutes waiting for you, he says, laughing.

Adi can see him in the mirror. She tosses the braid down her back, goes over to the bed, and lets the nightgown fall on the yellow bedside rug. A little shy, she holds her hand in front of her breast.

They kiss.

Fritz bends her head back. Take hold of me, he orders gently, and she does.

She closes her eyes. When the bed creaks and he grows too loud, she holds her hand protectively over his mouth, or they press down deep into the feather cushion so no one will hear through the wall.

A light in passing flits across the ceiling, across the feather bed, the cushions, the gown on the rug.

●

Dearest Adi,

My female acquaintanceships and friendships are not so close that you need have apprehensions. Here, too, the vanity of

9

the "man over 40" plays its part—the last hurrah before true old age. You know, it is such a joy (and so proud are we) to come off as the "victor" in so large a stable of males. You have no idea how frantically this girl-crazy bunch chases petticoats, probably out of sheer vanity. And in the final analysis, just so they can give one another a poke in the eye. You understand this sort of thing because you know the male soul through my openness, and with me it really is that way. A big dog that barks but bites very little. So set your mind at rest and permit me my little pleasures on the side, which really do you no damage. You, my good heart, you belong to me and I to you!

You are so full of love! My only ray of hope is that here I can ride my horse every day. But in spite of this I still sleep so fitfully and briefly, in contrast to life at home, where I can sleep like a bear. It's probably the missing vis-à-vis in bed.

Oh, stop, war! But mustn't whine. Sleep well with your flock of children, and kiss everyone. Good night, my darling, my love. A heartfelt kiss and devotion from yours,

Fritz

Two photographs fall into my hand from the folds of a letter, black and white, blind with age. One is Fritz silhouetted in profile, with a cigar, a puff of smoke curling, two Aphrodites next to him, laughing past him into the camera. *The friendly L. sisters, Agnes and Louise,* I read on the back. My father is certain they and Adi will become friends after the war. In the second photo a young woman sits on a chair and looks into her lap, or down at her folded hands. Her blond hair is parted in the middle. There is something of the Madonna about her.

This is Anna, rather sad… Anna made such a heartfelt plea that I remain her good friend. She is so alone, and no one advises her

when she needs counsel and care. She trusts me and would like
me to be hers, even though she must know it would be a "useless"
love. Is that not moving? I do not know what girls see in an old
fellow like me. If you were with me, I wouldn't give a damn about
this war I can do nothing about, but that just isn't how it is. I love
you very much. Stay young and pretty and gay and glad, for your
children and your biggest child.

Is the lady in the photo embarrassed? Does she dislike being photographed?
Does she have ideas, hopes, that a direct gaze could betray? Is she really sad
because she *would like him to be hers* and *love is useless*? Or did she try it anyway? Were they having an affair? One that makes her sad? *Without a future*, as
Fritz quotes?

My mother had the wonderful quality of not burdening herself with inalter-
able situations. Later, when I was older, she and I discussed the male clan, the
male rituals, the way men tumble around in the society of men. How in male
precincts there was not much analysis. More boasting, more whacking on the
shoulder, no admitting weaknesses. Then there were the silent observers. In their
faces the muscles played the alphabet of what transpired in the brain. Sport occasioned the most agreement: a well-aimed blow, maximal velocity, good condi-
tioning, stamina. We would double ourselves over with laughter talking about it.

My very dearest,

Just got your letter, thanks a million. You are the most rea-
sonable soul in this wretched world. Accept my thanks, my kind
love! Did you get the money? For you to make yourself thoroughly
elegant. Don't have so many inhibitions next time! By the way, in
S. I saw pretty dresses lying in the window of Häuser, the ladies'
clothiers (at the foot of the Königstrasse, on the left). Will you
write me which one you wish to permit yourself? I embrace you,
my dearheart, and kiss you and our three children.

My enthusiasm grows with the reading of the letters. A caring father, a husband who longs for his wife and wants to buy her a little dress, despite his sorrow and despair about the war and their separation. Because of his upbringing, which was prim and loveless, he is reserved, but then again not, not with her. And he shows himself soft, and vulnerable, and trusting, that he is vain, and like a dog that does not bite.

I remember how often I despised my father in my teenage years, when he was already ill. I wanted a different model, not the crippled pessimist cared for uncomplainingly by my mother, who paid no heed to his utterances, bitter as gall. In my mother's heart was the Fritz of yesteryear. She had remained young, or stood still in her youthfulness, or simply refused to back down; in any case she was glad and optimistic.

But back then I could not see it that way. I reproached my mother for not defending herself against the unfeeling monster. And him I reproached for being ill, for not wanting to live anymore, for not rising up against the illness, for giving up instead. The tyrant, as I knew him—a benevolent one, to be sure, somehow good-natured, who often regretted his own ways, who got on his own nerves—all that now fell away. Mother and I had to make all the decisions. He no longer felt like it, he did not want to decide anymore. I reproached him for this, too.

What kind of father he wanted to be, or not be, I could no longer find out from him, since long before I took an interest in him and became conscious of any such thoughts, he had died, spiriting himself away.

> *My very dearest,*
>
> *You know well how disgusting I can be when something goes that hard against my grain. Well, my mood stinks, especially when I think of you all alone in our little bed. Oh, Adile, it is dreadful. How long must we go on separated from one another, taking in our love only in little doses? Be glad you are sitting in H.*

Rumor has it that life in the big cities is less than delightful in every respect.

Now for some glad tidings: starting April 1st, reserve officers are to draw the pay appropriate to our rank, in my case about 450. Now if the estates just go on paying my salary (500)—and I assume they will—then please order coal for the winter, and given the auspicious financial constellation you can keep the nanny as long as you like. I will also "organize" a "Viennese" summer dress for you after Easter. The latest models are rolling in. I will push aside your leftover shopping inhibitions from 1939, because I want you young and pretty and fresh and slender (so I do not get any silly ideas!). This does not mean we have to become spend-thrifts; we want to set something aside even so. I am delighted about this financial change. Did I not show a good nose for money when I refused public support? This purely private and voluntary income is no one's business, off the books. All in all it is just a fair solution, since we reserve uncles in professional life were badly damaged; everyone complained they would not be able to make ends meet. Now all that should come to an end. But say nothing to anyone. The envy is too great. Are you happy about all this?

As a child one cannot recognize one's parents as people, outside their role. Later one gets to know the other side of them, a side scarred by life itself. One does not wish to know them earlier, since one is too preoccupied with oneself. Unconscious of inherited character, or indifferent to it. Or one is convinced one is quite different, and shoves these parental affinities away entirely.

But now, having the privilege of finding my father's love letters, I understand my mother, who nourished herself mainly on memories, drew strength from thoughts of her Fritz. Through this small, valuable packet we become allies. Two women who love the same man, each in her own way and in her own time.

> *I plan to start my vacation in H. on the 6th of April. On the evening of the 7th a sleeping car to B., in M. on the 8th, 9th, 10th, 11th, back in H. on the 12th, heading back into "the field" on the 13th. Though we will not get to see much of one another this time, I have reserved eight days later on, when the two of us can travel somewhere together and enjoy eight days "in inmost pleasure and joy," without the entourage and all—just as we have dreamed so often but never managed.*
>
> *You can see, Adilein, I am bursting with the joyful prospects near at hand. Spring seems to be the cause, or the long separation. Or the restoration of your "normal physical condition." But enough of all these exciting allusions, or you and I will both be unable to sleep, and it will get hot in bed.*
>
> *How are the children? Is Beatrix flourishing under the tutelage of Sergeant Klara, who controls and directs not only Beatrix, but all of us (when we are around). I am missing out on Uli's report card. Tell him to stay good and gallant, always be and remain inwardly and outwardly proper. Now I wish all of you a good Easter Bunny, a good baptism without me, and gladness of heart in these serious times. Greet the whole household and our respectable neighbors, and be embraced and always beloved by your sometimes very stupid but true and hotly loving,*
>
> Fritz

•

This letter stands out among the rest. On its envelope: DELIVER BY MESSENGER.

> *My dearest Adi,*
>
> *The state of war continues, and with it departs all hopes for a bearable future. God knows "they know not what they do," or perhaps they do, in which case their crime is all the greater. Nobody wants war, and every reasonable person asks: why, what for? Personally, I am perfectly desperate. A good thing there is still wine to drink. But I need not go on about it. You know how I regard what has taken place over the past six years. Furthermore, I have declared my withdrawal from the Party—without giving any reasons. I am curious as to whether there will be cross-examination as to Why and How, since I just joined so I could help our friend Karl K. I am glad I can now so easily use the war and my status as conscripted soldier to withdraw from this "community," which I detest thoroughly enough. Hopefully you and the children will not feel any side effects.*

Soon after the war broke out, my father could no longer reconcile his conscience to the Party's ghastly doings. He left the Party amid the general chaos, using it to his advantage.

Uli, who had taken his own path, wanted to get away from my father's authority. He, like all the others, had run off with the raucous gang of the Hitler Youth. It was so seductive, so magnetic, they were like rats following the Pied Piper.

Father had been shocked and furious at Uli's enthusiasm for that "heap of swine." Often there were quarrels; Fritz would fly into a rage, for Uli was slipping out of his grip. Father was beside himself with fear and powerlessness. He had lost his son to an ideology whose machinations he had despised for the last six years, an ideology from which he feared worse to come.

Nevertheless, Uli ascended to Flag Leader. One day he was confronted by his superiors about his father's departure from the Party. Uli answered them quite cunningly: Fritz Ost was, above all, a dedicated militarist. Military service was going to be taking up all his time, so he would not be able to fulfill his Party duties satisfactorily. Luckily enough, and with the help of the all-around chaos, this response satisfied them, and nothing more was heard of the matter.

Long, long after the war, gathering snippets of conversation, I pieced together the reasons why Father had joined the Party in the first place. He had wanted to ensure the safety of his Jewish friends—signing an occasional document, organizing a passage to America—and so had made himself inconspicuous and helpful beneath the Party cloak. Of course, Father's good deeds had to be veiled in secrecy. After the war, several friends and acquaintances he had helped to "magically disappear" resurfaced amid great rejoicing. I clearly remember two of them.

One was Uncle Karl Kienan, a tall, elegant man from an old banking family in Frankfurt, whose property neighbored ours. My father with his foresight had convinced Kienan to get out of Germany in '39. Father oversaw Kienan's agricultural affairs in his absence, advising his Aryan wife, who had stayed on through the debacle. In the early '50s, Uncle Karl finally returned from Argentina. I got to know him then.

Another was Herr Rossbaut. During the years he was in hiding, his grand piano dozed upstairs in my parents' bedroom beneath an exquisite silk throw with tassels spilling over the golden lettering: Bösendorfer. After the war, Herr Rossbaut returned. He visited us several times at Goldachhof and amused me with magic tricks. At the climax of each visit, he went to his grand piano. The household assembled downstairs to hear his playing wafting from above. My mother held up her hand, arching her brows in admiration. Psst, she said, intolerant of any interruption. Her head cocked slightly sideways, she whispered: a virtuoso!

The Bösendorfer left us one day. Many strong arms carried it down the steep curving staircase with the utmost care. Mr. Rossbaut accompanied it, parting from us with his assurances of eternal gratitude.

In the last letter, my father writes:

> *I live with the hope that this war will be over in a few months. If I have one wish, it is only to be able to be with you and the children once again. But that still seems far off. Only this wish, this wish keeps growing. Human inadequacies can go to the devil. I am holding on to my young, glad heart, and greet and kiss you long and heartily.*
>
> *The opposing troops are almost within sight. How remarkable people are: despite the visible terror such a war brings upon a country, and despite the impressions of the last war, such a misfortune for us, preparations are being made for an even greater blow than the events of the last weeks. Hopefully there will then be peace, whose fruits our children can enjoy in a long peacetime.*
>
> *When you get this packet, with rationed coffee seized from the enemy, I will be many hundred kilometers away from you darlings. Do not worry, distance can never ever part us. As you well know, referring to one's location in correspondence is forbidden, no matter how well worth knowing it would be for you.*

On the back of the letter, in my mother's hand: *Fritz in Bordeaux until fall, then to Schwent on the Oder—there I could visit him one more time.*

Then his regiment was sent to Africa.

HEMMINGEN CASTLE

Once, my parents had lived a truly magical life. In the early years of their marriage, between the wars, they lived with their friend Baron Wilhelm Farnbühler at his castle near Stuttgart. The Baron had his own wing; my parents, with Uli and Anita, had theirs. In the great hall, in a cage, there dwelt an owl, who preferred to eat living things: rabbits and mice. His lame wing folded into a crutch, he shrieked into the night and rattled the bars.

I was born there, at Hemmingen Castle. My father was in charge of the Baron's agricultural affairs. Wilhelm and my mother made ceramics and studied botany.

In an abandoned glass house they set up a pottery studio. Adi, in a leather apron, produced useful and useless things out of clay. Wilhelm sat at the table, creating imaginary landscapes and abstractions—blue and multicolored—on tableware and vases. He was experienced in glazing, and he knew the proper temperature of the kiln.

The three of them went hunting in the surrounding woods. They drove in an open car to the neighboring castle, brought a freshly killed deer as a present.

The Baron loved his neighbor, Countess Alix, but he could not marry her. Why not? I asked my mother. Hmmm, some people are not made for it, she said. More a child could not extract. Homosexuality was barely even thinkable then.

The idyll—which one might call happiness, since everyone involved made splendid use of the situation in which they found themselves—the episode of rural simplicity, lasted only a few short years. Then came the shock. My father and Wilhelm had to prepare themselves for the war.

My mother slipped on her felt hat, buttoned up her striped wool suit, planted a calm, dutiful expression on her face, and accompanied the two men to the train station. On the way home, at the gate, she could no longer contain her tears. As if seen through much too strong a lens, what had been a clear drawing liquefied, became a watery sketch with abstract contours, its perspective reaching no farther than the trees of the park.

Very soon after the first weeks of the war came the news of Wilhelm's death. It was over. No more botany studies in the garden. In the greenhouse, orchids spread out air roots. A mouse family nested in the cold kiln of the potter's shed.

The sack of clay burst, eaten through by bird droppings. A storm blew out a windowpane. Rain mingled with dust. The material for an entire banquet of plates froze into lava.

With the war, the dream had collapsed. My father, who did not believe in happiness, had his confirmation.

You'll see soon enough, you with your optimism, he'd said to my mother.

AFRICA

Over and over, my father would tell stories of Africa. Benghazi, Tubruq, Aidabiya, Darnah. I still taste those exotic names in my mouth like bonbons. Perhaps, at first, he was thrilled to be there. Away from the familiar names, away from the artificial enemy, the love of his Adi warm in his heart, accompanied by the illusion that it would only be a matter of months now.

Numbed by the general intoxication and uproar around him, he arrived with his comrades at the harbor of Benghazi. My father was named City and Harbor Commander of Tubruq, giving him a quasi-civilian identity. Perhaps they had placed him in this responsible post to be rid of him on the one hand and to keep him busy on the other.

In photographs he stands before a tent, the shadow of his tropical helmet hiding half his face. The moustache sits smugly on the swing of his upper lip. His chin has its dimple in the middle. He wears a short-sleeved khaki shirt and khaki shorts, his hands dug into the pockets. Behind him a few figures sit on the floor in the tent's dusky interior. He has stepped into the sun to be photographed.

He loved sun. He liked the heat that jumps at your throat, pressing the wind out of you. One needed only dress reasonably, preferably just like the Arabs—in a caftan.

In these photos he still looks happy, smiles. There must have been wine, for he often wrote how glad he was at least to be able to rinse down the misery.

Africa spoke to him. He took an interest in the city, indulged his natural love for people, strolling through bazaars, giving in to the enchantment of colorful carpets, keeping in mind the exotic effect they would have on the wooden floors of cold Bavaria. He brought back oil lamps, metal jugs, ashtrays, water pipes, side tables that mingled with the baroque and Jugendstil in our rooms. My war booty, he rejoiced.

When he stepped into a shop, the owner would call for strong hot coffee with lots of sugar. My father would sit in the middle of the situation, attentive. No word, no gesture escaped him. There was a pow-wow, demonstrating the best wares, examining materials, rubbing wool between one's fingers, enjoying the quality of the design, listening to stories. For Fritz, the situation must have been exotic, like his later horse dealings with the gypsy Buchs. The protestations, the extravagance, the mimicry, the gamesmanship, the cunning close of the deal.

And of course the fun of taking one another for a ride, at least trying to, or simply sitting together, smoking, nodding.

Fritz was very gregarious and had a fine instinct for making himself liked. He was easygoing, and it was easy to forget his uniform. And Fritz was a paterfamilias whom the shopkeeper had to convince, who had to fall in love. He must not return from the hunt without prey. Unwritten laws, unwritten rites. This was about the head of a household, the master, the patriarch of the clan, furnishing his rooms without input from his wife. He had to be served in a fitting manner. The largest possible purchase had to be concluded.

Fritz took great pleasure in bargaining, forgetting the hated war. In these hours he was happy, sipping his coffee, so strong and sugary that the teaspoon stood upright in it.

Later he told stories about it all, with ever-changing elaborations, drawing in new characters, living out his impulses as his mood dictated. Only he had been there—and he was a superb liar.

•

My father stood on his balcony. Africa, you untamable bird. On the coats of the camels, on palm leaves, the dew gathered. The cold of night saluted the dawn of heat. A red sunball labored across the hills beyond the city of Tubruq. A pink cloth fell across the desert. In the oases the dogs shook themselves dry and stretched out their paws. The yard below swarmed with swallows. The muezzin climbed the tower. Someone came running from the harbor, bringing the general cacophony with him.

Fritz remembered the dream of the previous night quite clearly. He ran through it again and again.

In their bedroom at Hemmingen, Adi has been startled from the marrow of her sleep. Sirens force their way across the city to the park, the ponds, through the gaps in the blinds. In his powerlessness he clearly hears the noise, the

21

howling. He sees Adi reaching for her coat spread across the foot of the bed, her feet searching for the boots that stand ready on the carpet.

She runs into Anita's room. Wake up, child, we have to get to the cellar. Quick, pull on your coat. She bends over and laces up her daughter's little boots. Uli is already standing in the doorway. Adi takes Beatrix gently from her cradle and wraps her in a blanket. Beatrix gives a start at the howling of the sirens and cries all the way down the stairs, down through the door to the cellar, farther into the arched, dungeon-like shelter.

Strangers and neighbors have already found their way there. Benches and chairs, a folding cot. Whispering. Uli sets the suitcase with their valuables next to him. He runs up the stairs once more. I'll just step outside quickly, Mama, to see what there is to see in the sky. Adi shakes her head, powerless against "the man of the house."

Boundless, deafening noise. The ground trembles. Up above, the low-flying planes drone toward their goal. Whistling, the crackle of fire. A bomb falls quite nearby. Vroooooooom. Trees break free of their roots, smash into one another. Basement windows shatter. Screaming. Air pressure forces the people flat to the stone floor. Uli storms back down the basement stairs, out of breath, eyes bulging, laughing like a maniac. Adi rocks Beatrix back and forth as she drinks at her breast. My Adi, always so composed. Anita, swaddled in a blanket, lies on the cot and cries. Flashes of flak fire run along the cellar walls.

On the balcony Fritz wiped the sweat from his brow. Between his shoulders ran a sticky little brook. He gulped into his dry windpipe. Beneath him, in the courtyard, jasmine bloomed; a little breeze carried the scent up to him. An orange fell with a thud onto the tile floor. A camel dozed in the archway; behind it the street ran off into jacaranda blue, a woman balancing an urn on her head. White doves hovered in every direction. I have to get dressed, he thought, have to shave, have to tell my boy to have the car ready at eleven sharp. Have to get down to the harbor, have to . . . A spider lowered itself from the banister to the sill. He watched it for a long time, motionless.

Fritz sat in his office, the bottle of red wine next to him, taking swig after swig, looking at the world map on the wall and shaking his head. Ants were running a sugar caravan across the desktop. By evening he had scared off the dream, swallowed it down. Eventually night fell, and sleepless sleep. Here it was again: fear, impotence, a panicked jolt, howling of sirens, clattering, blood seeping through uniforms, saturating epaulettes, medals, SS emblems. The German flag devoured by flames. Dead eyes. Mouths distorted with fear. A child without legs. Adi's forehead bleeding. Little Beatrix, crying in the snow. A tree sinking into a crater. Nothing left of the house but bricks and dust clouds. Uli marches with the cannon fodder, laughing in lockstep, his boyish thighs straining his trouser seams. Red heaven above riderless horses.

My father had nightmares—every night. During the day he dutifully did his dutiful duty, procured wine, visited his friends in the bazaar, drank coffee with them. As an enemy he didn't amount to much: that, everyone noticed. But the sleepless nights of a pessimist have profound consequences. In the end, he must have been quite mad.

Over his many months in Africa, my father became friends with Field Marshal Rommel. Then something happened. The year was 1943. They must have been alone, standing before the big map of the countries, my father crazy with homesickness and longing for his Adi. He and Rommel were studying the conquests and what remained to be conquered. Whereupon my father supposedly said to Rommel: If you look at the map, Herr Field Marshal, you must admit that the war is lost.

Rommel slowly turned to him, the story goes, looked him in the eye for some time, and said in his Swabian dialect: You know, my dear Ost, at this point I am really supposed to have you shot. My father surely met his gaze and shook his head. Perhaps Rommel laid a hand on his shoulder, then turned away and left the room without saying another word, leaving my father behind like a red warning light. Then the unexpected happened, as if the one man had read and silently accepted the thoughts of the other. Fritz Ost was simply sent home by the fastest route, without any further attention. Nervous breakdown.

GOLDACHHOF

In the middle of the war, in 1943, my family moved from Hemmingen Castle to Goldachhof, the estate of my childhood.

Among my earliest memories are my father's daily routines. In the morning, as his second task—the first being wake-up call—he went into the den to the grandfather clock, opened the glass door, drew his watch from the red slit of his vest with his left hand, pried open the gold lid, checked, compared it with the dial above—Ja, richtig—then his right hand pulled the cone-shaped weight up by its chain. Sometimes he gave the minute hand a push forward, when he had a premonition that his wife would be unpunctual. Then, he would lecture.

Since the beginning of the last century, since rail travel began, time has been standardized everywhere. That goes for you, too, my love.

I stand in the room, smell the familiar things, hear the ticking of the clock. The impatient clop of horses' hooves outside. My father pulls the peaked checkered cap over his head and puts on his overcoat. His stockinged legs peer out from underneath; he is wearing lederhosen. My mother hurries through the tiled corridor, tak tak tak tak, sticks her head quickly through the kitchen door, and calls out an extra order for Olga, our cook.

I need to go back there. The urgency is getting stronger, catching hold of me. I dream a dream.

I am in the house of my childhood. It is raining. So hard that it presses my umbrella down on my head. I run to the garden. The little stream is a raging river. A dog swims toward me. He looks like a rat. I must, must get across the current, but I cannot see the riverbank.

Voyage

LIKE SUPERMAN, we overcome time and space. We are sitting in the airplane. Ludwig, my husband, has fallen asleep. He twitches sometimes, like a dog who moves his paw or his leg in a dream, who runs away from something or runs after it. He emits little sounds, as if he were barking, giving a speech. Behind his trembling eyelids a dream plays out. Released from reality, the images flee through imaginary situations, thoughts made flesh spring hurdles, the impossible pulls away from the logical. Wishes become reality. He pulls up one corner of his mouth, purses his lips, then rises with a start and murmurs something incomprehensible. His arm falls heavily to his side. No one else knows him like this. This is almost as intimate as the act of sex. Does he resemble my father? In what way? It can't just be the moustache over the curl of his upper lip.

Later. We are sitting in a Hertz rent-a-car. Ludwig, having finally escaped the American 55-mph speed limit, drives full throttle. We whiz down the autobahn.

We wanted to vacation in our city, the one we both grew up in, the one Ludwig was born in and never left until we went away together twenty-five years ago. He had looked forward to this trip with great anticipation. He knew some of my childhood stories, those colored by Adi's fabulous sense of humor, her words, her gestures. The way she dealt with temporal distance and spatial details lent her anecdotes the feel of a movie.

The estate I grew up on lay thirty kilometers north of the Munich city limits, on the little river Goldach—hence its name, Goldachhof. It stretched out for a thousand acres. The property was like an island. One could arrive from any direction and be woven into the insular framework of order—as a visitor, as one seeking protection, as a family member, or as a stranger speaking an unknown language. There they had all landed, or been stranded, and shared life until the next ship sailed. There were few ships back then, so many people stayed for years.

In the dark glass of the car window I see the reflection of a little girl calling me: Do you remember the sirens, 1945?

Here, stop, we have to get off the autobahn and ask directions. I call out, just in time for Ludwig to slow down before the turnoff at the Hotel Erdingerhof exit. I ask a dark-skinned man in a green apron the way. His German is fluent, but one hears a trace of a Slavic accent. He gives us partial directions, then we stop to get the rest from someone else. The second man could be from Turkey, from Egypt or Morocco.

This is Hitler's nightmare come true, Ludwig says with a grin. Soon it will be as motley here as it is in America.

The wintry landscape is so familiar, greeting me like an old friend, yet everything seems crowded more closely together, the land more developed: more streets, underpasses, overpasses. In between, new housing developments thrust forward, surrounded by rectangular fences. The old walls of a farm surface in the cool light. The stable leans crookedly in the winter air; steam rises from fresh cow manure heaped up behind. An ancient moated castle, regal, painted golden yellow with dark green shutters, is visible between the pines.

The land. Altered and yet easily recognizable, as a whole if not in individual details. Flat northern winter light, sun without shadow. An old love, very warm, slumbering in my bones, climbs forth from childhood: a love of the familiar, of my Muttersprache, my Vaterland. Grand words. One rarely uses them. In fact, never. One is ashamed. And yet when one lives abroad and looks toward the Heimat… Another such word. They come up, after all, perhaps just as literary echoes.

Quick mental images alternate with the momentary impressions racing by.

In spring the storks found their messy nest. The horses at the Goldach River drank in their shattered reflection. My father, when he was in the mood, showed me the white trembling heat across the wheat field, the alphabet of the heavens and clouds. Told me that gold lay at the end of the rainbow. In one of Father's books, Zeus devours his son. My nasty grandmother boxed the chambermaid's ears. Squares of paper for the loo were cut from newspaper. In the stables one heard moaning and then a window shattering. Card games. Drunken quarrels over money. Sleigh journeys to neighbors across frozen fields, tin canisters filled with hot water beneath one's feet. Churning butter by hand, the howling of the circular saw from Tafelmeier's workshop across the courtyard. Total stillness in the den, interrupted only by the yapping of dogs in their dreams and the buzzing of two copulating flies. Grandfather turning pages— Sssschip!—his hand moving a sheet through the air like a blade slicing an apple. The hue and cry when the maypole is finally up. Olga's voice, in broken German: You best one.

Stop—that's my schoolhouse! And there's the stall where Anita left her horse every day.

I am quite beside myself. Now we pull over to the left, past the cemetery. The wall that rings it is lower than I remember and looks freshly painted. Black marble scrolls with gold lettering. Angels cut from white stone spread their garments protectively over the dead and the past. Perfectly straight gravel paths separate the graves.

Just the way orderly German houses protect themselves with garden fences, I laugh.

Here I remember trees and meadows; now there are bungalows with little gardens in front. Thank God the rest of it survived the building boom.

Oh well, says Ludwig. Landscape doesn't change; cemeteries, definitely not. And the fields of cabbage out there were a local industry, even in your childhood. We are the Krauts, after all.

The old train station is still over there. When we would call in from the farm, the operator would have the train wait a little longer just for us.

The road leads over a narrow bridge. On the other side, a new assortment of

27

houses has been cleanly laid. I have an exact memory of this street, which we children traveled on foot every day between school and farm. This road from the farm to Ismanning is still unpaved. On both sides the embankment falls steeply, dangerously, into the gardens and fields. Slowly, slowly—I want to see everything exactly, enjoy it sip by sip. Thoughts are like champagne bubbles, my mad Uncle Erwin had always said, on his way to alcoholic nirvana.

We reach the tree-lined avenue leading to the estate. Fields border the street on both sides. On the right, our neighbors' farm, with a little turret like a warning finger. We roll closer, dip beneath the roof of the avenue trees.

Drive slower. Stop!

Before us, on the right, stands a burned-out ruin: our house, or what is left of it. Black charred beams, window frames devoured by fire. Our stately house, the adjacent stables, everything is destroyed.

Tears well up and flood my eyelids. I see my father's stern face clearly in front of me: Don't ever smoke or play with fire. Never, you hear me? Never near the stables with your damned cigarettes. His eyes jet from visitor to visitor. A sharp furrow crosses his brow.

The story was told in a warning tone, accompanied by the rap of his walking stick or, when he was telling it at the table, by the pounding of his fist, the rattling of the silver, to lend fear dramatic emphasis. At the end one had to promise to be extremely careful.

It had happened almost twenty years earlier. The screams of the farm lads who released eighty stallions from their tethers, drove them out of the stables. The whinnying, the stamping, the fear in the horses' smoke-reddened eyes. The farm dog, forgotten, burning on his chain. The granary, full with the fresh harvest, devoured by fire, all scattered up into the night. The insane, raging heat, the firemen who spent a week extinguishing the blaze, who doused the house in the middle of the farm with a constant rain to save it.

This great fire burned down the state horse-breeding operation my father ran in the twenties. He lived in constant fear that it could happen again on his

own estate. Someone might throw away a burning cigarette, children might repeat the deadly sin of playing with fire in the hay.

I am completely still. Across the courtyard to the left, the little house where the König family lived stands untouched by fire. Frozen geraniums hang from the window ledges on both sides of the entrance. Next door stands the little chapel where I celebrated my childish Mass, degrading the Virgin Mary to a mere mannequin in my theater of the sacred.

The wind must have blown from the west, carrying the fire from the house to the stables to the cow stall with the hay above. That was why the little house was spared, and the chapel next to it. My father's nightmare had come true after all, four decades after his death. Did he conjure it forth? Do places have predetermined fates?

Why had the idea of visiting the estate not gripped me two years earlier, when it was still intact in the flat moors? But I, too, would have been a different person. My childhood would not have held the same burning interest for me. And only my mother would have read my father's letters.

Across the courtyard from the ruins, a woman's face appears in an upstairs window.

God bless, we call out, and wave up to the stranger. I grew up here fifty years ago. This farm belonged to my father. I gesture in the direction of what's left of the house.

Mai, you're nowhere near that oyd, the woman responds.

You bet I am, I say.

The woman shakes her head good-naturedly: Aye don't believe yaw.

All three of us have to laugh: she down at us, we up to her.

Go ahead, park here, take a gander, she says. Wherever you like. Jus' look out if yaw go in there where it done burn.

She gestures with her chin across the courtyard. It looks like the aftermath of an air raid, like the bombed-out city houses in my memory.

We sit down on the bench in front of the Königs' house. There is no one else in sight.

God, it's quiet here, I say, breaking the silence. A little breeze bundles a few leaves together and blows them into a nervous swirl.

My grandfather Theodor, Fritz's father—I loved him immensely. He was simply there with me. And when he died it was because he was old, very old. I was richly favored by my grandfather. And that is why I never missed him very much. When you have been greatly enriched you do not feel the loss as keenly as when much is still lacking. I can see that now. My time with my grandfather appears much longer than it actually was.

Here on the little bench I am in the land of Non Sequitur. In memory my thoughts stand on their heads; the unexpected reigns.

The big house stands across from us. The geraniums my mother always loved so much hang down from the balcony over the entrance. The hall smells of horsehair—the stable is built right onto it. The banister ends in a soft curve, just right for sliding down.

Like trembling leaves in a labyrinth of branches, private idioms flickered through our everyday speech. Waterfalls we called "fallwaters." The glow worms had "explosions," my mother said. To my grandfather, anger was "katzenjammer." Hagenreiner's delivery van was called "Nugelpinne"; that term came from Aunt Julia. Grandmother's farts were her "howling wind," that one from Father, as was "freshman bladder," for when someone often ran to the toilet. "Someone shit in your head" was also Father's: that meant you had a dumb idea. "Now the light goes on": one understood. "Don't be so sanctimonious" was said when someone concealed something. Tattling was forbidden in every case; it was dishonorable. Even I, the smallest, was not allowed to do it.

Petze, Petze ging in den Laden	*Tattler, tattler went into the store*
Wollt' für'nen Fünfer	*For a fiver he wanted*
Petze haben	*tattle galore*
Petze, Petze gibt es nicht	*Tattler, tattler we're sold out*
Petze, Petze ärgert sich	*Tattler, tattler jumps and shouts*
Pfui!	*Phooey!*

When someone was sly he was called a "Holzfuchs," a wood fox. When someone always knew better, he was a "Klugscheisser," a smart shitter. If some-one had done something naughty, he "needed a headwashing." If someone got annoyed, a louse was running across his liver. If someone was cunning in money matters, he was surely a Jew. For messiness: "It looks like Russia around here," or "the Hottentots." Charming as a Frenchman, cowardly as an Italian. No one was politically correct yet. And when Grandfather did not want to hear any-thing more out of his wife, Marie-Louise, he turned away and mumbled: Get off my back.

Part Two

You cannot explain the taste of salt
to someone who has never tried it.

—Tibetan proverb

Breath of a House

GRRRRRR! Get off my back, grumbled Grandfather Theodor, mostly to himself. He towered above on the stairway landing. A green satin vest showed beneath his suit jacket. From the buttonhole to his vest pocket swung a gold chain with boar's teeth, weighted with an eagle's claw at the end, where the round gold watch casing sank into the red lining.

The stairs creaked beneath his feet, crrrk, crrrk; he grew toward me with each step. When he arrived at the foot of the stairs and stood next to me, I barely reached his waist.

Get off my back, he said again. This time he winked at me, gesturing upward and over his right shoulder with his chin. So I knew he meant Grandmother, whose dress I had just caught a glimpse of, or the air between us.

What's up? he asked with a friendly grin, taking my small hand in his big, paper-dry one.

Something new, Grandpapa!

At the end of the hallway, tied-up boxes and leather suitcases were piling up. The front door stood open. Umer, the Hungarian coachman, hauled another load of luggage into the dusky house. His woolen trousers were deftly tucked into his riding boots. Looking about the hallway in search of unused space, he skillfully heaped his load into a gap in the mountain of suitcases that had gathered there. Politely tapping his gray cap, he took a little bow. I tapped my forefinger to my forehead, and we both smiled.

Grandfather and I strolled slowly through the hall, to the front door. Our curiosity had been whetted. Just at this moment Aunt Julia and her daughter, Alexandra, stepped through the doorway. They were the family members we

knew little about. No one had ever mentioned them until a letter arrived, revealing their place: Julia had married a cousin of my mother's. The desperation described in the letter was harrowing. They had been bombed out of Breslau, forced to leave everything where it stood. Only at the last minute had they managed to save themselves and a few suitcases from the Russians.

How horrible, my mother had said, making a sorrowful face. My God, those poor things! And on top of all that, Oskar is dead!

Alexandra was two years older and a head taller than me. Right away I noticed how beautifully she was dressed. Dark blue coat with cherry buttons, a red cap perched over her ear, black patent leather shoes. Oddly, she looked at me with only one eye. The other listlessly observed the unpacking of the luggage. Later she showed me that the second eye was glass. She took it out of the socket, rinsed it with water, and deftly stuck it back beneath her eyelid. Now I knew. My child brain spun a tragic war story. I did not believe she had got unslaked lime in her eye. No, no, the eye was pawned. It was waiting for her to claim, like all the other things. Should she find her way back to her old life, she could trade in the glass eye for the real one.

Aunt Julia, in a veiled hat and high heels, glanced nervously about her and peeled her gloves from her hands.

I must look dreadful after the long journey, she apologized.

The little group looked about in embarrassment.

Grandfather bowed stiffly: Honored.

G'day, she replied. Alexandra, too, said g'day, instead of God bless. She spoke Prussian and was thus, like her forebears ever since the war with Prussia, one of the Saupreussen—the Pig Prussians, as they were called in Bavarian. A string of Prussian word beads followed. Finally my mother appeared, her hearty greeting shooing Grandfather's awkwardness into the dusk of the vestibule. Prior to their arrival my mother had planned how to situate everybody. They got the Yellow Room. Olga, our Russian cook, was ordered to clear the jars of preserves from the floor and the armoire. Thus were Aunt Julia and Alexandra given a little foothold in our house.

Alexandra's arrival marked the start of an endless drama about hair. Long, or short? Alexandra wore a practical pageboy; I had braids woven around my head. My mother loved my coronet hairdo, but Aunt Julia felt short hair was more practical. My mother went along with her, and to my horror, I, too, received the chop! But as soon as my hair was cut off, it became apparent that it would have to grow back to a certain length after all, so the unruly tufts could be decently combed back.

If only you hadn't cut them off! Now the stringy mess is forever getting in your face, my grandmother hissed.

Alexandra had the stricter mother. It was never, What do you want? Just, Do this, do that. Hair got cut when she said. End of story; no talking back. Quite unlike my mother, whose philosophical contribution was: Really, it's just hair.

Yes, and if it were curls? Well, then! clucked my grandmother.

Upstairs on the second floor of the great house were the Blue Room, the Green Room, and, next to it, the Yellow Room. There was also a drawing room, and next to it my parents' bedroom. Then the room I shared with my sister, Anita, plus a linen closet and the only toilet. Atop a steep staircase sat the majestic attic, with a round window pigeons flew through just as they pleased. They built their nests in the beams under the roof. Beneath them their droppings piled up. When you opened the attic door, dust and feathers flew at you with the draft. Right at the start of the morning, before the sun came up, we could hear the pigeons' amorous cooing coming from the floor above.

All the way downstairs on the main floor was an office and, next to it, the room where the lads slept: my brother, Uli, his student friend, Georg, and Dieter Brün, who had saved Uli's life. Across from that was the only full bathroom in the house. Then there was our spacious kitchen with its pantry, adjacent to the large dining room, and beyond it, the cozy wood-paneled den with its tiled stove, in whose crevices the dogs slept.

Provisions were difficult to come by in the city, and the bombings became increasingly frequent, making it too dangerous for my grandparents to remain in their home. So they, too, moved to the farm, into the Green Room. A string of tobacco leaves dangled from corner to corner to dry.

Grandfather lifted me up. Along the ceiling of his room, I was to tie red ribbons between the clusters of leaves, to ration them out for the season so he would not become too extravagant before the next harvest. From this point to that by Christmas, up to here by Easter, and so forth.

My grandmother hated the smell and opened the window all the way. You can't breathe in here, she fumed.

That was the moment Grandfather Theodor lost his otherwise endless patience. Get off my back, he grumbled, muttering further heresies through silent lips as he trundled off.

Then there were the Brüns. General Brün—tall, blond, with beautiful blue eyes, erect gait, and ever-helpful manner—settled in to the Blue Room with Auntie Brün and their twelve-year-old son, Peter. The other son, Dieter, stayed downstairs with Uli. Dieter and Uli were both nineteen, and both already veterans. They belonged to the Kinderenthusiasten, that youthful excitement Hitler had hoped would conquer Russia for him. Dieter had carried the wounded Uli through a snowy minefield to safety. That was in Murmansk, in Russia.

Oh, we must be so infinitely grateful to Dieter, my mother mused. So when the Brüns arrived in an open cart and stood homeless at our door with a few suitcases and boxes, the Osts took them in without a moment's hesitation.

We called Mrs. Brün Auntie. She looked so friendly with her blue eyes, her blond curly hair, her rounded figure. But I somehow knew better; I saw her hidden side. Auntie was short-tempered. Her hand was quick to fly out and land audibly on the cheek of the sinner Peter, often merely because he was a little slow. Snatches of Peter's screams would carry downstairs, and a little while later he would appear with a red imprint on his cheek. But my mother excused Auntie. Somehow she could understand her. They had lost everything, lost the roof over their heads, all but lost their minds.

Mrs. Brün told the story of the bombing of Berlin. One night, wrenched from the marrow of her dreams, she found her house in flames. All she could do was wrap herself in a wet blanket, drag Peter out of bed, find her way to the back stairs, flee to the street. The glaring heat all around left only one escape route. She joined the fleeing mass of people who had mindlessly found their way together. Sobs, shouts, barking dogs, and the whistle of the falling petrol bombs. Then, somewhere, an open bomb-shelter door: a hand, a dry coat, a place to sit down.

My mother accompanied Mrs. Brün's story with her eyes wide open in fear and sympathy, making us all doubly horrified at the unfolding catastrophe. In the subsequent silence I asked whether she could tell the story once again, for me, to give me an exact idea. I always asked the same when fairy tales were read to me. I couldn't hear them often enough; they were horrifying and fascinating in equal measure.

The tales and the voices flowed into one another and made Peter, who had experienced it all, a hero. But Peter never talked about it. Nothing made it to the outside, not a word slipped past his lips. He did not want to relive the terror, and when I pressed him, iron silence.

The things that boy has been through, my mother said, running her hand through his tufty blond hair.

Red spread from his throat up his cheeks, into his ears, burned there for a little while—the fire of embarrassment. She drew Peter to her breast, held him there, and finally, finally, released him from public scrutiny.

I quickly took his hand, tugged him along to go play. His embarrassment made him docile and willing to participate in one of my favorite activities: sliding down the banister. He had to catch me at the bottom.

Well, all right, just once, he said, casting a bored look down at me from his twelve-year-old height. After one catch, he turned and left me standing there. He strode outside, looking around the courtyard for the older boys, who called him Pig Prussian. He would rather be with them.

The house was now bursting with people. A shelter for the shelterless. Sometimes a queue built up at the door of the one bathroom. Whoever could not wait ran through the door at the end of the hall, to the stables, and found a place to squat. One had to be alert lest one frighten the beasts and receive a kick, or a moist snort from a curious nose. I always went to my favorite, the calmest one, a brown workhorse with thick bunches of hair on its haunches.

In the mornings Justa, the Yugoslavian chambermaid, trudged upstairs, her face contorted from sleep, the hair at the nape of her neck a stringy mess. She knocked at each door, and regardless of whether one answered, she brought in a pitcher of hot water, carried it to the washstand, and, oblivious to anyone in the room, fished around under the bed for the chamber pot, or looked for it in the night cabinet, to take it downstairs if it was full.

Once a week Aunt Julia organized baths for everyone. Alexandra and I waited, each with a large sea sponge in hand, until we were allowed to climb into the tub. Then one of the mothers scrubbed us. When the bathwater took on a gray tone it was replenished. On bath days everyone had to keep the wood stove going so the next person could enjoy a hot bath, too.

Then the holidays arrived, and the bathtub turned into a fish tank. There the carp and trout were kept fresh. I dangled my chin over the rim and watched them flapping their gills. In this narrow space I could touch their slippery skin. Their round glassy eyes glided along the white porcelain like marbles. In a perpetual circle, an oval, they searched for the outdoors, for green reed-grass, for the blue mirror of sky. They opened and shut their carp mouths. What were they thinking about? The delicious pond lettuce, the teeming grubs, the swarms of plankton, the mossy stones, seeds, gnats' wings?

BREITREITER

There was plenty to eat on the estate: vegetables from the garden, and turnips, potatoes, and cabbages from the fields. What we urgently needed was coffee. Not ersatz coffee, not Muggefugg, grain sludge—we needed the real thing.

My grandmother was mixed up in certain deals to obtain the beans and sugar we longed for. She had spun a plot with a character from the city who would show up at our place in a curious postwar contraption. Trade coffee for food? He wouldn't take it, didn't need it. Had plenty. It had to be something more refined, something special, something from us personally. A piece of our home.

A white billow in the distance. Who was producing all that steam? Who was that coming up here? A strange vehicle rolled nearer and nearer, until we discovered it was one of those do-it-yourself cars they called Holzgassers. It ran on steam rather than gasoline. In the back, on a platform behind the driver, sat a stove with a stovepipe and wood or coal heaped up next to it. When the power started to flag, the driver hopped out to top up the stove.

The cloud rolled over the bridge and curved into the courtyard. My grandmother pushed the curtain aside. Aha, there he is. She was already hurrying through the hallway. Just as the carriage stopped, with a creak of its hand brake, Grandmother stepped out the door.

Get out of the way! she said, annoyed, shoving the dog aside. Then, like a break in the clouds, a sweet smile flashed across her face.

So, what lovely surprises have you for us today, Mr. Breitreiter? she laughed in greeting.

Thus began the ritual. First, one acted as if the visit were a great surprise. But here only one thing really mattered: coffee, the delicacy that could not be found anywhere else. Grandmother's eyelids fluttered. Her hands clapped, setting the mood: she stepped closer, leaned on the strange conveyance, folded her arms beneath her bosom, cocked her head, crossed one foot over the other. There she stood in the starting gate, all at once quite young again. The negotiations could begin.

Mr. Breitreiter had His Plan, how much coffee he was willing to leave in the house after his visit. My grandmother, too, had Her Plan. For there was never enough coffee. Uncertain when the spring would bubble forth again, she wanted to negotiate the most out of Breitreiter and titillated him with a baroque silver box, a Chinese snuff bottle. She did it so consummately that no one could see anything, skillfully holding the treasures in the folds of her skirts. If I was too eager to be part of it all, and came too close to her, she shooed me off. Go away, you cheeky devil! Grandmother had to concentrate.

My mother, too, stuck her head through the door and looked into the courtyard. In a single second her glance took in the whole space. Then, like the lens of a camera, her attention honed in on Breitreiter, vehicle, grandmother. My grandmother, for her part, paid no attention to my mother: Breitreiter was her turf.

Let's go, my mother said to me, taking my hand. She pulled me through the house, down the stairs on the other side, and out into the garden.

Will we be getting more coffee? I asked.

Without a word my mother took two watering cans to the stream, bent deeply, plunged one can into the water as if she wanted to drown someone. When the gurgling tapered off, she jerked it back up, heavy with water, practically lost her balance, then repeated the whole process with the second can. She lugged both to the rose bed, her face red with exertion. I did not ask any more questions. I searched the roses for bugs, turned the petals over the way my mother had taught me to. Mother watered devotedly: here a bush, there a languishing shrub.

Eventually Breitreiter's Holzgasser rattled off across the bridge, through the foliage. My mother looked up. A strand of hair clung to her moist brow. She sighed, trailing the cloud of dust with a dark frown, until the noise of the motor was lost in the vanishing point of the tree-lined avenue.

Later my mother noticed that a small patch had been cleared in the dust on the mahogany chest of drawers. A rectangle. That was the box. In the glass case, a dust-free oval. That was the snuff bottle. Once again Breitreiter had taken with him part of what my mother called "our culture."

The war changed the value of all things. In the hour of need, intrinsic value seemed irrelevant, uprooted from its meaning. What was hard for one person to get was traded for what others could easily find. The value of the objects exchanged was unequal. Scarcity premium for scarcity premium. Everyone was more or less addicted to what they could not have. My grandmother was forgiven her bartering so long as times were bad. But when luxury goods were once again available on the open market, the family feuds began.

How on earth could my mother-in-law give that gouger all those superb, irreplaceable things? Adi lamented. He has enough of our estate to open an antique shop!

Over time, the family heirlooms—exquisite objects of ivory, part of the snuff bottle collection, fine small furniture, too—disappeared piece by piece into the Holzgasser. But in exchange we had real coffee, and my grandmother was in a better mood.

•

Sometimes as I sat with my grandfather, someone would say within my earshot: Yes, it's quite true, quite obvious from the side. One can easily see it: she has the same profile.

What profile? I would ask.

Well, your nose and your bearing. Just like the Empress Sissi.

And what about this, they exclaimed: Beatrix is not even six, yet she is already binding up her waist!

Indeed, to the general amusement of our household, I was often seen with my smocked jumper tightly bound at the waist with one of my father's cast-off red ties.

My grandfather, vintage 1860. His background was taboo.

Theodor Ost was the illegitimate child of Max of Bavaria, the king's brother and Empress Sissi's father. As an elderly gentleman Max had fallen in love with a beautiful maiden in Freising, where the royals went hunting. My grandfather was raised in Professor Zirngiebel's house, where his mother worked. He attended the Maximilianeum with the children of the aristocracy, spoke ancient Greek and Latin, studied history, and became a professor. He had never known financial worries; he received a royal stipend. His suits were sewn by a Czechoslovakian tailor with fabrics from England; his shoes were made to measure in Italy. An air of mystery suffused his quiet existence. The backs of my grandparents' wardrobes and chests of drawers, the undersides of chairs and table legs, all boasted the royal Bavarian coat of arms. Silver tableware was hidden in the finest pig-leather chests; the wondrously exotic collections showcased behind glass also came from Grandfather's "family." During the war years, the furniture had been evacuated to our house, along with my grandparents, to await the return of peace. In twilight, collectible objects stacked behind panes of glass were admired as a legacy. The furniture, too good to use, dozed away in the upstairs hall. These pieces were my grandmother's domain. She dusted them, oiled the old woods, and forbade the children to touch them. She tied ornamental cords across the arms of the chairs so that no one would sit on them. A coverlet shielded the tabletop's fine veneer. Only Grandmother could lift the cloth: at the base of the table, on a wooden stone, a boy played his flute at a wooden brook. I reached out to touch it with my finger.

Cut it out! she hissed. You look at valuable things only with your eyes, not your dirty fingers!

Hunger

SOMETHING TERRIBLE HAPPENED on the neighbors' farm in the last days of the war. The young German workers who were all off in the military were replaced with forced laborers from the conquered countries in the east. The forced laborers on Herr Grub's farm were not happy. He did not pay them as much as his own Bavarian crew, and on top of that, he gave them less to eat. In a rage, someone had bestially killed him.

Naturally there was talk. Would the trouble spread? Umer, our coachman, said with conviction that it couldn't happen on this farm. No, not here on Herr Ost's place. He treats everyone fairly.

A few days after the murder of Herr Grub, a Bavarian policeman sent by the Americans came bicycling up the tree-lined avenue. He stopped in our court-yard.

Where is Herr Fritz Ost? I have a warrant for his arrest.

What? What is this all about? my mother demanded.

Illicit slaughter, the policeman stated slowly with an air of sure authority.

How was it possible that someone had the power to order Fritz Ost off the estate? True, since the end of the war, slaughtering was controlled by the American authorities. But who could have blown the whistle on our farm? Surely one of our forced laborers. A Pole, the dirty bastard.

My father was enraged, but then his mood shifted. What could they possibly hang on him? He loftily ordered the horses harnessed up. My mother prepared his leather overnight case. He mounted the carriage. Umer sat on the box, my father next to him, puffing on his beloved Virginia cigar. The policeman climbed on his bicycle and led the way, pedaling in front. The carriage rolled lackadaisically behind. So they went, all the way to Ismanning Jail.

My mother and I waved until the group was lost in the distance, a cloud of smoke trailing behind my father's cap. Away from us, becoming smaller and smaller, like a toy from Anita's play farm, with its small carriage an exact replica of a real life-sized one. And that tiny bicycle policeman.

I stood in the courtyard and bawled because I didn't really understand what had happened. No one had had time to explain.

At first even my mother seemed confused, but then something changed. She lit up. I saw it written on her determined face. That calmed me.

She stormed to the telephone and called her friend Eugene, a lawyer in Munich. Adi called Eugene her spiritual anchor. Before she married Fritz, Eugene had fallen in hopeless, undying love with her. He loved her still.

You have to get him out of there right now! Only you can do it! she wheedled. We can't get along without him here. All these people, the forced laborers, only Fritz can deal with them.

Then she stopped and listened. After a few minutes, her features grew calm. She even smiled. He must have said he'd help her in any way he could.

At the end of the conversation, my mother said: All right, tomorrow I will go get him.

And that she did. They had not been able to prove anything. The proof had long since been turned into sausage and eaten as schnitzel.

The next day I sat on a stone, waiting until the carriage curved once again through the gate into the courtyard. This time my mother held the reins and my father sat next to her. We were so glad he was back; without him we would have had to invent our own rules.

At Goldachhof Fritz established the agenda; so be it, Adi confirmed. This pattern was irrevocable. Best to give in; it simplified things. There were no ifs, ands, or buts with him.

Fritz was the authority figure, the Almighty. He gave his orders in a clear, loud voice. They practically showered down from his towering figure, or they came from the tip of his cane, when he pointed out unacceptable situations. Bitingly clever, he was. Just, cool-headed, transparent blue like ice, but furious when something went wrong, when an order was not carried out well or promptly.

Imposingly tall and slender, he always held himself upright, rather stiffly. Military upbringing. A bit of it would do anyone good, he said, although he hated the military. There are quite a few useful things you only learn through drills. He always had a goal in mind, always looked directly and alertly at whatever he was naming, or the person he was addressing. Eye contact.

Yes, my father had regal manners. He was as just as he was strict. He loved order, and logic, and courage, consistent thinking. He himself was the largest of larger-than-life characters, with his stern face, the attentive look, observing everything. Everyone's knees knocked in his presence. But no one who felt at home in his own skin needed to defend himself when something did not suit my father. You could argue well with him. Those with a guilty conscience had a hard time. That he could smell. He had a nose for it.

Respect and love are quite close together. Umer was very respectful but not at all subservient. On the frequent occasions when my father was nervous, Umer did not let it irritate him at all. With complete composure he laid the reins and girdles around the horses' bellies and the bits into their mouths, scurried around the carriage, tightened the wagon shaft.

Growing impatient, my father called out: Umer, hurry up!

Can only do slowly, are nervous animals, he said. That calmed my father, since he knew Umer was clever.

You're right, you're right, I'm always taking off, just like the horses. We'll make it up by letting them gallop on the straightaway.

Umer he never called an idiot, a word that otherwise lay happily on his tongue. Umer knew his craft, and my father knew it. Between the two there was room for a real love.

49

Fritz also has a great sense of humor, my mother pointed out. Come on, Fritzl, where's your humor? she sometimes had to remind him.

Earlier it sat more lightly on him. Before the war his nerves were better, my mother said. She wanted everyone to like him, her Fritz, to include in their image of him the young Fritzl only she knew. Often she functioned as the softened echo of his harsh order, when she repeated in her own words something everyone had understood perfectly well. Then she took his arm and looked laughingly at whatever or whomever had caused his fury to well up. Adi always wanted peace, while Fritz never ceased to stew. Somehow he needed conflict as fuel. His nerves, my mother said.

Because of Father's bad nerves, it was always my mother who drove the car. In the office hung a big photo of our neighbor, race-car driver Hans Stuck, sitting in his white car, my father next to him. Both were wrapped in white dusters, with caps and racing goggles parked on their foreheads. They looked like twins.

We looked at the picture, Uli and I. Who is at the wheel? he asked.

Hans Stuck! You know Father can't drive. He's the passenger.

It was also my mother who was allowed to drive into Munich in Hans Stuck's little white racing car, with Hans on the passenger side. Upon their arrival in town the car would be surrounded with gawkers, not just because of the famous race-car driver, but also because of my mother. Back then a woman at the wheel was an unusual sight.

Stuck was inevitable fodder for neighborhood dinner gossip. Mrs. Stuck could no longer bear seeing only the legs of her husband. When Hans was not at the racetrack, he spent almost all of his time under his car. Because of the love affair with his car, and because of the whispering about other affairs, she finally left him. Adi did not understand how one could leave one's husband. In her picture of things every man needed a woman at his side, preferably a strong one. That was just the way it was. Otherwise, people would be built differently.

HYACINTH

It was always Adi who had to cope with difficult tasks. Heroic, fearless, eventempered, never moody, she was sent into action, or sent herself.

Once again we were in a tricky situation. My mother prepared herself.

Please, please, Mami. Can I come with you?

It was already getting dark. Umer had hitched up one of the four Arabians to the gig, our small carriage. My mother took the reins; I clambered up and sat next to her. Off we lurched toward the moor. The knotted willows along the dirt road thrust their fists into the shroud of fog. The horse obediently trotted along. It felt creepy. I concentrated on the horse's hindquarters; the play of its muscles distracted me from the blurred twilight world, from the vague outlines that gave wings to my fantasy. A knight with his sword was leaning over there on the tree trunk. An elf was springing up the embankment. A dark animal scurried across the road. The clip-clop of hooves and the creaking of wheels sounded out through the stillness. Here lived the Nightschratz and his helpers.

We reached the moor. Narrow paths between canals. The fog crept along the waters. Here small rectangles were cut out of the moor, stacked atop one another, dried in the wind. The towers of peat, for winter heating, looked like a village of huts. In the fog they were floating above the land, suspended on a gray, airy foam, swinging hither and thither like my thoughts. Anything was possible. Startled awake by the clatter of the hooves, the spirits from German fairy tales stepped forth from their pages, thrust themselves in front of reality, which had long since cleared out and made room for horror. Horror was practiced as an educational method. I'll teach you what horror means. A threat, casually tossed off.

I clung to my mother. There stood the elfin king. His spirit garb swam in the foam of fog. Doubtless he would carry me off through the night air any minute now.

Mami, where are we going?

To Hyacinth, she said, tapping the horse's back with the whip. To Hyacinth, our shepherd.

The horse snorted and tore at the bit. The carriage creaked. In my terror I forced myself to think about the peacock egg in the chicken coop. The egg, a present from the neighbor, was packed up for us in wood shavings and brought in a crate. Now a mother hen sat on it, believing it her own. Her three eggs in turn lay silently under an electric bulb in the peacock-egg box in the kitchen. The shavings make a beautiful nest, I thought, and concentrated with utmost precision on recalling every detail. The lamp has to hover over the center. If the power goes out there will be a catastrophe. The egg could not survive it.

I looked up at my mother: squinting, her body tense, leaning into the misty vapor. She gripped the harness with both hands, held it so tightly that the white of her bones peered through the skin of her hand. Consumed with fear, I meditated on my sins. Never again will I snort back snot. It makes you dumb, Grandmother says. Just take your handkerchief and blow your nose properly.

The horse pulled; my mother drew the reins tighter. The stillness was so still one could hear it. Noise came only from the carriage, the snorting horse, the trip of its hooves: in the fog chamber every sound was thrown back twofold.

Suddenly the road curved. We drove between rows of trees. Off flew a lone crow: caw, caw. I trembled and swallowed a scream. But then I felt my mother's calming strength next to me, and I started to feel a little better.

And there it was! The shepherd's cart materialized out of the mist. Slowly we rolled closer. The sheep's heads bobbed behind their sheepfold like little balls on water: toward us, away from us, here, there. A figure detached itself from the cart. Hyacinth. A breeze swelled his loden cape as he moved toward us. He reached out his hand to my mother, taking the horse by its halter. The dogs whined all around us.

Do you have it? my mother asked, gesturing with her chin toward the sheepfold.

Hyacinth nodded, signaling wordlessly.

The sheep behind the fence danced and jostled each other nervously, first into one corner and then into another. Dogs circled the flock.

The transaction went quickly, like a well-rehearsed pantomime. While Hyacinth went off toward a cluster of rosebushes, my mother opened the flap beneath the seats. He returned carrying a heavy load: one dead sheep slung over his shoulder, plus two more, one in each hand.

Hyacinth unloaded his cargo into the gig; each landed with a thud. He pushed them close together and covered them up with the flap, pulled a kerchief from his trousers, wiped his brow, and gave my mother a small smile with a farewell nod.

And off we went with a jolt. It almost hurled me from my seat. Hyacinth, his white hair, the cart, the sheep, the dogs—everything disappeared, reclaimed by the fog.

I clung to my mother's arm, so strong and calming. Yes, from restraining the beasts. She also had another strength, the strength that allowed her to drive off into the moor, the strength with which she rebuffed my father's grim premonitions, took away their inevitability and fatefulness, simply lent them a different coloring. For her there were no catastrophes. Everything was just an event that had to be dealt with.

Lately, there had been much whispering at the dining table: procurement methods, sources, deals. Meals were the constant theme of conversation at meals: where to get them, from which hat one could pull the rabbit, how best to preserve meat. How to make marmalade without sugar, like using sugar-beet syrup. Conversations and remarks, arguments behind closed doors in the house, in corridors, in rooms. Outside in the courtyard, at the little bridge, side glances, whispers behind the backs of hands, high fives.

The household was once again without meat, putting my father in a bad mood—hence, our meeting with Hyacinth. The foggy, dreary night was perfect for this secret adventure.

We turned onto a gravel road, broader and safer. The wheels ground on the pebbles to the steady rhythm of the horse's hooves. Suddenly I felt my mother's body tensing. Right before us, a figure on a bicycle emerged from the mist.

The stranger pedaled alongside us. He wanted to hold on to our carriage, he said. What a piece of luck that we had come along, in this weather, and so late at night. He just wanted to hitch a little ride.

Yes, sure, said my mother. Just grab hold. What else could she say? There was no choice. But when she looked back, she noticed to her horror that blood was seeping out from under the flap where the sheep were lying. The man could be a black-market informant. He could turn us in, or worse: the price of his silence could be an entire sheep.

The stranger shifted his grip between my mother's seat and the curved board that blocked the spray of mud from the wheels. His head danced back and forth like the heads of the sheep. I felt my mother's uneasiness, fear and tension in the tone of her voice, her nervous laugh.

So where are you coming from at this time of night? she asked.

Yeah, I hardly see nuthin'. And you with the rig and all, where d'you come from? What you got back there? he brashly asked. And then, with a broad smile: This horse see in the dark?

Yes, my mother said. It knows the way. Horses have instincts.

Yeah, animals got the jump on people. Sure is shitty weather for you all to be out in, he kept drilling.

We'll be home any minute, and someone's coming on a motorcycle to meet us, my mother lied.

On a motorcycle, aha! And a mean, sly smirk lit across his ragged face. Oh yeah, yeah. So long, then. See ya next time.

The stranger pushed off from the carriage. He swung onto a little path and gave a final tap on his cap. For a moment we still saw him sketched in gray, then the fog swallowed him.

My mother cracked the horse's rear with her whip. It took off at a fast gallop. I hid my face in her coat.

For God's sake, she said. Let's get out of here.

The fog laid itself across the horse's hide like cold sweat. Behind us drizzled blood, the clue linking the deed and the scene of the crime to the perpetrator and his hideout. But we had gotten away with it.

OLGA

On the blackboard that hung on the kitchen wall, written in chalk: Potato soup. Olga, our cook, slowly deciphered my mother's orders, glancing at the clock above the door.

Mne nado poiti nakopat' kartochki v ogorode. Vsyo rabota da rabota. I have to go dig up potatoes in the garden. Nothing but work, work, work. She peered through the window into the snowy whirlwind.

Ah, ya, she groaned. You want come along to garden?

Yes, I happily nodded, already climbing into my clammy leather boots.

Going out with Olga was a privilege. Olga was an authority. She was still young, in her mid-twenties, with a strong peasant's build, her broad face typically set in skepticism. She obeyed only my mother and father. Not promptly, not immediately, more slowly, in her own rhythm. Olga's Siberian tempo, my father called it, and had to laugh, since he liked her.

Olga alone had the key to the icehouse, and sometimes she took me along. To lock in the cold, the door was reinforced with layers of peat. Inside stood row after row of preserves. Frost covered the glass containers; meat and innards, wrapped in cloths, were frozen on ice-covered shelves. In tin buckets trout and carp stared open-mouthed through ice. Breath steamed up, and freezing fear crept into my heart at the thought that someone could lock us in. But Olga always took the precaution of sliding the key, fastened to the end of a wooden spoon, into the side of her boot. No joke this! she would say sternly.

In the farm kitchen, the oven sat solidly in the middle, and in the middle of the stove, framed by the fire, was the hot water cistern. Every morning a regiment of cockroaches scrambled about in search of food. Great hordes of hungry insects scurried soundlessly across and around the cool stove. Da chort poberi! Olga cursed. The devil take it! First she tossed a load of hot water at the creepy-crawlies. Then another, until the kitchen floor was flooded. She pulled up a chair and observed the roaches in their death throes. In one hand she held her mug with hot grain coffee; in the other, the ladle, reaching into the steaming kettle. Elbows propped on her knee, lost in thought, she stared blankly ahead. Olga's morning meditation.

The kitchen door opened, and my grandmother poked her head in. No reaction from Olga.

Hrrrr. Olga is back with "the Russians," my grandmother grumbled, using the Bavarian folk term for roaches, and threw the door shut.

Olga and my grandmother waged incessant war. Yet again that Russian tramp is not listening! she would say. When Olga simply did not wish to hear Grandmother, she rolled her eyes to the ceiling and groaned. Then my grandmother really got cross. But Olga remained unmoved, stoic and solid. Sometimes, at that crucial moment, Justa, the chambermaid, entered the picture. To unload her frustration, my grandmother gave her an undeserved box on the ear. Olga clattered loudly with the stove rings. Justa held her cheek. She was like a little dog, forever plagued with pangs of guilt and language problems. Somehow she regarded every box on the ear as just what she deserved.

Grandmother left the kitchen with a huff.

All Justa could say was: Stupid cow.

You stupid cow self! said Olga, brandishing the knife through the kitchen steam. Why you say nothing? Not hit me! Ya, Russkaya! pounding repeatedly on her breastbone. She underlined her point with a poke on Justa's forehead.

Now, with my leather boots laced up, the coat pulled about me, I was ready to go out with Olga. She was already fully dressed in her Russian military fur, felt boots, fur cap with earflaps, fingerless gloves, and the basket.

No, you not enough warm, she said. She lifted my skirt to pull on a scratchy pair of baggy Bleyle tights, just high enough to cover the holes in my stocking knees. Far too large for me, these tights hung formlessly from beneath my coat. But warmth was the main thing, so I did not protest. I wanted to be with Olga.

Thus we set out across the little bridge, on past the frozen rock garden. Mounds of snow revealed bushes and shrubs; rectangular markings meant frozen vegetable beds. We trudged further through the sleeping orchard, leaving behind Grandfather's tobacco row on our left. Its remnants leaned in the frost like scarecrows. A thin cut of black earth sliced the field in two. Rows of snowy mounds spread before us. We had arrived.

When fresh turnips, potatoes, red beets, or celery root were needed in wintertime, Olga ventured out to hack up these frozen mounds. She shoveled the earth aside, revealing a thick layer of straw beneath. There, protected from the frost, slumbered the fresh vegetables.

Vsyo rabota, da rabota, always work, nothing but work, Olga groaned, and dug.

How come you don't talk like us? I asked into the cold, between Olga's lunges. Olga stopped.

I not German. Ya, Russkaya, Russkaya, Russkaya, I Olga Vlatinova. Rossiya, moya rodina, Russia is my homeland. You not understanding. You, best one, best one, she said, digging further. I speak language, that my mother, home, she said, laughing, and pressed me to her chest with her moist earth hand.

I helped gather vegetables into the basket, and above all, a few celery knobs. My mother had taught Olga to make one of my father's favorite dishes: cooked celery knobs, finely sliced, mixed with minced apple, walnuts, pepper, salt, oil, vinegar, and mustard.

Fritz be jolly, Fritz be gay
Today is celery salad day

My mother sang her little tune, hoping the celery would perk him up. My father chuckled briefly.

You have no clue.

Yes, I do, more than you think, she replied gaily.

Adi never got cross, and that got on Fritz's nerves. As he silently spooned up his food, charging the air with unspoken tension, my mother simply left the room.

THE GLEANERS

It was gray, evening coming on early. November fog lay low across the harvested potato fields, mixing with smoke from the fires. Old roots and dried shrubs were piled up and burned. Cold crept along the ground. The white dust of the frost encircled branches and brittle leaves; spread itself across frozen puddles, over molehills, into hollows; lay in the air between the land and a pale sun.

In the distance, knots of people stood together around fires. Others moved along the potato furrows. They hauled sacks, bending deeply, fishing for the last potatoes, the overly small ones, those forgotten or left behind, those no one bothered to harvest. Collecting went on all day: bend over, stand up, bend over, stand up. They looked like crows pecking for seeds. They made their pilgrimage from the city, from the surrounding villages, into the surrounding fields. Mostly they were women of all ages, but children and old men were there, too. The women wore trousers beneath their skirts to keep warm; the men, boots or wooden shoes with thick socks, and old army jackets.

For us children from the farm, it was an adventure. We blew warm breath into our fists, hopping from one foot to the other, warming ourselves at the fire with the hungry people from the city. Potatoes rolled into the glow. We fished for them with sticks, poked around. The hungry held their red hands above the heat, chatted a little until the potatoes were done, then shared them.

In the evening, having picked the fields clean, they tied their sacks behind them on their bicycles and pedaled homeward. Or they pushed a cart, freighted with sacks of potatoes, a child perched on top with a skinny dog for company. One pulled in front, another pushed in back. So it went all the way home.

They came again at the end of the summer, after the harvest. Hungry figures from town visited the wheat fields. There were always some with only one leg or arm. They leaned their bicycles on one another, traversed the field in search of gleanings, made bouquets as if they were flowers. At the end of the day their harvest was painstakingly bundled up and strapped to the bikes, so it could be transformed into bread at home.

Sometimes they lingered. My mother, passing by in the carriage, stopped to chat with the women. She asked them where they came from, or how many mouths they had to feed, or she said: Do come around to our door when you're done. I'll give you an egg or two.

The gazes of the hungry children pierced through me, the well-fed child, like buckshot.

There, at the edge of a cornfield, grew the social framework for a new society.

Did you see her delicate features, those tender hands? my mother said. That one has seen better days.

From beneath the woman's apron peeked a ratty old dress. That, too, told a story of better days, of summer, of strolling through town, of coffee under the coffeehouse umbrella, of a fiancé's kiss at the door.

The gleaners. Naturally, they were forgotten by history, along with everything else, in the circus melee of the postwar years and the economic miracle that followed. Their newfound affluence slowly swallowed the old hunger. They did not want to be reminded. No one mentioned it anymore. Don't even think about it, push it away, make room for a new world.

·

In late autumn, during harvesttime, Dieter was dispatched into town with the tractor, wagon in tow. He was to fetch a group of young teenage girls from a girls' school, to help with the farmwork.

Thanks to the war, the girls had grown up very fast. Surviving many bombings had made them very bold, and despite the lost pleasures of their childhood, they had sustained their joie de vivre. Dieter glanced back furtively. It seemed to him the girls were wearing the latest fashions, especially compared with his shabby army outfit, so often mended by his mother. Lined up on two boards along the sides of the wagon, they sat and swung their legs, showing them freely, laughing about anything and nothing, embarrassing Dieter. And so they rattled along the road until they arrived at our potato fields.

The girls trudged along behind a plow, collecting potatoes in sacks. When the sacks were full, they were tipped into a cart. It started to rain. The girls sought shelter under the one available roof: the potato wagon. But the rain got through between the narrow planks, and after a short while, they were drenched. Their cheap dresses rode up above their knees, clinging to their thin bodies. Little rivulets of color ran down their legs.

All alone with what was now a silenced, freezing crew of girls, Dieter made a chivalrous decision. Take your seats, he told them, I am taking you home early.

Holding the spare sacks over their heads as tents, their short skirts pulled down over their knees, packed together, they rattled along the paths to the road toward town. All was quiet on the cart. No more giggling. They were once again just little girls who'd had to go to work far too early, who'd lost their childhood to a Führer, traded away their carefree liberty.

THE TAFELMEIERS

The farmyard spread out in a rectangle, with the farm buildings and stalls on three sides. Opposite our house lived the workers. A short way down the road stood the little house where the Tafelmeiers lived. Behind it was a perfect green piece of meadow, dotted with black molehills. There were always moles, lots of them.

Josef Tafelmeier was our carpenter, a tall, lean, muscular figure who smelled like pine sap and chewing tobacco. To make sure we children would not play with his dangerous tools, he looked up from his workbench with his earnest, inquisitive stare, a thin sickle of white appearing beneath his eyelids. His wife, Maria, helped out in our kitchen and in the chicken coop. Whatever time remained she spent in my mother's garden—or wherever she could spread her silly chatter.

Maria Tafelmeier, her robust figure wrapped in wide skirts, childless and ever driven by insatiable hunger for gossip, divided her world into two categories: Strangers and Us. Strangers were everyone outside her familiar order, hence incomprehensible, the rebellious forced laborers above all. With those people one had nothing, really nothing at all in common. They came from the eastern countries Hitler had conquered first. There were about twenty of them on the farm, from Hungary, Poland, Yugoslavia, Romania.

My parents belonged to her world of Us. Even though their actions were often hard to fathom, when it came down to it they were nonetheless Bavarians. The Osts were in the same place as Maria Tafelmeier, spoke a German comprehensible to her. We didn't sound suspicious, like those Prussians. We were not to be persecuted, gassed, or driven away.

Despite Maria's ingratiating servitude around Goldachhof, it was clear that she didn't fully approve of my mother. Frau Ost was too friendly, too compassionate. She didn't understand my mother's kindness, the fact that Mother didn't make much distinction between social classes. Maria Tafelmeier simply submitted to Frau and Herr Ost out of duty and proletarian humility.

FATHER'S GARDEN

Just behind the field where the Tafelmeiers' little house stood lay the moor. And farther to the east, saluted every morning by the first gold of daylight, stood the black shapes of our forest. My father, a passionate naturalist, loved his moor and his woods. Both had to be preserved and cared for. Throughout the cold months, the fires in our stoves were fed with the peat we harvested from our moor and the carefully planned cuttings from our woods.

On our Sunday walks we strolled in the greenish light, along a shadowy river toward the patch of forest. Trees clawed their way up the riverbank. Willow boughs stroked through the water. Delicate mosses padded the rail of a stone bridge. Now and then a bird plunged into its watery reflection. And there we arrived at my father's garden. The pines stood in rows of columns, like a military unit. Underneath, in their shadow, grew the untamed blackberry and raspberry patches.

On these walks my father loved to quiz us. He knew the Latin names of mosses and trees. He could look at animal scat and tell you everything that was going on in the forest simply by which beast it came from, where it was dropped, its consistency and form. From these facts he composed an entire forest history, gesturing this way and that with his cane, posing questions. Then he quizzed us about mushrooms. We had plenty of poisonous and edible ones: Toadstool? Champignon? Teubling? Chanterelle? To confuse us, he would point at the right mushroom, then at the wrong one. Then the subject proceeded to trees. Beech? Ash? Linden? Fir? Oak? Birch? His cane flew about, his eyes flashed with excitement. It was a game he played in earnest.

We would leave the woods and stroll in a wide circle into the moor to look at its ragtag assortment of animals. Billows of warm fog surrounded the garden apartments of batrachians, salamanders, and snakes—even poisonous ones, sometimes sunning themselves on mounds of peat, letting the heat of the sun drive their blood like a motor, only to slither away when human steps echoed across the yielding ground.

In the deep black swamp, storks eyed the water from reed grass ledges, rings breaking the sky as they fished for frogs. Dragonflies zigzagged the air. An owl dozed the day away in a hollowed tree trunk. Below, on both sides of our path, like onyx, quite still yet inviting, gathered the swamp water where the Moorschreck waited in its depths to suck us down, never to let go of us should we fall in. Indifferently, the black water swirled, the summer flowers bowed, the wind bent the willow. Oh, what horror stories the grownups told.

Grandfather's Extravagances

THEODOR WAS EIGHTY-FIVE when he became my grandfather and I his little Trixilein. Although he claimed he was already withering into his grave, his figure was still upright and youthful. A precisely cut, full beard surrounded his chin. Narrow, aquiline nose, blue eyes, high forehead. A sparse wreath of hair crowned the well-formed head. He invariably wore a suit with a vest. Theodor is a handsome chap, said my mother. She liked him very much.

One of Grandfather's incessant behavioral rhythms was his smoker's ritual. He probed the lower pockets of his jacket with his long, slender fingers—Ah, there it is, my tobacco—then drew out a pouch. Actually, it was a wooden toad, an antiquity from China, with a frog sitting on it as a lid. A wonderfully polished ivory pug hung from a cord as weight. The pipe nestled in his breast pocket. Now the pipe cleaner had to be found. He tapped around for it. Ah, 'course. There it is, next to the pipe, just where it belongs.

Grandfather kept a tobacco plot. The beds lay a good way off at the end of the vegetable garden, just before the fields began. He visited his crop every day. If it was raining he used a gigantic lawn umbrella, which one of the lads, Dieter or Georg, held above him like an imperial attendant. He had to inspect his plants, check them for aphids and any other creepy-crawlies. He loved that. It was a kind of duty, self-imposed, that gave important structure to the day: Grandfather, beneath the umbrella, or without it, as the weather decreed, between four and six o'clock.

No one likes your poison, no normal person, nagged my grandmother. Only you and the boys, who are much too young for it. Really! She would leave the room shaking her head, fussing with her thin arms, as if she had to wade through a tedious swarm of mosquitoes.

When you smoke you can think better, he would call after her with a grin. Plenus fumus studet libenter.

Grandfather was a contented snob who seldom expressed an opinion. Mostly, he smoked and read. Good morning all around, he'd say, greeting the assembled company, adding a vague gesture of his elegant hand as he strolled toward his armchair, his feet whispering along the floorboards. Then, glancing out the window into the sky: When the sky is scaled like a trout, it'll rain in twenty-four hours, no doubt. Always the same, tempora semper idem. He slowly took his seat, looked around the room, drew at his pipe, and fumbled about for his book, nodding lovingly in my direction: Now I must read and you must play, he said softly.

And that was it for the morning. He opened his book and sank into it. The carryings-on around him disturbed him no more than the fluttering of moths in a cupboard. What moved him slumbered between the pages. When something happened, when a dogfight carried into the room, red and loud, he merely registered it: lifted his watery gaze, squinted into the situation, drew at his pipe, blew a smoke ring, then another, put his pipe back in his pocket. His eyes made the rounds—rested languidly on the exhausted fur ball, lingered on some object, a person, perhaps—then he sank his head back into his book and read further. In Grandfather's presence the course of all activities slowed down. His day dozed along, sleepy, like the dogs that gave themselves over to dog dreams, lulled by the heat near the oven. When it grew dark and he could no longer see, he resurfaced from his book in slow motion: How'd the time slip away yet again?

Perhaps he despised the world. Disenchantment, or repeated confirmation of his belief that nothing really changes, only time itself, circumstances and locations. That generally everything repeats itself, like a hamster in his wheel, roundandroundandround. No, he never felt distressed. Bored is more like it, cured of curiosity. In his history books whole peoples hastened toward their fate. The repetitious game of world affairs could not impress him. This last war too he filed away with the other senseless slaughters. His utterances resounded with Buddhist equanimity; rereading history was his daily meditation.

Grandfather and my father were highly educated, each in his area; but otherwise, except for their profiles, one could find nothing in common between them. For both, love and tenderness existed only in letters and literature, or on the heroic scale: love of nature, love of fatherland, love of music. Fritz called his father by his first name, Theodor. This did not mean they were bohemians, nor modern—far from it. It was unusual, strange, in this kind of family, which made it all the more striking, for they were not close; rather, divided by a tender inability. Only sometimes, perhaps when Fritz had mislaid his facts, did he ask his father: Heh, Theodor, when exactly was Napoleon's march on Russia? The answer shot back as if from a pistol. Fritz's response: That's right, just as I thought.

And to me? This grandfather was a great father. Later I had no regret at having known only this side of him, no longing to have known him some time in his youth, nor under other circumstances. He belonged to my postwar period, was a symbol. He was isolated from the goings-on on the farm, from the doings of the group chance had thrown together in the house. He and I shared many great events where we stood unnoticed in the thick of things, like the time when the horse had to be shot because it had broken its leg, and we both saw behind the barn the blood pudding that had pressed the gigantic cadaver into a form; the horseflies in their glimmering enamel could not decide where to begin their feast, and I was not to be pulled away.

Practical matters were foreign to my grandfather; he couldn't care less. Such unconcern was part of his innocence. Once, drenched with the downpour of an April storm, we looked over from the bridge at the electricity shed into the foam of the waterfall in which one of my shoes danced and vainly struggled to get loose. As I tossed in the other one, Grandfather nodded in agreement. You can't do anything with just one, anyway.

To tempt him from his book, I fiddled with his page, traced the veins on his hand, pinched a bit of skin between thumb and forefinger, tugged at it, let go, until he finally noticed me.

Yes, sure. He surfaced from his book.

They called Alexander "The Great." Know why?

I gestured upward.

Nah, nah! he shook his head. 'Cause he was a Personality. King of Macedonia, a pupil of Aristotle. A historic figure, not just a number. Superb! Three, Three, Three, at Issus Agony. That's where he beat Darius.

Now I had his attention.

Sing something for me, I begged, and ran my finger along the stripes of his vest. He smiled and cleared his throat. In a wobbly voice he sang one of his soldier songs, the ballad of a youth torn from life by an enemy bullet.

Again! I cried when the bloodthirsty tale was at an end. He patiently sang it one more time, skipping a verse, for by now he wanted to get back to his book.

My grandmother appeared, angrily shaking her head.

You and your eternal singing. The child doesn't understand a word.

Grandfather and I gave one another a look.

I understand everything, I said.

She understands perfectly well, Grandfather said.

With the rustling of her dress, Grandmother's overbearing character had barged its way into the room. There she stood, an exclamation mark: peaked, thin, strict, in a black silk dress. A high collar surrounded her wrinkled throat, a brook of white lace crashed over her breast. Her wardrobe had not kept up with fashion; everything was as it had been long ago, when she was young, frozen at the fin de siècle. It was the same with her ideas and strict rules.

There was laughter behind her back; everyone knew. You could hardly still call it a secret. Out of prudery—many things were passed over in silence in those days—there was not much talk in the house about Grandmother's past, nor Grandfather's. Too scandalous. Grandmother had been married once before, before her marriage to Theodor. An elderly cheese manufacturer had asked for her hand, and although she was still very young, she quickly said yes. Simply felt like being the richest woman in Kempten. People called her Käse Marie, Cheese

Marie. But soon her spouse was confined to bed. Marie-Louise grew bored: sick old husband, no child. Then somehow a good-looking, well-fixed history student drifted in and rented part of the big old house for his stay at the town's university. She must have bewitched him quickly, for although he was quiet and studious, he succumbed to the seductive arts of Marie-Louise.

Suddenly she was pregnant, and even before gossip could confirm all suspicions, the husband died. Grandfather Theodor married the pregnant Cheese Marie, and she promptly gave birth to twins. How she tempted him into her arms remained a mystery, although she supposedly had possessed a ravishing charm—she must have been very pretty.

But that was all too long ago. One could no longer discern how she had once looked. Naturally, not only time but also her character was at fault here. As if she had bitten into a lemon, her facial expression scrunched up in the middle. Thick, dark eyebrows lay too heavily above the piercing blue eyes. She had something of a bird of prey about her. Her eyes moved restlessly until they caught something, then slipped themselves free right away to find the next victim. Her pursed little mouth cannot have been soft and curvaceous, either. In long-ago photos everything was too small, the faces tiny, retouched in generally unsuccessful color. Well, she has a lovely nose, and had superb skin, said Adi, to add an upbeat note.

After both grandparents died, my parents stopped being embarrassed about the double affair of Cheese Marie and the twins' less than immaculate conception, of Grandfather's royal emergence from the forests and meadows. Now there was talk. One was allowed to know about their past, roll one's eyes, raise one's eyebrows, put on modern airs, laugh and wink. My parents too had emancipated themselves from their moral corset.

•

Ah, childhood winters. They were so cold. Ice flowers bloomed on the windows. With my warm fingers I sketched streets into the panes. The dogs came back into the house with ice knots on their paws. My feet were always cold in their thin leather boots. I constantly had a runny nose.

One day snow had been falling since morning, through the day and into the approaching night. High snowdrifts were piled up along the sides of the road. Protected from the wind, the street blended seamlessly into the field; the icy surface was smooth. All afternoon long we children built tunnels and caves. The dogs dug along with us, sniffing for mice. It got dark early; by five o'clock the sun had already disappeared into the folds of milky sky. We were freezing. Our gloves were wet from digging in the snow hills, the cold had chewed its way through our shabby shoes. Snot froze from nose to lip. We did as Uli had taught me: hold one nostril shut, exhale powerfully through the other. In the heat of play we never noticed the cold until it was almost dark.

So white, the snow. Give me your hand. There are the trees along the avenue, the kitchen light. Ah, the warmth by the stove, in the room.

My father stood at the door as we scraped our shoes and shook off the snow. He gazed into the turbulent sky, checked the thermometer at the window, whistled for the dog.

There you are! Come on, leave the cat alone. Now come in, children, it's damned cold. Well, tomorrow we will be completely snowed in. Then, almost as an afterthought: Has anyone seen Grandfather? He scanned the yard beyond us, worry in his voice.

The news traveled through the house like wildfire. Grandfather was nowhere to be found. Where on earth can he be? His days were all of a piece. Only brief walks punctuated the routine of sleeping, eating, reading. Surely he won't be in the attic—what for? No, and not in the stables, either. Why should he? Nor in the cow stalls, where it smells of fresh milk. Doesn't interest him. Where in God's name is Grandfather? When was he last seen? Who spoke with him last? What did he say? His coat too no longer hung on its hook. His boots were gone. Oh, my God, bawled Grandmother. The icy night, the dreadful storm. Is he out of his mind?

My father pounded the gavel for a meeting.

We must search outdoors, there is not a second to lose. Dress warmly! Take torches! And the dogs, too!

A few more workers were summoned to help. Divided up into small groups, they set out in every direction. Leaned against the storm. Probed with their eyes and feet into the formless raging. He could have gone to the four carp ponds, or perhaps just to the chicken coop. Or to the orchard. Or he lost his way and wandered off toward the moor.

Alexandra, Peter, and I stayed inside in the warmth. I rolled into the empty dog burrow under the tiled stove. I always crept in there in moments of despair. Outside, the storm howled and rattled. Inside, my grandmother sighed, her brow furrowed in the middle. She stared out the window into the chaos.

Beatrix, dear, give me your hand. She bent over and took my warm little hands into her cold ones. Now everything was permitted. I was even allowed to be there under the stove.

If only my Theodor does not leave me, not leave me, not leave me, lamented Grandmother.

I was still. Peter and Alexandra sat dejectedly in their chairs.

The vehement storm rattled and shook the bull's-eye pane in its round lead frame. Suddenly stillness, a pause for breath, then the storm roared away again, sprinted around the corner of the house, raced around the chimney, caught in the door frame. Thick, round fabric sausages filled with sawdust lay between the double windows as insulation. But the storm forced its way through the finest fissures and smallest cracks, powdering everything sugary white.

Oh, oh, oh, oh, oh, lamented my grandmother, and tried to peer outside through the white mass. Noble soul, noble soul, she whispered, where are you, Theodor?

Outside, white on white, the courtyard was gigantic, the house across the way dissolved. Somewhere a light hung, with two others farther below. The outline of the linden tree, then a white knife cut between them.

My God, we survived the war, whimpered Grandmother, the air raids!

Suddenly there it was. At first quite delicately, through the violent ballet of the storm, we heard the dogs return, howling and barking, then voices. I scurried from my cave, and we all arrived simultaneously at the door. They pressed through from the vestibule, bringing with them the cold and a gust of snow. The dogs, my mother, my father, two or three people carried Grandfather, pushed him on into the warm and laid him down on the bench by the stove.

Ahhh, he grunted, and looked confusedly about him.

Just imagine, under a snowbank, snowed in! At the edge, right behind the barn, on the way to the ponds.

My grandfather, peeled out of his frozen coat, lay slender and still. But Grandmother, recovered from her fright, mutinied, even as she examined his feet for frostbite.

Theodor! How could you...?

She tugged irritably at his shoelace. Love, fear, reproach, everything bundled up into one.

To me he looked like a troll: red cheeks and a satisfied little grin on his face. His beard melted and dribbled on his chest. He cared little about all the hubbub, folded his hands over his stomach and gazed wide-eyed within himself. He had no wish to talk, nor to justify himself. He simply said nothing to all this questioning, closed his eyes, pretended to sleep, kept it all to himself, his secret.

My father bent over him and touched his arm.

How are you, Theodor? How do you feel?

No answer, just a sleepy rumbling and a feeble dismissive gesture.

Rag-and-bone man, thought the old man. Under my feet, like plowing, and so tired. The fur flaps whacked his face. Centaur of Ixion. Just not the intellect. As long as you can manage, don't do it. Animus caelestis, because of the blue. Ahh.

He veered from the path, on past the bush, after a white hare, and sat down.

I sat so close to my grandfather I could feel his body, and laid my hand on his, normally so warm. I thought about where he had come in from. He had headed out into the white adventure with an idea, knowing what he wanted. I have a good idea, he always said. When he grew tired, he sat down and reflected. Sank into the soft white pillow, just as I always did, letting myself fall into the snow.

In the distance appeared a figure in a long coat with heavy boots, coming nearer and nearer. Grandfather squinted. When the two of them were practically touching, he recognized the soldier. He was the friend from the song, the one hit by the bullet, the one who collapses in battle. The sad story. The soldier recognized my grandfather. They embraced. The soldier had not died after all, the way the song says. No, a beautiful woman had bestowed new life upon him with a kiss.

They found Grandfather under the snow tower and robbed him of the ending to his story. The adventure was over. They shook him, freed him from the snow that had wrapped and cradled him like a protective house, pulled a fine fur over him to repel the cold, gestured to him, tempted him gently into another world. Freezing, the white death. That'd be grand, he had often said to me. That would be my favorite. I don't want to outlive my wits. Anything, just not idiocy.

Later on, when I told him my story, he said: Yes, yes, you're right. I was hoping the rag-and-bone man would fetch me, but it was your grandmother Marie-Louise. She wouldn't let me go. Got nervous. He gazed about in his customary manner—impartial, one might say—at me, the dog, the lines of his book, a fly, a cat mirrored in the window. Death, and life, closely intertwined.

Screaming from on High

THE MANOR HAD NO BASEMENT. The watery moor pressed up from beneath. So the house rested on logs, like the houses in Venice, and there was no underground refuge.

In the last month of war, when the howling of sirens from the city sliced through the day like a knife, the farm went into electric overdrive. Everyone left the sheds and stalls where they were busy, left whatever was in hand, swallowed back any half-uttered sentence, and ran out into nature, away from the buildings.

We children ran under the little stone bridge at the end of the tree-lined avenue. Resi König, too, with her brood and some of the women who worked in the garden, sweating and out of breath, made a mad dash down to the watery hideaway. There we all stood close together on stones, pressed against the moist walls, and waited. The water rats stared from the water with their black button eyes, ran zigzag, panicked, dove, and swam off.

And here it came. It roared over our heads like artificial thunder onstage. Mission of terror. The air vibrated, the stream trembled. The curious rats resurfaced; confused by the terrible noise, they sought refuge on a rock, near a shoe. The big boys shouted deafeningly against the brutal howling above them. Powerless, terrified, yet compelled to do something about the situation, Xaver, the oldest of the König brood, dropped a stone onto a rat. Bull's-eye! The rat tilted forward, went into spasms, and the flowing water tugged it off. Xaver hurled himself in behind it, grabbed it by its thin tail, and heaved it up. Red dripped from its open mouth.

Papa König stuck his head under the bridge at the very moment Xaver was dangling the dead rat in his sister's face. Roserl pressed herself against the moist tunnel wall, covered her eyes with one hand, and screamed. With a practiced grip, Luggi König wrenched Xaver aside and punched him in the face.

You get the real thrashin' later, he said. He took his little girl onto his arm and shuffled off, up the riverbank.

The whole scene rocketed by in a single gasp. Xaver held back his tears, still holding the tail of the rat.

After the all-clear that carried from the city of Munich, we made our way out of the moist dome. The women looked up at the sky. Had the tumult left any traces, had it imprinted a portent on the clouds? Peacocks sat on the gate. Doves swung down from their tower onto the parked wagons and pecked at scattered seeds. Workmen lounged around in the courtyard, leaned beneath the linden tree, smoking, letting off steam through their lungs. Yiiiii, Yiiiii, Yiiiiii, Wooom! They drew up the accounts on the disaster that had come crashing in upon greater Munich. Looked to the southwest to get a fix on the billows of smoke.

Oh, man, there'll be nuthin' left of the Frauenkirche.

Nah, they done blew that one to hell day 'fore yesterday.

Luggi König stood off to the side, wide-legged, observing. He had his own ideas. He never took cover, always remained wherever he happened to be. Mostly on his tractor. In the middle of the courtyard.

Fritz shook his head in exasperation: Luggi, you idiot, hit the deck. They'll mow you down!

But Luggi wanted to irritate the enemy, wanted to show he was fearless. He played the hero. His shirt was open down to the fourth button no matter what the weather. Nestled in the red hair on his chest was a medal of the Virgin Mary.

Ain't you freezin'? he was often asked.

Nah, he grinned.

He fished for a little white snuff bottle, tipped a pinch of black powder on the back of his hand between thumb and forefinger, held it to one nostril, snorted it back. A loud sneeze followed: Luggi's gloss on the art of conversation. He passed the bottle around and with an encouraging nod allowed the others to participate in his nasal intoxication. When they had all sneezed, one after the other, Luggi stuck the bottle back in his pocket, lifted his shoulder up to his nose, rubbed first his right and then his left nostril on it, and set off, satisfied, grinning.

Anita's Love

ONE DAY MY FATHER's horse-trading gypsy friend, Buchs, appeared with a new horse, a gift for Anita's birthday. It peered out from behind the covered wagon, which it had been obediently following.

In front of the house, my mother sat on a bench in the sun with the young lads, Georg, Dieter, and Uli, waiting for the spectacle to unfold. When the horse discovered the waiting group, it raced away with a start, leaping and bucking, into the middle of the courtyard. Umer ran and grabbed it by the halter.

Terrified of horses, I ran for cover, toward the house, up the stairs. This way I could save myself with just one quick leap through the door.

Anita jumped up and down with excitement. Buchs grinned. My father smirked, laughing, his legs set wide apart, hands in his lederhosen pockets. He got a kick out of the wild creature and was the first to mount it, courageous, just to show everyone. After a few seconds it reared up and threw him off.

Uli, his long legs cockily stretched out, could not hold back a snicker.

Before the war he and my father had often quarreled at the top of their lungs. After the Hitler Youth, Uli was determined to join the SS.

They've shit in your brain, you idiot! Brainwashing! shouted my father, threatening that he would forbid him ever again to cross the threshold if it came to that. That he could guarantee.

Now Uli was very glad he had obeyed his father. A little bored, he lounged with Georg and Dieter on the bench, smoking roll-ups. The sun shimmered in his dark mane. His arm, shot through with shrapnel, hung in a sling like a broken bough.

My mother, too, could not resist a laugh at my father's comeuppance, though she half-hid it behind her hand. Dieter and Georg grinned. Uli went over to clean the dust off Father's jacket.

What a beast, said Father breathlessly, admiration in his voice. Anita, you've got your work cut out for you.

Before too long Anita had tamed her Bella. For weeks she had carefully approached the wild thing in its stall, with an apple or a piece of bread on her flat, outstretched hand. Bella munched, rolled her big eyes, snorted distrustfully through her dilated nostrils. Anita conversed with Bella. If Bella stepped forward, she went backward. Her voice was always close to the horse's ear, whispering intimately. I sat on the feed trough in safety and watched mutely. I had to be quiet or she would chase me off. When Bella permitted herself to be touched, even combed with the brush, she was rewarded with another piece of apple or a handful of oats. So it went until they were ready to head outside and Bella, on a training line, grew more obedient and companionable by the day.

Then came mounting, likewise rewarded with apple and bread. Finally Anita sat in the saddle. Father held the long line. Right turn: good Bella; left turn: good Bella. Mount, dismount, reward. Then without the line, at a trot, at a gallop. Then out through the courtyard gate, down the avenue, off across the fields.

Anita combed Bella's coat and cleaned her hooves with a stick. She cared for her animal like a stable boy, her long dark braids bound together in back, apron at her waist. This was serious business for her. She had got her first pony when she was little, three or four years old. Now she was sixteen and had outgrown her second horse. Bella was the third. Anita was a little heavyset, already almost a woman, with a well-proportioned oval face and large, rather sad brown eyes; her nose lightly curved like my mother's. If she had had her way she would have been sleeping in the stall. That was pushing it too far!

I also had a passion, a little piglet I wanted to take to my down bed with me; I got as far as hiding it beneath the bed frame, but it squealed too loudly and my

mother found it. Around our house there were not too many rules to break, but this was out of the question.

Since Anita spent her time with her horse instead of romping around with the other children, she drew close to the grownups. She had a direct line to my father, who loved animals, his horses above all.

I was still too young to go to school. I stayed behind with Grandfather as the troop of children headed off on foot each morning, satchels on their backs, a sponge for wiping the blackboard tumbling at each of their sides in the open air. Anita was not in the same age group as any of the farm girls, and because she rode, she did not fit in with anyone at all. She looked down from her horse, her saddlebag with her schoolbooks behind her; looked out across the courtyard, across the bridge into the avenue. The children gaped up at her.

Every day, when the troop had to walk the four kilometers from the farm to school, Anita sat high above on her Bella. This was a provocation. So the older boys cobbled together a conspiracy. Anita was to be brought down from her high horse; indeed, tumbled off it.

They hid behind the avenue trees in the embankment undergrowth. They drew a string across the avenue. When Anita approached, they planned to pull it up, draw it taut, trip the horse and send her flying through the air. They painted themselves a malicious and boastful picture of what would happen. Their revenge for her snobbery.

The preparations complete, they lurked in the bushes, awaiting the right moment. But Anita noticed them at the last minute, saw the rustling in the bushes, and became suspicious. She tore Bella aside, down the embankment, and galloped away across the field, her heart pounding. The boys shouted and whistled.

As luck would have it, this was the cue for one of the wagons that pulled into Ismanning at random intervals during harvesttime, pulled by a tractor or two workhorses, piled high with a pyramid of cabbages. The driver refused to stop, but the brigands hopped on in back nonetheless, slipping beside the round cabbage heads and holding on to the side planks.

Anita came bawling to tell my mother about the boys. But there was always some drama going on, and no one particularly cared about children.

Louts will be louts, said my father; he cursed them but did not really want to get involved. The farm children were forever being beaten anyway. The smallest incidents sent their fathers into violent rages. The business with the horse was not really so bad, and it ended well, my father said, comforting Anita. He wanted to spare himself a big blowup until there was a real reason for it.

•

In those last war months no one could see where it would all end. A fine net of fear lay across the deceptive stillness on the farm. The hacking, scraping, stomping of hooves, the creaking of wagon wheels, the sputtering motor of the tractor: they were all familiar. These sounds accompanied the rural stillness unperceived. The occasional sawing and knocking from the carpenters' shop was also silent in its familiarity and lost itself in the haze, along with sudden screams and cursing.

But then unannounced the nemesis came shrieking in from above, at breakneck speed, with a loud, piercing screech, threatening, unfamiliar and yet immediately recognizable, out of the distance at first: the howling of the sirens. The shrill tone raced across the fields, across the nearby forest, across the courtyard, into the house. And there it was. Fear.

Sometimes the bombers raced toward the city, sometimes they were after the radio station near the estate. Or the city water reservoir. Terror had wormed its way in like a cancer. If a bomb hit the dam, the farm and its flat surroundings would sink beneath an epic flood.

Anita was riding home from school. Suddenly the air around her swirled on all sides with the howling of sirens. It could be low-flying bombers again, and they could be firing simply because something was moving. It happened. One was never certain.

Anita leaped from her horse. Already spooked by the noise, Bella galloped off. Anita ran down the embankment and threw herself to the ground between the rows of potatoes and cabbages. There she waited, breathless, until the insane racket above the fields ebbed away.

Later, when the ruckus was over and all was quiet again, when their firepower had been concentrated on the city, one caught one's breath, breathed a sigh of relief, saw a butterfly, noticed a cat; those beneath the bridge scrambled up again, others climbed down from trees, ran back across the meadow, crept out from behind the bee house. Everyone gathered, and there it was, the clip-clop of Bella's hooves drawing nearer, until she arrived at the patch of grass at the farm gate and started grazing.

Then Anita, too, slowly came trudging up the avenue, exhausted, her jacket encrusted with dirt, her braids untied, the ribbon lost, her brown eyes searching about. Ahhhh, a flash of recognition, happy and reassured. There she was, her Bella. She kissed her on the nostrils, heartily slapped and stroked her. Passing me, she went through the gate, her hand on the horse's back, across to the stable. She seemed a little sad.

She doesn't like me, I thought. How long was she lying in the ditch? She's dirty. Was she caught in the drizzle? Or did a tree protect her this time? Did she scrutinize the soil, observe a centipede? Had she already been at the brook?

I did not know. She never caressed me, never took my hand. Never anything but the horse, the horse. The giant, unpredictable beast—her she loved, with her she spoke. Stinging tears welled up behind my lids, and I blinked into the dark tongue of shade to hide the lump in my throat.

One could say we sisters were strangers our whole lives long. In childhood it was a horse. Later half the globe lay between us.

More on the Königs

SEVEN KÖNIG CHILDREN. Xaver, the oldest. Then came Rita and Xeni, li'l Lenerl, li'l Roserl, Maxi, Josef. Rita and Xeni were older than the twins, Roserl and Lenerl. Josef, the youngest, was known as Pepperl. Xeni was cross-eyed, with one eye fixated on the base of her nose. After the war she finally got glasses that conditioned away her zany look.

The König brood. A red-haired, freckled, pale bunch. Trousers with patches on the seats. Pullovers with holes big enough for elbows to poke through. Dirty necks, earwax spilling out, shredded skirts, undies hanging between scabbed knees. They brawled and whacked one another over the head with their satchels. Only Lenerl and Roserl could read properly. Rita was going to be a hairdresser. Don't need to read nuthin'. She'll learn quick enough how ya twist a curling iron!

Mother König had no authority. She stood powerless amid the tornado of their antics and quarrels. They threw stones at beer bottles, shouting when the glass sprayed out; aimed their slingshots at birds, taking to their heels when a grownup showed up. If a brawl started, everyone looked on, like at a boxing match. Oh dear, oh dear, Mother König whined, I'm gonna tell Daddy. But by the time Luggi got back from the fields it was all forgotten, the bloody nose had dried, the blue horn on the forehead was old news.

In my memory the König children multiply into an entire classroom. When Father Luggi blew his stack, he just pounded right in on them. Then we would hear their screaming across the street, up into our house. Father König called thrashing the boys a prophylactic measure. But the storm quickly died down. His anger flew away and he was sorry about it. Grinning helplessly, he wanted to make some sort of amends, so he pampered and doted on the girls.

That place has turned into a monkey cage again. The poor woman, said my mother, and sent Aunt Julia and Justa to the König house for a thorough cleaning. They tried to bring a little discipline to the ragtag bunch, and to support poor Resi as a women's team.

The little König house had three rooms. The bedroom was crammed with small beds where the children all lay jumbled on top of one another and a large bed against the center wall where Resi König slept with her husband and always with one of the babes who crawled in with them.

The next room was stuffed with junk: mousetraps, bicycles without wheels, mountains of clothes, shoes, all kinds of stuff that people donated to them when they did not know what else to do with it. Resi gave a friendly grin, ceremoniously accepting the deliveries, but most of it would end up in useless heaps, gathering dust in corners.

Two wondrous sofas inhabited the third room, both for sitting and as impromptu armoires. Early in the morning, when the order came for the children to get dressed, the hunt was on. Articles of clothing were whipped out from big holes in the seats. That belongs to me, screamed one of the children. No, it's mine, bawled another, prying a flowered shred of skirt from one slit. This brought something striped into view. Out with it. But that's mine! They shoved and punched one another, tore out one another's hair. Pieces of clothing flew through the room, found an owner, or not. When all parties had gotten their hands on something, the rest was stuffed back into the cushion slits, the springs recompressed, a towel laid across the top. Now one could sit down again on the sofa-armoires.

This room also served as kitchen. Resi sometimes warmed milk at the stove or brewed grain coffee. That was about it. Resi couldn't cook. The little ones clung to her breast as long as possible, the rest ate sandwiches. Luggi sat at the table, his legs apart, before him a gray stein of beer. He would meditatively take a deep draft, poke his knife alternately into a piece of bacon here, a piece of blood sausage there, tear a corner off a loaf of bread, then take another draft. This was followed by a satisfied belch. Sometimes he would make a little fire behind the house, squat, spear a trout on a stick, and watch it sizzle. He sat on a stone like a philosopher, mutely turning the fish between the forks of a branch above the fire and staring into emptiness. When a thought was done, he spat into the glow.

Resi was sweet and always friendly, but she never fraternized with our female workers. They looked down at her because she did not work, just stood around all the time amidst her brood. In the farm-worker pecking order Resi was on the lowest rung of the ladder. Cain't even handle them brats, they gossiped. Shoulda thoughta that earlier. Now she's got the whole lot of 'em. They said it out loud. Resi heard it or not, gave a friendly grin, sat on the bench in front of her house in the sun, in the midst of the roughhousing little pack, herself a child among her children, above all, an uncategorizable individualist. And sometimes, when the sun shone pleasantly and some pleasant apparition crossed her mind, she stuck a feather or flower through her unruly reddish bun like an arrow.

When Resi could not find anything more to eat, was broke, payday still far off, her head appeared in the door of Olga's kitchen.

So what's cookin' t'day? she probed with a grin. Some of her hungry brats peeped from behind her skirts.

Olga already knew the story. Resi was in trouble again.

Sit, she ordered.

Resi nudged one of the children and motioned with her chin toward the door they had just slipped through. Immediately the child turned and raced outside. Five minutes later the whole brood pushed its way in.

Olga ladled from the big pot, slid a loaf of bread across the table, a stick of country butter next to it. Licking their lips, smacking and slurping, they hurled themselves upon their booty. Resi grinned thankfully.

●

On the estate one had to be completely self-reliant. There were no fast cars one could use to go fetch something, only the horse-drawn carriages. Medicines were poured together in kitchens, brewed, boiled, recipes compared, for animals as well as humans. There was nothing to buy anyway, only to get. Via detours. From neighbors. In exchanges with friends. Someone mentioned something one remembered later on. A medicine for the stomach, baldrian, also effective for headache, for rubbing in once heated up. For sore throat, linseed wrappings. Cat hair for rheumatism, and, naturally, good old chamomile, gathered in summer.

Once Lenerl König stuck her arm into a threshing machine. A dreadfully bloody something hung at her side where the arm had just been. Shock imprinted astonishment on the small, pale face. Cries for help. Where on earth was Mother König?

Mummy, Mummy, I screamed, Lenerl has no arm anymore.

Everyone was already converging at the scene. Someone carried Lenerl into our house. Silent tears ran down her dirt-smeared face.

The entire König brood congregated in the den under the horned stags. Lenerl lay on the bench. Blood everywhere, on her dress, on Georg's shirt—he had carried her. It dribbled onto the floor. Quickly Olga threw chamomile into the boiling water that constantly bubbled in the cistern of the stove, next to the glowing heat of the oven. My mother daubed a cloth with chamomile, as hot as possible, on Lenerl's arm. It indeed stopped the bleeding. Then she poured some red iodine on the wound. Stillness had fallen on the room, except for the busy rescue of the child, the ripping of linen for bandages, and the consoling whisper of my mother. Lenerl whimpered and Mother König stared helplessly at her child.

The shredded arm was firmly bound against Lenerl's slender body, and she was placed in a rucksack with two holes cut for her legs, its top drawn closed at her throat. Georg swung the sack over his shoulders, jumped onto an old bicycle, and raced off. It was five kilometers to the nearest doctor. The bicycle was the quickest and surest way to get help. The sidecar motorcycle must not yet have been in the picture, or perhaps there was no gasoline, or no tires or…who knows?

Lenerl's wound healed, but a large scar remained, with her upper arm a little thinner. Never again would she do a handstand or cartwheels. Lenerl became more reserved and kept her distance from the children's constant scuffles. Mother König's darling, she clung to her skirts and always stayed behind her twin, Roserl. In the summer, when arms went uncovered, it was easy now to distinguish the two.

HAPPY DAY

Luggi König. Come payday, long awaited, he washed and shaved, put on his Sunday best, and climbed onto his bike.

Has Luggi gone to the city again? my mother inquired.

Resi nodded and smiled, looked down at the ground, past my mother, into the sky, said nothing.

Luggi had gone off to get loaded. Generally he would be out of sight for two days. By then Resi would grow uneasy and could no longer stay in the house. Then one would see her standing on the bridge, even in the cold and rain, with her youngest on her arm, keeping an anxious lookout for him.

Resi leaned against the stone wall and gazed down the tree-lined avenue as if she wanted to hypnotize the dust.

She's got nuthin' to do—like it's Sunday, the farm women remarked venomously. Ah, Luggi is off the leash again.

Resi stared and stared in the direction where he had vanished. That is where he would have to reappear. He had to, always had. And truly, as if conjured forth by magic powers, he appeared, quite far in the distance, at first no more than a dot, swaying back and forth on his bicycle: the rascal, the beloved. Finally.

When he had almost reached Resi, a shy grin flitted across her face and she gave herself a little heave off the railing.

He slowed down. Wobbling, he brought the bike to a stop and climbed off, grinning, unsteady on his feet—his legs were not entirely willing—handed the bicycle over to her, took the baby from her arm, and cuddled it. Thus he maneuvered himself back into normal family life.

Resi held the bike quite firmly. Always at a loss for words, now she had none.

The scene quickly livened up. The other children were swarming around their father, tugging and tearing at his rumpled jacket. Their dirty hands, in search of a treat, dipped into his pockets. He good-naturedly patted his litter, like a beast of prey home from the hunt, sniffing, licking all of them and then conjuring forth his booty, happy to be back among them. Luggi König was home again.

Thank God. The Lord must love drinkers, said my father.

The children, large and small, sat on the stoop, licked lollipops, blew on kazoos, and burst balloons. The twins wore new little red caps over their tousled hair. Later they wore their caps to school on a rainy day. Little red rivulets ran down their faces, and reddish traces stuck to their hairlines long afterward, commemorating a happy day.

Coffee and Elegance

THE SIMPLEST THINGS KEEP US ALIVE. Love would be quite simple. But love always wants to be nourished by something.

Looking out from the kitchen window, behind the house, through the trees, past the brook that slipped through the garden like a snake, one saw foxglove growing, and knapweed, rows of roses, lilies, larkspur, everything my mother had dreamed together and squirreled away, also her beloved rock garden. Farther on, embroidered into that colorful rug, stood a little house overgrown with ivy, where the crippled chief cattleman Beni lived with his wife; and farther still, in the field, stood rows of fruit trees, and my swing, right next to Grandfather's tobacco garden. It was a paradise. An autarky, like a rain forest. A living order ruled the chaos. Sunflower oil from sunflowers, pressed in an ancient press that looked like an instrument of torture. Carp and trout swam in the waters. The river generated electricity. Bees. The usual fruit. All sorts of berry patches. From the fields, corn, potatoes, cabbage, milk, animals for slaughter.

The sounds of the farm. A stillness within which everything could be clearly differentiated: horses' whinnying, Pluto's barking, the cry of a bird of prey, frogs croaking from the ponds, chickens cackling, workers cursing, the wheels of a carriage on the gravel. In the house all the steps creaked. There was lots of tittle-tattle, novelties lasted only minutes. There were loads of bugs to coexist with, moth-eaten woolen suits and sweaters to live with. Malice and benevolence side by side.

At night, while we all slept, the pine martin went about his business up among the beams. Hedgehog families drank milk from the cat bowl. Once it hailed so incredibly hard—hailstones as big as eggs, ripping apart the joints in the wood of the spring vegetable beds—that the stream in the garden became a river and carried off the tomato vines and all the other vegetables. And sometimes there was fresh red beet juice to drink, squeezed from the same torture instrument as the sunflower oil. When I looked across the farm the full moon hung there only for us, laid his shadows like blue skirts about the farm implements and trees.

Then someone observed a shadowy figure crossing the yard—and the whispering began again, grinning gossip. I was too small, but I caught wind of all these dramas—everything. I saw Justa bawling in the kitchen, and I knew it had to do with her love life.

We were always waving farewell after someone who left his story behind on our landlocked island. Do you still remember when V. was here and told stories about Africa, and came back in the end after all, even though they were supposedly Jewish? Well, what about G. with all her excuses? You will never convince me she was just a civilian.

The afternoons revolved around coffee, often with delicious cake. My grandmother was not the only addict. My mother certainly was, too.

Behind the house, out where the gardens spread forth, where a bridge led across the little brook tumbling through like gossip coursing through society, stood a birch pergola. A group gathered in the open air around a long table, with benches extending on three sides. On the fourth a rose entwined itself up and around, down onto the path. Fragrant shadows bent across the gravel. Perhaps it was Sunday. Or a Catholic holiday. Or the June birthday of my father. Or just a visit.

Bird droppings were scratched from the table, white lace laid across it, topped off with the floral Meissen and baked delicacies from Olga's kitchen. Marmalade spreads on platters. Sweet odor. Bees humming.

My favorite was the poppy roll with the crispy black seeds. When Grandfather ate a piece, Grandmother handed him a toothpick.

Clean your teeth, she commanded. That is just dreadful, what a horrible sight, those black seeds! she ranted.

Politely he accepted the little stick, parked it in a corner of his mouth, and chomped on it. Just as you wish, Marie-Louise. Politely he made fun of her.

Marie-Louise wore her hair "undulated," as she called it, perfectly lacquered, with a place for every strand. It was singed yellow in places.

Mother, you set your curling iron too high. I smelled it, my father mocked.

Ah, what do you know? she replied, annoyed that it had happened again. But now she was in a good mood; the coffee was her invitation. Gesturing with the forgotten napkins, she hastened across the bridge. How many of us are there? Fourteen, and one half. The half is you, Beatrix. She had permitted herself a joke, completely forgetting Alexandra, who sat there next to her mother.

For no discernible reason poor Alexandra had been banished to a dark corner of Grandmother's psyche. Like Justa, she was a lightning rod for Grandmother's frustrations. Whether she sensed their weaknesses, or smelled their fear, no one knew; but Grandmother often vented her anger on these two innocent members of the household.

The spoiled brat! one could hear her spitting as she pinched the child's arm in passing.

Alexandra was terribly afraid that her mother would die before they had a chance to make their getaway. Away into a life better than this one in the country. A city life I had no clue about. Back where they were before the war. There their lives played out in the big house where they had a whole sprawling floor to themselves. An elegant étage with as much hot bathwater as they wanted, with golden taps and bath salts. Her mother, Aunt Julia, going out to dinner parties every night, leaving her with a French-speaking governess.

I listened to Alexandra's descriptions with open mouth, and could not imagine what was superb about having a French governess, least of all an Etage. Two concepts too unfamiliar to fathom.

Alexandra's chin twitched, close to tears. She showed on her arm the bluish

stain of Grandmother's pinch. Without her mother's protection she would not survive Grandmother. She would rather die.

The scent of Grandmother's coffee hovered above the table.

We've got it good, said Mrs. Brün, drawing the scent into her nostrils, expectantly ironing the napkin in her lap with her hand.

Dipping through the shadows on the narrow path, my grandfather approached, decked out in his well-worn white linen suit, Borsalino grazing his brow, polka-dot bowtie round his neck, in the elegant handmade shoes he always polished himself. Every step was accompanied by the creaking of his soles; they sing, he said, because I still have debts at the shoemaker's. He loved his shoes. They came from Italy, all the way from his regal days, before the war.

On days like this Grandfather was in his loftiest element. Rhythmically, with his walking stick, he cautiously set out across the little bridge. Someone must have tipped him off. Or the scent of coffee had tempted him. Mirza and Lexi wiggled around him, since his pocket smelled like bread crumbs. In passing, he grazed the Borsalino across my hair.

Happy to have arrived in time for the gathering and a cup of fresh coffee, he lifted his hand in a general greeting. This afternoon we two were part of things, he the oldest, I the youngest. Often they excluded us—from delicate discussions, in particular—imagining that my grandfather could not hear and that I would not understand.

In a professorial mood, he launched forth without a moment's hesitation.

We are making history even as we sit here.

He lowered himself into a creaking garden chair. Because he seldom said much, everyone perked up their ears.

The gods—here he cleared his throat—the gods are deliberating the fate of Germany as never before.

Since he was hard of hearing, he did not wait for any feedback. He had to let it out. He hit his stride.

Germany is being put in its world historic place. History registers every act, without exception. Above all, criminals and their deeds. Good and evil beaded together like a pearl necklace. Ah, that is the history of a people. Veritas semper ad lucem venit.

He cast a watery gaze about him, took a gulp of coffee, and went on.

Today certain people are embarrassed that they exulted over Hitler. Yes, exulted over a certain Adolf Schicklgruber. Just imagine. The women voluntarily voted him into power.

He paused.

Grandmother, red with outrage, protested: Not me.

Ja, well, that's just coincidence, he dared to say, gesturing as if swatting a fly.

He had another point on his mind, and leaned confidentially across the table: So, Herr General Brün, what was your position on the Jewish question? I assume you protested the so-called Final Solution.

The General looked up in terror from his cake; he was almost choking on the crumbs. It was too direct a question, like a punch in the stomach.

Yes, no, naturally—horrifying. For a long time none of us knew anything about it. One had one's duties and one's orders. That's the way it was, unfortunately.

Aha. Grandfather took a sip, grinned, and said in closing: Yes, well, it was best when one saw and heard nothing. I am glad I was too old for the war.

He had not yet had his whole say, but he politely restrained himself, leaned back, the chair creaking, fumbled for his tobacco, and closed his eyes.

My father sat at the other end of the table. Coffee did not much interest him, and he did not want to hear his father's views on the damned war. When something is over, it's over.

Today he had on his knickerbockers and a striped linen shirt with a linen vest. The requisite knee-highs were knitted by Justa in deep adoration, and fear. Sitting on a stool at the kitchen stove, her legs crossed, knitting needle in mouth, she would count loops. Should my father stick his head in the kitchen door, she would interrupt her knitting and freeze. If he bellowed an order into the dusky room, she would jump up, the knitting needles falling to the floor; she was at his service, somewhat mindlessly.

Olga, even slower than usual on account of Justa's nervousness, would put down the pot, dry her hands on her apron, and ponder what to do first.

Ja, ja, doing already, okay, doing already.

UNCLE ERWIN

One day everyone got to know quite another Olga. She had just put a great shock behind her, was quite beside herself. She burst into the office, whipped her apron over her head, tossed it to the floor, and stomped all over it. He or I, she shrieked in rage. She was raving.

My father stood up from his desk, held out a conciliatory hand to calm her down, but she recoiled, repulsed by everything masculine. My father took a step forward, offering soothing words; Olga stepped backward, scolding in Russian.

Who would have thought it? It was about Uncle Erwin Müller. Skinny, middle-aged Uncle Erwin, weathered by the South American sun. Having just arrived from Argentina, he was making a stop at the estate, and he stayed many weeks to carry on his research.

Behind the barn, near the river, stood a group of trees, like black lace against the sky. Uncle Erwin sat beneath them, leaning on a trunk; through a small metal straw he sipped his yerba maté from a tin pitcher and peered out into the countryside, lost in thought.

What are you doing? I asked inquisitively.

I am meditating. That he was, more strenuously than any other visitor. In his mind, maté was the gold of the future. A ruined country like our Germany, a desolate people at its political and economic nadir, would be prepared to adopt a new national drink. And what pleased the Argentineans—bitter like Bavarian beer, yet alcohol-free—could be a smash hit here, too. His garden in Frankfurt, which wound its way around a tower, was not suited for large-scale planting. You had to hit the big time right away. He saw here on these flatlands The Opportunity of the Future: yerba maté.

Fritz, who tormented himself with potato cultivation and wanted to grow even larger heads of cabbage, could enjoy swifter and less strenuous hopes of maté millions. Particularly now, with workers standing in line, harvesting would be no problem at all; the people had grown modest, like the Indians. Over there, behind the large garden, tea planting was to begin.

For his part, Fritz found this idea totally moronic, the tea appalling, Erwin a crackpot. Now and then my mother took a polite taste from Erwin's tin pitcher. Yes, yes, quite aromatic. But Uncle Erwin assured all listeners that though the habit came slowly, it embedded itself firmly, predictably, into the human organism, an addiction like cigarette smoking. Then came the millions.

Uncle Erwin stayed and stayed. The only little unoccupied corner in the house was the laundry room, where a bed was pushed in for him. He wanted to spend a sustained period studying climatic conditions, since in Argentina this national treasure grew on mountain crags, and here one was likewise at the foot of the Alps. He was not to be dissuaded, even if it snowed twelve inches in April.

The plants would grow acclimated, he said cheerfully.

There he stood before us, tanned and wrinkled, a wiry Jewish cowboy, brown Indian-knit cap on his bald skull, rhapsodizing. We had grown used to Uncle Erwin and his drivel about golden maté. But then came the sudden blowup with Olga. No one had any clue that Uncle Erwin had entrepreneurial interests in other fields, too.

Uncle Erwin had harassed her a little bit, then more and more. At first she thought it quite charming, only flirtatious teasing. That she tolerated. But then he got fresh and, at an unexpected moment, grabbed at her breast. There she drew the line and slapped his face. But he grew ever more impudent.

On staircase grab me by ass, she screamed. Today night show me in kitchen prick, very big. She was outraged and stunned: How a fine gentleman act so?

Olga, he just likes you, my father said, wanting to tone down the indictment.

No, she shrieked, you knowing nothing like all man.

Olga was deeply offended and horrified that a gentleman of a higher class, and a guest in this house, behaved worse than the yobs in her village. She was somewhat afraid of being at his mercy and was suddenly no longer certain of her power.

Summoned by Fritz, Uncle Erwin laughed.

Hell, they're all a bunch of Indians, he said, winking.

From then on Olga no longer let Erwin into the kitchen to brew his tea. She threatened him with a red-hot poker if he so much as opened the door a crack.

Now Uncle Erwin sat with us in the grove at coffee hour, casting a melancholy gaze out into the fields and hills behind the garden, farther beyond, where he, but not Fritz, could see endless rows of maté dancing in the wind and millions in his bank account. Perhaps Uncle Erwin would have to look for something new.

•

Friends were visiting from a neighboring estate: Tony Schmelzle with Rita, his latest acquisition. My father greeted Tony with a jovial slap on the back and a wink, to acknowledge his friend's youthful conquest. Rita did not really suit Uncle Tony—much too young. Her dog, a wire-haired dachshund, had to be held off the ground so our dogs would not mistreat it. My mother compared this to the poor besieged hens, the harassment they had to put up with from the roosters.

Both visitors were fabulously elegant: he in summer linen, she with painted red lips. Her acetate dress, fashionably puffed up with shoulder pads, barely covered her knees. She wore cork pumps, crossed her legs, and smoked. I could scarcely gape my fill. Although Uncle Tony was the same age as my father, who already had gray at the temples and a chrome dome, Uncle Tony's hair and moustache were mysteriously still jet black.

He looks like a rug dealer, said my mother with a laugh.

Rita kept nervously powdering her nose. There was much laughter, and my father, too, was carefree, happy.

The most beautiful of all was my mother. In the green dress with shoulder pads, pleated at the bodice—in her decollete one saw the lace of her slip. Her coal-black hair was knotted at her neck. Red lips. Decent, she had said once she was made up, pressing a kiss on loo paper. Around her neck she wore a green malachite necklace. This Fritz had brought her from France during the war, together with Chanel No. 5. She had hidden a cotton ball misted with scent in her brassiere, between her breasts. She leaned back gaily and enjoyed her cup of coffee. On her left hand she wore a ring with a rose-colored stone, engraved with her family's emblem. Rossbach—Steedbrook—had been her name before she married my father, and the family's coat of arms depicted a horse springing across a brook. Above her light green eyes arched her dark, lilting brows. Her lightly bent nose reminded my father of a racing dog's. A borzoi, he laughed. She was very beautiful, everyone agreed.

But she was modest when it came to her beauty, blushed when her old friend Eugene visited, kissed her hand. Ah, Adelheid, you look wonderful again.

Whereupon my father, like a collector priding himself on his rarities, put his arm around her and pressed her to his breast.

Aunt Julia had sewn the green silk dress with drapery across the middle, buttons on the side. She became our seamstress as soon as she moved in with us. Julia reminded us over and over how different her life had been before the war. She had studied medicine, gotten as far as doctor's assistant. Then came the war. Otherwise she would be a doctor today. Alexandra's birth had merely delayed her studies, not put an end to them. There'd been no lack of staff in her posh apartment in Breslau, she had not had to sew, her suddenly deceased husband had provided for every eventuality. Except a war, naturally. Who could have seen that coming?

Since he was dead and no one knew much about Julia's marriage to my mother's distant relative, no one said anything. People exchanged glances. She just put the information out there as a fact, not up for discussion.

Now you are here, said Adi affectionately, wanting her hand.

But Aunt Julia quickly pulled the arm and herself away. Sometimes Julia's tears welled up when she talked about the past. She described her flight in detail: Alexandra on a rack wagon, perched atop the suitcases with the silver and a few valuable pictures, everything they had been able to toss together in their haste.

It all happened so quickly, she said, and groaned.

It will all get better soon, said my mother optimistically.

No, it will never be the same again.

As soon as we get a roof over our heads, we want more, whispered Mrs. Brün.

Julia dried her tears. No, she did not want to be ungrateful. They simply had no idea here in the south, in the country. She could not accept their sympathy, since they were not in a position to appreciate the extent of her loss. They were illiterates of fate.

Aunt Julia also sewed clothes for Alexandra, Anita, and me. Somehow, from somewhere, silk arrived, or another piece of fabric was traded for eggs, honey, vegetables, a hen. What luck. Alexandra's dresses were the ones I always preferred. Aunt Julia, Alexandra, and Anita talked me out of it, or tried to, or said: You spoiled brat, you don't need to have everything.

Not everything, I shrieked, pulling at the skirt. Just this dress! I cannot stand it!

I never won, had to put on what Aunt Julia produced for me. I had to, even though I convinced Grandfather that the fabric itched and the color looked like shit, brown. He nodded in helpless agreement.

When the times are better, he consoled me, when you are a little more grown up, then you can go to the city on the train and buy what you like. I'll give you the money.

Don't talk rot, interjected Grandmother. Children have to wear what grownups put on them. Where would it end if they were allowed to decide everything?

Not everything, I blared, just not Aunt Julia's dress. Are you all deaf? Alexandra's is much softer, and blue.

Angry tears streamed down my face. But the women were hard as steel. And for once, finally, my grandmother and Aunt Julia were united, in condemnation.

ANTON

After Aunt Julia had lived with us for a while, a telephone call came from Berlin. This was it, the call, the news, the urgent news she had been waiting for. Everyone else, too. Thank God, the call was from her fiancé, Anton Reznick. Finally. Amid the chaos of war, at some stage of her flight, Julia had managed to find a man, a fiancé no less. No one had really believed her, but here was the proof. Who else could it be? Julia went running.

She returned quite flushed, her cheeks red from expectation, from the call itself, and from hope. She hoped she could speak with Fritz and Adi, hoped they would understand. Hopefully his stay with them would not be all too long. Beaming, Aunt Julia approached my mother, took both her hands.

Oh, Aunt Adi, I am so deeply in your debt.

Grandmother scowled, throwing glances like lightning.

And shortly thereafter Anton Reznick appeared. A dark-haired, elegant man, very shy, quiet and utterly polite, mysterious from the start. He and Aunt Julia shared the Yellow Room. Alexandra's bed moved into the room with my sister and me.

Everyone on the farm and in the house had to earn his bed and board. Anton's talents included horses; he rode in the war. He had a knack with people, too, experience, he mentioned. If he has the time he will work for Mr. Ost on the farm.

My father looked directly into his face with piercing eyes.

You will have to make time. No one here cares where you come from or what you did in the war. No questions asked. You will be put to work. You will join us at the table. Everything else will be decided day by day. You understand?

Jawoll! Handshake, slap on shoulder.

Right, then. You will bring a load of potatoes into the city.

Jawoll, naturally.

Here is the address. Do you know the way?

Jawoll!

Do you know the city?

Jawoll! Once again Anton clicked his heels together.

No goofing around, my father warned once more.

Jawoll!

Anton drove off with a load of potatoes.

The day came, the day went. We waited. Evening came. Still no Anton. We could all feel the suspense. At the table the only sounds were the scraping of cutlery, chewing, and the ticking of the tall clock in the corner, cutting away time. Aunt Julia's chair was empty. She had excused herself with a headache. My father could not bear even Adi's calming hand on his arm. He was boiling mad.

When Anton finally returned, late at night, my father flew into a rage. Every word bored through the walls. He stomped back and forth in the office.

Unbelievable! Unbelievable! Sabotage!

Something fell. His fist at the desk, perhaps. As it turned out, he had good reason to explode.

Anton stood rigidly in the door frame, knees clicked straight, and let the bellowing wash over him.

Anton had driven into the city; however, before he had arrived at the agreed potato address, he had detoured into a quite different area, to tend to his private affairs. Naturally no one had suspected any of this. The wagon with its taut sacks of potatoes he had left sitting there. Only five minutes, he swore, but as every child knew, that was enough time to liberate anything unattended.

I will cover the loss, Anton claimed.

My father shot his steel glance at him: Sure, when pigs fly.

And from that day on, the household suspiciously eyed and monitored the quiet Anton.

When Aunt Julia did herself up after work to get ready for her appearance downstairs at the table, or when she was expecting Anton back from a trip, she stood before the high mirror in the room Anita, Alexandra, and I shared. Perched on wedge heels, she observed her legs while she tied the sash of her blouse, which fell down over the silk lingerie she had hand-embroidered with her initials and a leaf. She studied her legs from the right side, then from the left, then from behind, to check for runs, but also just because she enjoyed them. A black seam parted each leg into halves. She assured herself that it ran straight, whistling, then singing, with intermittent, absent-minded gaps:

. . . steht sie noch davor,	*. . . she's still standing out there,*
tra la la la la	*tra la la la la*
So woll'n wir uns da wieder seh'n	*That's how we long to meet again*
Bei der Laterne woll'n wir stehen	*We want to stand at the lantern*
Wie einst Lili Marleen	*As Lili Marlene did back then*

She plodded contentedly through the door, went into her own room across the hall to powder her nose and her high cheeks in the small mirror. With a wire brush she teased her blond hair up from her neck. Rraach, rrrach, sang the brush. At the end she sprayed a little perfume from the atomizer over her shoulders. I wanted some, too, and stretched out the back of my hand. Aunt Julia shook her head. Anton didn't give it to her to fool around with, she scolded, tapping my nose reproachfully.

Wash your dirty paws, she ordered Alexandra and me. Afterward we reluctantly followed her loud step downstairs.

Julia had to struggle for everything. She had to work hard even for her place at the table. We said nothing at all. What was there to say? She never felt like answering our questions anyway, and most often she was in an impatient hurry.

Seven gold bracelets tinkled on her wrist like bells—everyone knew when Aunt Julia was coming. She was the one with the most beautiful legs in the house, just like Marlene Dietrich's. General Brün pulled the corner of his mouth downward to put his monocle in place. Shifted his face left, grimaced right, pursed his lips, finally the round eye window sat in place. Now he cleared his throat, wished to say something on the subject.

Julia's legs are her best feature.

Everyone agreed with him. Hmm, tja, nodding.

Thrilled at this initial success, he abandoned his otherwise so thoroughly correct general's posture, adding with a grin: Doubtless she used them to make her way here.

Clearing of throats. A moment of silence. Then laughing applause.

For certain, he repeated, red in the face.

A citron butterfly sat down on the poppy roll at the coffee party. With its rolled-up proboscis, it investigated what it thought was a flower. Mistake. It fluttered up, hovered in the mirror of the coffee cup, over to the sugar bowl, on the flower-sculpted top, realized its error, flitted off into the roses. The air was moist with sweat. Some fumbled with their napkins, fanning their foreheads.

The silent Anton, always at a smiling distance from the others, smoked a pipe of my grandfather's tobacco. Elegantly he leaned back. He looked directly at no one, just gave an occasional polite nod to the conversation. Something was missing: the cake server. Straightaway Anton jumped up and went running, to make himself useful, or to absent himself. With his zeal he achieved exactly what he wanted to avoid: everyone wondered about him, and speculated.

Pah! What is he really up to?

The policy of the household was don't ask, don't tell. Fritz Ost liked it that way. Who would reveal the truth?

Will he marry her? whispered Auntie Brün, looking across to my mother, avoiding mentioning names.

Well, remarked my grandmother, she is not exactly making herself scarce. She shook her head.

Yes, I think he will, said Auntie. I tell you, she is so diligent, and showers him with attentions.

And more besides, added the General.

Auntie blushed. Oh, you with your...

They laughed.

With what, I inquired, so I could laugh along with them. But they had already buttoned their lips.

Mrs. Tafelmeier, our vox populi: Neah, he'll never marry her. Not with Alexandra and her glass eye. Mrs. Julia ain't young enough for that dapper Mr. Anton. He's on the road all the time. Bet he's got a young honey in town, hunh? Bet she's loaded, too. She rubbed her thumb and forefinger together with a meaningful look.

In the kitchen Justa was endorsing Mrs. Tafelmeier's opinion: Beautiful man, too young for Mrs. Julia.

But Olga, the object of old Erwin's desire, laughed: Not matter, nothing too young.

I was bored. I had eaten my cake, lapped a little cream, no one was talking to me. Sliding from my place at the bench, with Grandfather's Borsalino on my head, I went to the brook, took off my wooden shoes, and swung my legs in the water. The brook had already flowed through the shadowy fruit trees on its way into the garden. It ran cool and fresh between my toes. Mirza joined me. Down below, little fish haunted the water, nervously crisscrossing through the reflected sun. A largemouth gudgeon wallowed along the river bottom, obscuring the play of light. Bubbles burst, trembling swamp grass dipped into sky blue, the water babbled. Mirza, her ears perked, looked attentively at the motion below her, letting out small whining notes, wagging her tail.

I was wearing one of the pleated dresses my mother had brought back from a trip to Bulgaria for Anita, when she was still little. The dress drove me crazy. When I bent over it fell over my feet. To keep it in place, I had bound one of

Father's ties, a red one, tightly about my waist. I was also convinced it looked better this way.

Beatrixchen, sing us a song, Uli called across to me from the grove. Because of the difference in our ages he was a kind of second father or uncle to me.

Perhaps, I said. I slowly stood up, dried my feet, and enjoyed being the center of attention. Everyone peered up toward me on the bridge with slightly bored faces. The lazy afternoon, the electrical heat in the air, made room for every sort of amusement. A dogfight, or speculation about a stranger's bicycle leaning against the fence, would be a welcome intermission, or a bird shriek leading to ornithological observations.

But now they all looked expectantly in my direction, nibbled at their sweets, and drank their coffee. Uli, Georg, and Dieter smoked and chatted with Hilde, a young girl from the city who was about to start working for us.

I could do a handstand, across the bridge rail, swinging over, but I would need help, I thought. Or I could sing.

I dawdled, laboriously put on my clogs.

Come on now, sing something for us. We want to hear something from you, begged Dieter.

Come on, you sing sooo beautifully, flattered Uli.

Yes, Beatrix, sing, my mother said, already clapping.

With all that urging, I slowly stood up, went away from the stream, to the pergola. I positioned myself before the assembled company, on the black gravel, and holding my skirt for balance, I let loose:

Könn' se nich nen	*If you could use*
Hund jebrauchen—komm se	*A little dog—come on out*
Doch zu mir	*See me*
Jartenstrasse wohn ich	*I live on Garden Street*
Parterre Numro vier…	*Up on the fourth floor*

Gleich wennse reinkommn	*Just as you come in*
Erste Türe rechts	*First door on the right*
Könn' se Hunde kaufen	*You can buy a dog or two*
Beiderlei Yeschlechts	*Of either secks*

Who had taught me the song? Perhaps Aunt Julia, or Auntie Brün. They spoke Prussian, and the song surely came from there. My family spoke Bavarian. Worlds apart. The Bavarians saw Prussian almost as a foreign language, and the Prussians themselves as domestic foreigners. The Prussians by contrast loved the Bavarians and found them southern, almost Italian.

That was delightful, too funny, you sang wonderfully, Beatrix. They laughed and clapped.

Beiderlei Yeschlechts, mimicked Uli, howling with laughter. My father even dried a tear from his cheek. That I had made him of all people laugh so heartily made me proud. My mother beamed too, at him, her Fritz, otherwise so earnest.

After the applause I did a few more cartwheels on the hard gravel path. My dress flew across my outstretched legs, fell over my head. Once more I twisted through the air, propped on my spindly arms.

Bravo, bravo, bravo!

The afternoon dozed along. Thick clouds gathered in the west.

We could use some rain, said my father, who stood up and played conductor to the weather with his cane. He strode into the black gravel path, away from the party, as if he had had enough of a good thing—or did he want to inspect his seedling potatoes at the edge of the garden? He came to a stop by the berry bushes, a silhouette against the charged sky.

Grandmother was aghast: a coffee stain on the fine linen cloth.

Oh, God, the Meissen. Careful, please!

Now the coffee afternoon was folded away; the lace had to be soaked. Justa came running with a tray.

We, too, have to get going—hopefully there won't be any rain with our open carriage, said Tony Schmelzle, patting his pretty Rita on the cheek. She still had to freshen up a little before the long journey.

My mother accompanied the guests across the bridge to the house. Uncle Tony whistled for Umer, who had parked his carriage in the shadows of the linden tree in the middle of the courtyard, next to the Maibaum, the maypole, which was adorned with garlands of dried flowers and bundled gleanings, with the symbols of agriculture stamped in tin. The maypole overshadowed every building on the farm.

Hmm, I doubt the weather will hold. Oh, well, perhaps it will veer off into the mountains, said Uncle Tony.

By the bridge I threw a handful of pebbles into the water. A school of red speckled trout burst forth from the river grass.

Grandfather, here, your hat.

Oh, I almost forgot it. He sat it on his head.

Through the mint leaves the carriage rattled past. Uncle Tony and Rita waved. I squinted into the last ray of sun, just as a cloud descended.

Sepp—A True Fairy Tale

IT WAS ALWAYS ALMOST DARK WHEN HE CAME AROUND. Black from head to toe. Dark. Black, as if he were the chimney sweep. His clothes stiff and soiled. In dark slow motion he pedaled into the courtyard, in from the moor, past our house.

When my mother was standing outside the door, he climbed down from his bicycle, tipped his soiled black cap, and grinned uneasily.

So, how goes it, Sepp? What'd you catch today? she wanted to know.

My mother found the denizens of the farm interesting and took advantage of every opportunity to chat with them. People liked her. You could ask her for advice, or tell her something from the bottom of your heart. She really listened. She was not just friendly but your friend.

On both sides of Sepp's bicycle, next to the seat, hung dead black moles. Thirty or more. Like little satin pouches. Pink nose dots, strung together. Pink little paws paddling the bicycle wind. His day's haul.

When my father showed up somewhere in the courtyard, Sepp just tipped his cap and pedaled on. He did not climb off. For fear of him? Out of respect? Did he have black thoughts behind his black ears, beneath the black cap?

He came to a stop at the cow stalls, leaned the bike against the wall, and, with an unsteady grin, tin can in hand, approached the chief cattleman Beni Reitmeier, who ran the milking operation. Not a word was said; Sepp stood with Resi König on the lowest rung of the rural pecking order. He dawdled a little at the periphery of the warm stalls and watched the evening milking. Hulked in the entrance, glanced into the courtyard in the direction of the house. If the coast was clear, he lit a cigarette. If someone appeared, he twisted his cigarette inward, into his palm, pinched the glow from the shaft with forefinger and thumb,

111

stubbed it out, and let the butt slip into his trouser pocket. Because of the ban on smoking.

Beni positioned a round milking stool with three legs at the udder beneath the cow's belly. Sat down, squeezed a bucket between his knees, took two teats in his hands, and wheedled the cow.

Ho, ho, ho, c'mon, let's git goin'.

His cap sat wrong way 'round on his blond shock of hair. He pressed his head against the cow's belly. The milk spurted rhythmically first from one teat, then from another. When the bucket was full to the brim with warm foam, he poured it into a container with a lid. When one of the beasts did not obey, the silent Beni cursed and started in on her with a stick. The sticks leaned at several places against the sweaty stall walls, so he always had one right at hand. Sooner or later, wordlessly, he stuck his hand out from beneath the cow's belly.

Sepp handed Beni his tin canister.

Because of his terrible fits of rage the children feared Beni almost as much as Sepp, just in a different way. Another kind of fear, less symbolic. Once Beni had grabbed Peter and heaved him up onto the massive bull. He was always threatening to do the same to the other farm children. So we kept a safe distance. These were very concrete fears. The fear of Sepp, by contrast, was full of mystery. It had to do with the darkness of night, the wind in the trees, a flock of ravens, deep moor waters; with stealing our child souls, or with a magic spell to stunt our growth, cut it short at our current height. Never would we be able to make a mannerly gesture across a table; our noses would bump into doorknobs; we would always have to look upward as words rained down on us from beards; the beardless ones would snarl, their red gums like the fish that devoured Jonah. That was the kind of power he exercised over us.

One day there was a huge fright. We children had already long been playing in the hay, jumping down from the hayloft through a chute into the cow stalls. Back up the ladder, down the chute. Up the ladder, down. Evening approached. We had forgotten the time.

I jumped once more. As I arrived at the bottom, I saw, to my terror, Sepp approaching the stall on his bicycle. In fear and panic I searched for an escape route. The other children had vanished. At this instant all I could do was creep under a hay bale. Sepp was the bogeyman of my darkest fears.

Our workers, especially Justa and Olga in the kitchen, had fed the fire of fear with their stories. One day he'll grab you all up, you'll see. He carries children off into the moor, slaughters them and skins them. We would become part of his harvest, like the little black moles, laced together, hung up, nailed taut on the wall. Every few centimeters a nail would be driven into our skin, stretched, then the next nail, until like a tambourine, headless, we dried in preparation for tanning.

I had seen his hut in the moor. In rows beneath the rafters hung the furs of hundreds of little black moles, stretched out, nailed at their four corners. Fear raced through my tormented brain. As I lay petrified beneath my hay blanket, breathing at half my normal rate, feverish pearls of sweat accumulated on my forehead.

Sepp was just handing Beni his tin pot, a mere meter from my hiding place. He looked about. I was quite certain he was looking for me. I saw his black face all too clearly, the whites of his eyes, the red tongue he greased his lips with. On his belt hung a big knife in its sheath, for killing children. Me, Beatrix.

Finally, from far away, a voice calling my name. Oh, Mummy's voice, I thought beneath the hay that smelled of summer. The world had not left me in the lurch. I still belonged to it, to the dog, to the cat, to Olga's kitchen, to the down bed. They had not forsaken me, the adults. If only they kept on calling me, because they missed me—I often doubted this.

You are just a child. Sit still. Be quiet. You're not to speak at table, the adults said. Over and over the children were supposed to be invisible, not to exist. But then, when we were very quiet, because we wanted to hear the adults' conversation, we got noticed. This is not for children's ears.

But now my mother was looking for me after all. She must be worried, otherwise she herself would not be searching. She would send Justa or Olga, or Alexandra and Aunt Julia.

Mealtime. Where have you got to? she called, this time more emphatically. Beatriiiix!, louder and nearer. Have you seen her? she asked through the stall gate.

There they stood: Sepp, my murderer, Beni the milker, and the invisible me, frozen with fear, glad my mother had poked her head in.

Then she vanished.

Beatriiiix! Beatriiiix! Her cries dissipated further into the darkness. I hoped the milking would soon be over. Beni had to get home to his wife, his dinner. She scolded him when he got home late, that much I knew. Ya jes' gonna hafta eat it cold, she nagged. Ya ken wash yer own dishes too afterward. She sometimes grew suspicious, stuck her head through the stall door: was he there, or with one of the Polack women?

I was too scared. It was impossible to leave the hiding place in the secure hay. I had stopped breathing. Was I already dead? The horror story from last summer rushed through my inner cinema like an express train.

My friends and I had wanted to visit the moor. There at the edge stood Sepp's hut. We were certain he was not at home. A little while earlier we had seen him from afar, hunting his mole traps in a field. So we headed off toward the moor.

We trotted down the street, hopped over a puddle, plucked twigs from the bushes. Then we were distracted by a group of people in the middle of a field, standing in a circle, pushing their heads together, peering at something down below. What could it be? We needed to know. A bomb crater in the middle of the landscape. The deep hole had filled up with water. A metallic something, not clearly visible, lay at the bottom. The people were throwing pebbles at it.

After a while it grew too boring. I gathered my friends. Weren't we going to the moor? So we ran back to the road, followed a turnoff, and there stood Sepp's house before us, off to the side, by itself, in the middle of a meadow. Right where the moor began. An elderberry bush overflowing with white umbrella blossoms leaned over in the summer heat. The air trembled. Zigzagging dragonflies attacked the surface of a dark pond. We took cover in the long summer grass and slinked toward the hut.

I crept in front up to the door and prodded it slowly open. First a shrill squeak, long and mournful, then it fell with a sad whimper against the inner wall. The air was smoky. In the middle of the room stood a table with two chairs, a bottle on it, a plate with bread next to a jar of marmalade. Slowly, step by step, I tiptoed into the twilight. Pssst! Pssst! I gestured my friends inside. My eyes had adjusted to the haze. I looked around me. Just at that moment, just as I opened my mouth to whisper something, I froze. Inside. In the twilight, back there against the wall, stretched out across his bed, lay Sepp, smoking his pipe.

Come on over here, you little slut, he grinned, and beckoned with his dirty hand.

Here in his mole castle he was no longer silent. He kept watch over the mist in the room, the foul smell, the dead flesh, the little black coats, the horrified button eyes; at the border of the moor, at the dragonfly hole, he whetted his knife. This was his kingdom, amidst the sedge bowing in the wind.

I jumped as if from an electric shock, and ran and ran and ran. The others had long since taken off. I did not catch up with them until just before the farm, at the bee house. Out of breath, we threw ourselves onto the cement wall behind the Königs' house.

Did you see his eyes? He turned them right up into his head. His pipe spat fire. You all have no idea. You ran away. But I, I boasted, I said to him, How are you? God bless.

Now I was getting back at them. We jostled one another, let the fear out of our limbs. That he was a sorcerer we all agreed. How else could he be both at home and among the mole traps at the same time?

All that shot through my anxious head while I lay motionless beneath the hay. Finally, after an eternity, Sepp with his tin can sidled out of the stall. With a clothespin he pinched his trousers together at the ankle, tapped his cap—that was for Beni and his milking rhythm—climbed onto his bike, and disappeared into the night.

I crept out from under my hiding mound. By this time everyone was looking for me. Cries and whistles. Awoken from my paralysis to new life, I raced out into the courtyard. My poor mother, already close to a nervous breakdown, was overjoyed to have her child back and took me in her arms. No scolding.

I sat at the window. Moonlight outlined the linden tree. Exhausted, I dipped a crust of bread into warm milk, fresh from the stall. Like dust after an explosion in the gravel pit, the day's fear was laid to rest.

The sandman is coming, said Grandfather. I hear him already.

I don't notice anything, I replied, still fully present in the room with him.

After a little while my head sank onto my arm, my hand into the glass of milk. I had fallen asleep.

Bavarian Blues

FROM THE HAYRICK A BRIDGE ARCHED ACROSS A RIVER. The horses drew the heavy hay wagons this way when they came from the meadows. It must have been 1945, just when the war ended.

My father had ordered large rectangular ditches dug beneath the bridge, broad and deep, three altogether. Earth piled up on all sides, several wooden crates waited at the edge. Then the farmworkers came with boxes and suitcases to the ditches, dragged their possessions: pictures, mirrors, glass objects, here a chair, there a bicycle. All sorts of things were carted out of our house, too. Carpets, suitcases filled with silver, boxes with the beloved Meissen porcelain, a clock, a portrait of a lady painted by Ingres, the Rembrandt, and the twelve Carceri prints by Piranesi.

These I adore. They absolutely must disappear, said my mother.

A vase, a baroque chair, all packed up, swaddled, slowly lowered into the aperture. A protective layer of straw, then wooden planks. Finally the mountain of earth was shoveled on top, clumps of grass laid across, so it looked as if nothing had happened.

News of the war's end flew into the farm like a bird that had strayed into the room. No one knew what to think of it.

Now we're ready for them, said my father. He was talking about a new, different enemy, the people who had won the war. They are going to loot us. People had already got wind of this. By nature Fritz trusted no one. Intuition and reality shook hands with facts in the jungle of fear and experience. Thus everyone was somehow right. Each knew a story, a truth, a snatch of gossip, that gave wings to mistrust.

For my mother, her garden, the flourishing of the animals, and human welfare were more important, the war and the collapse of Germany somewhere else, not palpably at hand, nothing one could lay hold of and change. She was preoccupied with her smaller world, which made sense to her. What happened outside was like rain.

Don't be so negative, Fritz, she said.

You'll see, I'm right, came the bellowed retort as he looked past her with furrowed brow.

My father ordered white linen cloths hung from the second-floor windows. There they fluttered in the wind, only for one day and one night. Then they came.

The farm, just a few miles from the radio station, was overrun the next day by the Americans in their tanks. They rumbled down the tree-lined avenue, across potato fields, heads of cabbage, grain and corn, through the estate, through life as we knew it. As they thundered past us, we waved, fluttered white handkerchiefs in the air. Gingerly, uncertain, no one really knew; they were enemies, but at the same time liberators. One wanted to greet them, the new power. Fear cloaked in uncertainty.

Our forced laborers raved with excitement, pressed up to the passing vehicles, and shouted: No German, no German!

In the midst of all this tumult, the new chaos that paraded past, I saw a black face. Up above, on a tank, it peered out from beneath a helmet. The wide, laughing mouth, the white teeth. My eyes rolled along with it, until the helmet, a waving arm, the brown hand, disappeared around the corner at the tree. Not black with snot like Sepp's, not fearsome, no, perhaps like the whirlpools in the river, where one also is not quite sure and does not quite trust oneself to go. And where it is beautiful to look.

The harvest is buggered, my father scoffed. He looked through the window onto the dangerous spectacle outside in the courtyard. He greeted no one. The drama played on, down the avenue, toward the forest; one last curve, the chains of the tanks spat out the earth from the fields, then the last of them disappeared behind the hill. The air echoed their rumbling, then all was as before. Or was it?

We still stood together, even those who had screamed that they did not belong, chattering now in their own foreign languages, and laughing, looking at us, their unwilling captors. An apparition?

My father ordered night watches kept and Pluto let off his chain.

•

Quite a new style came over the house. The radio blared with pleasure. Jolly snippets of harmony: Ich nenne alle Frauen Baby, und das ist mir so angenehm...Or: You are my sunshine, my only sunshine. Sung, whistled, the new hit songs painted the beginning of a new era on the canvas of the future. I soon knew the lyrics by heart and warbled innocently through the house. Johnnie, wenn du mal einsam bist, and: Go and see what the boys in the back room will have...crooned Marlene, and I sang along. Even Grandfather kept time on the floorboards with the tip of his shoe. That was so new, so cool, so un-German. It had a lightness one no longer even knew after all the marching. It reminded one of the time before the war, of the shred of freedom between the wars.

A troop of American cars curved into the courtyard one day. Anita was ordered to go upstairs and wait there. Alexandra and I should best wait in the house, too. We could watch from the upstairs window.

My father had a very tenuous grasp of English, nor was he at all eager to exert himself. He still knew Greek and Latin, but English—no. So General Brün was summoned to play translator. They accompanied the uninvited guests, opening doors, the gate to the cow stall, to the stable. Anita, Alexandra, and I observed it all from our second-floor window.

From above, the brim of my father's hat hid his face. His emotional state could have remained hidden, but it vibrated. One could feel he was boiling. This intrusion still had to do with the war and all the cursed memories. The blessing of distance was still far off.

As his arm flew up from his body, his shoulders drew together, then he hid his fists in his trouser pockets and pressed his knees together. He strode a few times back and forth, threatened General Brün with his finger, paused, then shrugged his shoulders resignedly, turned with a start, and left the group, stomped up the stairs into the house, and slammed the door so vehemently that the upstairs windowpanes trembled.

Two young American soldiers emerged from the stables, each leading a saddled horse by the halter. As soon as Anita saw this she went out of her mind.

Those are carriage horses, not for riding! she screamed. Bawling, she tried to open the window.

No, no, you can't ride those.

But the two guys had already leaped up. The workers watched, slapped their thighs like idiots, and laughed stupidly. The irritated beasts danced, reared up on their hind legs, tried to cast off their burden, but the two stayed in the saddle, poked their heels into the horses' bellies, and zoomed off toward the pond, out of our windowed picture. Down in the courtyard hands shadowed eyes, heads turned to follow the drama.

An even larger mob was gathering. Umer tossed his cap into the courtyard mud. His face was red with anger.

Damned gangsters. The crowd stared at the Americans left behind. They smoked and grinned, passing cigarettes around. A Polish worker hesitantly took one, then others stretched their hands out. Jusef stuck one behind his ear. The König children gaped. Up in our room, Anita had thrown herself across the bed, faint with fear for her Bella.

One of the Americans pulled brown and silver packages from his pocket. He wanted to hand one to each child, starting with Lenerl. He laughed and gesticulated encouragingly toward her. Staring at him, she stepped back, took Roserl's hand for comfort. Distrust won out. There are such things as cannibals in the world, too. So foreign. They both turned and scampered toward the König house.

The older boys hung around the three Jeeps, probed them, jostled one another, laughed and grinned insecurely. Roserl and Lenerl reappeared, this time with Mother König, who dragged her Pepperl along on her arm. Resi did not hesitate, immediately stretched out her hand. Laughing, the soldier gave her the chocolate. Without looking at the packet, she immediately whisked it into her bodice. Maria Tafelmeier glanced disapprovingly across at her, made a quick gesture, thumb downward, as if sliding an imaginary object into the folds of her skirt.

She squirrelin' things away agin, she said, envy in her voice. Resi grinned.

And then down below us we saw Justa's hair gliding down the steps. She came to a stop, drying her hands slowly and deliberately on her apron. I immediately left my place at the window and raced downstairs. I just could not take it anymore, this stupid prohibition, while so many new things were taking shape down in the courtyard. Klip klap! my wood sandals resounded in the tiled vestibule.

Whish! My father's hand seized my arm so firmly that it hurt.

Ouch! I want to...

His eyes sprayed fire, his face had gone red, his mouth a small raging slit.

Get over there and don't move. He shoved me roughly through the open door. I almost lost my balance. The door dropped into its lock like a hard punch.

Grandfather, grown into his leather armchair, let the book fall to the ground with a thud.

Come over and sit with me, I'll sing you a song, he said tenderly, lifted both arms toward me like sheltering wings. But I was so enraged, offended and curious simultaneously, did not understand a bit of this drama. Voices could be heard from the corridor, loud and whispered. It was all a theater piece where the scenes had been mixed up and the actors strayed about in confusion. I began to scream, kicking against the chair, kicking into the air, until, exhausted with unhappiness, I surrendered into Grandfather's embrace.

More people crowded into the room. My father, bellowing in the vestibule, ordered them in. Justa, who had stood unhappily somewhere in the way, received a hard box on the ear in answer to her question. Everyone in the room jostled at the windows that gave onto the courtyard, where the Americans were unconcernedly shoving a bottle about with their boots. A few Slavs lounged around, gaping and laughing idiotically. They had not understood, or did not want to, until my father cracked his whip into the courtyard.

Get to work, you lazy riffraff! What are you doing standing around staring?

Very slowly they scattered, grinning, pranced across the courtyard, kept looking back, half-saluting and pulling faces in the Americans' direction, rebellion in their shoulders. They had never hesitated so long when Herr Ost bellowed an order. But now they were no longer quite as helpless as they had been, and my father was no longer so powerful.

Everyone was glued to the windows as Fritz entered the room, let himself drop into a chair, looked at no one. They tried to look neutral, exude calm, for on my father's brow, anger wrestled with its brother, impotence.

Yes, that's how it is when you lose. I saw it coming, he mumbled to himself.

The room let out its collective breath. One could empathize with him, show sympathy. He no longer shouted out his powerlessness, he showed it.

After a while the horses and their riders came back, exhausted, hot and sweaty, steaming as if after a cloudburst. The Americans were from Texas, they blithely told General Brün as they caught their breath. They had had no opportunity to ride for a long time, on account of the invasion. They wanted to thank Herr Ost, but he remained invisible.

Fritz leaned back, took off his glasses, and closed his tired eyes against everything outside. The tormented, sweaty horses, the childishly crude Texans, the fraternizing of the laborers, the slovenly disobedience, his own rage, and the slap across Justa's cheek: all that he found unpleasant. He never struck out, he yelled. His rage always remained in his breast, in his belly, never palpably discharged itself. What now? The scene really was as if on a disorderly stage, with my father tangled up in it all, a director without a script. The water rose; he could not swim; he saw the rat.

Years earlier, back before the war, when everything at least looked like it was supposed to, when only a few irregularities had forced their way into his ordered world—although he already sensed many things, and issued prognoses that no one bought into at the time—he came home one day from an outing in the city, quite beside himself. He had seen a sign on the back of a bench: Jews Prohibited. Like that of an animal that senses danger, his instinct was sharpened, put on high alert, in the presence of an injustice that could no longer be denied, a transgression never thought possible, against boundaries that until then had protected the rights of every man.

Here and now, in the room, in the chair, he felt himself powerless again, as he had then. He was always the master of ceremonies: I'm pulling the strings, the wires, the rope. In which direction should I take them now? But with this much confusion in the world, leadership was beside the point. Right now a swig would be the thing.

He stuck fast to the chair, his feet grew into the floorboards below. He closed his eyes. He whispered something, not more than a sigh, full of rage.

Shortly thereafter, soldiers—a horde, as my father called them—went fishing with hand grenades. Naturally everyone ran to the river, toward the noise, saw the dead fish drifting downstream, their gleaming silver bellies up. I immediately turned around and told my father. He went pale, had the carriage harnessed up right away, sat next to Umer, and drove into the city.

Within days, a highly decorated American officer arrived at the estate. A peaceful conversation was to take place in the office.

The office walls were full of photographs from Fritz's war years in Africa. One from Kilimanjaro, at whose feet lay the coffee plantation of his friend, my Uncle Fritz.

Sometimes, in anger, my father would say: I would like to leave this whole place behind and move there.

Africa? With us? I would ask, momentarily startled.

Yes, naturally! He stared morbidly into space. But then my mother somehow helped him find his "lost humor" again, and we stayed where we were. I had no idea what any of this meant, what our life had to do with his humor.

Today the office door stood open invitingly; General Brün, playing interpreter again, leaned in the doorway. I leaned on my father, listened to the sound of the incomprehensible and comprehensible words flying back and forth through the room, sometimes accompanied by laughter. My father took my hand and forgot it in his own. He accepted the American's apology and promised to forget the intrusions.

So. From here on there were new rules. Order. Fritz was once again the dominus. After great disappointment, accompanied by fits of rage, my father was in a forgiving mood, and the humor that so thrilled my mother returned.

When Americans came to visit they were not allowed to ride the horses anymore and had to fish like real anglers. There was chocolate for the children, cigarettes for the parents, cigars, too, for my father, but as a matter of principle he did not accept any of it.

Time went by. We got used to them and made friends. The children accompanied the soldiers to the carp ponds, the trout stream. We caught worms for our new friends. Impaled on the hook, the squirming creature flew out into the water in a high arc. I got my first chewing gum. Red and green and rainbow balls, much too big to put in your mouth all at once.

For Anita the time had come. She was taken to a boarding school, to the nuns. She was allowed to take Bella with her.

When my mother and I visited her, she was sad. Scarcely had we greeted one another when the thought of parting interrupted her joy and she cried, wanting to come home with us. Even the horse could not change her homesickness. It, too, wanted to go home.

But it won't work, child, you have to stay here.

Anita cried even harder. To my question—But why?—my mother responded: Well, you see, she is sixteen…But then she suddenly cut herself short and distracted me from further questioning.

That their music was so cool, that one would just as soon listen to it all day long, that she was worried about Anita because the Americans were a charming bunch, she did not want to confess out loud even to herself. The Americans were not the first to influence German language and culture, but from the beginning their occupancy had changed everything.

Back then Germany was so German, the outside influences so minimal, mass tourism still a utopian notion. Other cultures were accessible only to quite adventurous or privileged characters. People traveled to wars—the men. Later they remembered the others, the foreigners, who were a threat one defused jokingly. Whatever one did not understand was degraded to a joke, no longer dangerous. From far away one brought home shreds of language. As a present, as a memento of shared experience, the new words embedded themselves in every-day speech.

Many expressions originated in the war with France, which the older generation still remembered. Bavarians opened their "parapluies" when it rained, reached for their "porte-monnaie" to pay. Clothes hung in the "armoire." One washed in the "lavoir" or went to pee in the "pissoir."

Now we children played Yank all winter long as we sledded down the granary path on our Jeeps. We still had our "Judenstrick," ersatz cigarettes made from the winter-dried marrow of elderberry twigs, but we were infatuated with everything the Americans brought into our little world. They had landed among us with the exciting utensils of their exotic culture. Chewing gum. Nescafe. Powdered milk. Hershey's chocolate. Blue jeans. Johnson's lotion. Marlboros. Things useful and also symbols of hope, the end of terror. Our blue days were gone—long live The Blues.

Jitterbug

JUSTA AND OLGA WALKED ARM IN ARM along the riverbank. I tagged along curiously. They had dolled themselves up, wore flowerprint dresses with shoulder pads. Justa's skirt reached barely to the knee; Olga's was a tad longer. Both had piled their hair high above their foreheads. Justa had plucked her eyebrows to a thin line. They had to giggle all the time, everything was wildly funny. They pressed their breasts together as they folded their arms, crossed their legs, held their hands in front of their mouths as they giggled and at one another's ears as they whispered. They did not understand a single word of what the strange young men were saying at them.

Justa tugged in embarrassment at her flowered skirt, which kept wanting to fly up. She had to find something to do. So she started to unwind my braids. Nervously, with fidgety fingers, she tugged at my hair, laboriously braided it anew, clung irresolutely to it even after she had tied it back together.

Near Justa's feet, from out of the water, stared a fish, bringing on the dream that has kept creeping back in for several years now.

She has a knife in her hand, slits open the belly of a fish, lays it on a white cloth, and watches the red spread across the cloth like fat in a hot pan. She has stayed behind by herself. Her mother had to go visit her younger sister. Uncle Latzi and Mirko are the last guests in the pub. She dries the glasses. As she looks up, Uncle Latzi, swaying as if on a ship, comes toward her behind the counter. He does not look at her, stares past her, so that she confusedly makes way for him. But she already smells it, the liquor and tobacco, feels the old man's hand, feels the sweat on his fatty skin. Mama, she wants to cry out. But it sticks in her throat. Onion odor and cursing.

The first thing she sees as she awakens from her faint is the grease underneath the counter. A mouse sniffs at her hair. When they find her her hands are blue, so taut was the rope drawn. No one wants to hear anything about it. Everything unsaid is there to be read on her back, like newspaper gossip. Aunt Mirna, in Germany, takes her in, in exchange for work in the vegetable store. No one knows her there.

Justa's face with the flowery dress danced on the ripples. She was still tugging at my hair.

But you just finished braiding it, I said, pushing her away.

Justa still had to hold on one moment longer.

Jimmy came laughing toward her through the leafy door, took her simply by the hand, sat down on the grassy bank, and drew her to him, quite close. Too close. Her legs were bare. He touched her knee, ran his hand along her calf, drew a square in the air, gestured away from them, then toward himself.

You are going to get stockings from him, I translated saucily. Everyone on the farm wanted some, and Justa still had none.

She went red and hot in the face and almost cried, from weakness, and from the belief that she had not earned her happiness.

Olga's eyes wandered. She had not sat down and was not laughing anymore, either. She became quite silent and reflective, plucked a twig from a bush, wrapped it around her forefinger, looked for something in the river, hesitated a little while longer.

Come, she ordered, and wanted my hand.

No, no, I'm staying here.

The cuckoo called. Olga turned and went slowly off toward the farm. Joe whistled after her, but she did not turn, going faster through the undergrowth down the riverbank to the road that led straight to the house.

They were now our friends, Jim and Joe, Brad and Craig. Hershey's chocolate and Wrigley's chewing gum. The riverbank was the room where we met them again and again, not just we girls, but also the farm boys. One squatted on the bank and watched the fishing, dug for worms, made little ships out of chocolate wrappers and let them sway downriver.

Beneath the willow was my stage. Suddenly it was quite silent. Even the birds and frogs perked up their ears. The fish forgot their worm, the buzzing in the electrical shed went silent, the waterfall froze in mid-fall, I sang: *I'm a cranky old Yank in a clanky old tank, on the streets of Yokahama with my Honolulu mama, doing those beat-o, beat-o, flat-on-my-seat-o, Hirohito blues...*

I looked about me. It was still quiet. I took a bow as the roar of applause began. The waterfall fell, the birds chirped, the frogs croaked. Buoyed, I turned a few cartwheels. Finally the boys could wait no longer. There was shoving, good-natured punching, boxing. Their ears burned red. They held onto willow boughs so as not to land in the water. Clumps of American and Bavarian words flew back and forth, pretentious shrieking mixed with the song of the birds and the water. It was hot, superb, and thrillingly exotic. The foreign language sounded like soft rumbling, intoxicating, seductive tones from a foreign land.

The Americans danced the jitterbug with Justa and our new girl, Hilde. Breasts swayed and trembled, up, down, with the rhythm. Sweating, red cheeks, arms flying everywhere. Justa had no hair on her underarms.

Hilde was now Justa's best friend. Bosom buddies. Hildie the Wildie. Unbuttoned her blouse several buttons.

My father shook his head. She'll be the first one I get rid of. This fraternizing has to stop, it is going way too far!

I hid the American secret from my parents, from Anita and my grandfather. It was too beautiful, too exciting. A new freedom had forced its way in through the door of the old order. Unstoppable. We children ran alongside the Jeeps on their way down to the river.

But then, one day, Justa did not feel so well. She thought she might have to throw up.

Too much chocolate from the Americans, hmm? probed my mother. Justa blushed scarlet and dragged herself along. A little later, pale, as if someone had sucked all the blood out of her veins, she leaned against the wall in the hallway. Again she pressed her hand to her stomach. My mother pushed her into the room and closed the door. I hopped up and down the corridor, slid across the tiles; through the door I heard verbal scraps: How irresponsible...You are so young...ungrateful...don't wreck your life...

When they both reappeared, Justa was crying and slipped past me. Justa? I called.

We had wanted to pick strawberries in the garden. But Justa did not hear me. First she walked, then ran up the stairs to the second floor, to clean the rooms. Water sprayed from her bucket. The broom slipped, rattling down the stairs.

Beatrix, go play, said my mother impatiently. She peered anxiously upstairs, where we had just heard Justa's sobbing.

A few days later she and my mother climbed into the carriage with serious faces. They had to go into town. I was not allowed to come along, not under any circumstances. My mother drove. She did not need Umer. She gave the horse a lash with the whip, so that it sprang forward. Justa almost fell from her seat. Later, when they returned, Justa was even paler. She climbed slowly, puffing, up the narrow stairway above the stables, and before she closed the door to the cubbyhole where she roomed with Olga and Hilde, she waved to me.

Till tomorrow.

Are you ill? I asked.

The door remained silent.

•

Yes, and then? There was still something hidden. Before it was quite forgotten, sometime in some night, illumined by the headlights of a tractor, the buried treasures were lifted from their grave, the objects greeted like presents, un-wrapped, cleaned, dusted off. Admired, handed out, forwarded to their accustomed places.

For once it went well, said my father.

Fritz was seemingly his old self again, easily irritated and authoritarian. At least it seemed that way. Rectangular wrinkles sat on his forehead over the brows. They remained there, even when he was looking admiringly at the sky, toward the file of wild geese that gabbled across the courtyard through the sword rays of the late afternoon sun. He had second thoughts about everybody and everything, mainly worries. Quarrels great and small broke out incessantly within the seclusion of the farm. Someone poisoned someone's deal. Acts of revenge. Murder threats. In large matters as in small. He was a Schopenhauerian pessimist. It's all just one huge misery.

When I joined him for his private nibble in the living room, he forked down his meat, lost in thought, encapsulated in a cocoon. Without any noise of approbation from his throat, the boiled meat disappeared piece by piece into his mouth. Mentally absent, forgetting himself, he stared into emptiness, ruminating. When he noticed me standing in the doorway, it was as if through a fog. Did he see me at all?

Here, come over, eat, was all he said, pushing a little piece into my mouth.

My mother came into the room, stood next to him, ran her hand across his thin hair.

Fritzl, don't take it so hard.

He said nothing, chewed on.

What? I asked.

Oh, the farm and everything, she sighed, without further explanation. Eat up and go outside.

I chewed laboriously on the dry meat, through the silence, slowly, to stretch out my stay. Something hung heavily in the air. But both of them remained silent until I slipped down from the chair and went out.

The door closed but I remained leaning on the wood of the door frame, listening to the incomprehensible sounds within.

Perhaps he was sobbing. Perhaps my strong mother had laid his head on her breast, bent him out of his paralysis, toward herself.

You are not allowed in the room right now, I thought. I pushed off from the door with my foot, went down the steps into the courtyard, sat on the bench, and waited silently.

Perhaps throughout my father's life echoed his mother's horrid remark...a remark so cruel that one would rather not have known about it.

Marie-Louise had given birth to twins. Karl was the firstborn; then came Fritz, my father. Even as a little boy Fritz somehow played second fiddle, for Karl was their mother's darling. When Karl fell, right in the early days of the First World War, Marie-Louise let herself be carried away to the point of remarking: Why couldn't it have been you?

It fit her, and if one knew her, one believed it.

Yes, from childhood onward my father bore the tattoo of this mother; it was stamped into his existential passport.

Perhaps he had hopes? But essentially, he was unknowable.

Secrets

GO AHEAD, GO FOR A WALK, JUMP, GO PLAY, GET GOING, my mother would say, shooing me out into the new day.

The entire child kingdom was at my disposal. I could spend my hours wherever I pleased. My shoes, with my socks balled up inside, stood forgotten under the bench, proclaiming that I was wandering about barefoot in the cold weather. My dolls sunned themselves on a bench by the pig stalls. Surely I must be out rocking a piglet in the little cradle until it falls asleep. If I got hungry, or when the sun stood lower in the sky, I came back of my own accord. My mother, courageous as she was, never thought of dangers, and my freedom went so far that I sometimes wished I had to be home at this or that hour, like the other children.

But on some special days, for mysterious reasons, we were not allowed near the cow stalls. Why? The way my mother suddenly restricted my freedom made me curious. At any other time it was: No limits.

My mother shooed us children out into the garden on the other side of the house, off toward the brook, away from the courtyard.

Help Beatrix water the flower beds, take care of the weeds. Her garden needs it, much too dry.

We did not feel like it. In the distance, by the cow stalls, loitered a group of workers. We children wanted to be there, too. We escaped through the flowers, across the bridge to the stalls.

We found a place up in the hayloft. There one could peer through the gaps between the planks. From our box seats we could survey the courtyard and observe the goings-on down below. Several workers stood about, holding a powwow. We children made ourselves at home up at our peepholes. But then the big boys clambered up and shoved us aside. Now we had to make do with smaller openings in the wood. Through the slat window we saw a cow led from the stall.

Below us a thick iron ring hung on the wall, with wooden beams on both sides. The cow was led between them and bound firmly. Then the bull Jupiter appeared, the one we all so much feared. Beni led him using a heavy stick through his nose ring. A blond fur blanket enwrapped the knots of muscle running across his back, flowing into one another like soft gears with every move. Rolling slowly, aristocratically, with his goal firmly in mind, over to where the cow stood, he snorted and sniffed beneath her tail; then, determinedly, with unexpected lightness, he mounted her, thrust, dancing on his rear legs, pressing his massive head into the cow's back.

Now the boys in the hay went quite wild, tussled, and shrieked.

Give it to her, Jupiter! Oooh, now he'll never stop! Xaver and Louis raved with excitement, hopping about and shoving the older girls into the loose hay.

Wanna see a big one? they stage-whispered, red up to their ears with arousal. Already they were unbuttoning their flies. Wanna see?

The twins and I pulled closer together and stared expectantly. Somehow this scene was not really meant for us. More for the two boys, and for Xeni, Rita, and Luisi, the older girls.

They hauled out their stiff pricks from their flies and massaged them further, right in front of us, giggling and squealing, but also with a trace of fear sketched on their faces.

Don't say nuthin'! Hear? Louis threatened, buttoning his fly back up and holding his fist under Lenerl's nose. Sultry and forbidden, a sticky novelty that could not remain in the sweet-smelling hay.

I slid quickly down from the haystack and was oddly certain that only Louis, Xaver, and the watchdog Pluto had a pink thing like that between their legs. But Pluto's was pointier.

Eee! I'll tell my mummy, I blubbered.

I raced to the chute, jumped down, sprinted through the cow stall, then through the stables, into the house. Saved. My heart pounded. Inside me little loose clumps hopped like bullets. I knew I could say nothing to anybody. I was afraid and yet attracted. What was to become of this secret? What to do with it? Would it lie down under the linden tree, drown in the garden brook, rot with the plate scrapings in the chicken yard, calm itself in the dissection of a bug?

Not a word to my mother about what I had just experienced. No, no, she was very mysterious about certain matters. In the bathroom she gave me one towel for my face and another for "down there." I sat on the portable bidet as my mother washed my bottom. Then I dried myself with the "down there" towel. My mother looked on seriously, busily cutting off any questions with: You are still too little. Or a vague: You'll see when the time comes. One doesn't talk about that.

But Justa and Olga talk about it, I said. They do something with their tongues.

A moment of horror.

My mother, irritated: Those are proles.

For me everything was a gigantic chaos of secrets, forbidden unanswered questions. Somehow this theme was thoroughly unpleasant to my mother, revealing a prudish side of her otherwise so superb personality.

I, who spent most of my time unobserved among the servant folk, had sharpened my perceptiveness and intellect in a quite special way. For there the proceedings were not in the least secretive. A spade was called a spade. Bawdy stories were told without a trace of embarrassment. The most vulgar Bavarian idioms mated with foreign curses, even physical learning aids. Jealousy and hatred exploded when an atmospheric thickness, contracted to critical mass, was set off by verbal dynamite. I stood around and observed these deft theatrical entrances and exits with a child's cool, sharp understanding and enthusiasm for the dramatic.

•

One sunny afternoon I sat quite a long while, a child eternity, on the round boulder at the gate, passing the time by pushing a stone into the path of a mud beetle and watching how he was forced to creep now right, now left, around the monstrosity. No earthly power could divert him from getting through under the gate.

Finally the König children came back from school. Satchels flew in a high arc. Lenerl and Roserl begged part of my buttered bread. We sauntered behind the Königs' house, to the long cement wall, opposite the bee house, where it was cool under the lace pattern of leaves. We took bites of my bread, then hopped up and down, up, down, until we got really hot. Sweaty, with red apple cheeks, exhausted from being children, we fell into the grass.

Around the corner sauntered Xaver and Louis, hands in their pockets, their caps at a rakish angle above their ears, something threatening in their manner.

I have to pee, I quickly said, and started off toward our house. But Louis grabbed me by the arm.

Show us how far you can piss.

O terror! How did he know? I tried to rip myself loose, kicking his shin, but he held me quite firmly and would not let go. I tried biting into his hand, but he switched hands fast as lightning.

Ha! he taunted. I've been as fast as you for quite some time.

Oouuch! You shitty asshole! I screamed, frantically contemplating my next move.

Lenerl, Roserl, and I often met at the wall, dropped our panties, and squatted down. Then we pressed, peed, and pressed again. The longest jet was the winner. We dried ourselves with leaves, pulled up our panties, and measured.

But how did the big boys know about that? I stopped tugging, kept quite still. Louis' grip grew lighter. His attentiveness flagged. At that second I executed a lightning-fast turn, ripped myself free, slipped through beneath his arm, and raced off. Fear made me as fast as a rabbit.

Louis gave a whistle in my direction: I'll get you yet, you tattletale. He set off after me, but his aggressiveness was quickly diluted by a more exciting matter:

Rita, straddled on the wall, licking on a honeycomb, swinging her long bare legs expectantly.

NEGROES

In the heat of the day I had already freed myself from my socks and wooden shoes. These I hated because of all the noise they made. The gravel crunched loudly with every step, so when I came running, everyone looked up, knowing well in advance it was me.

We children had been messing around at the trout stream, by the waterfall, where the cows passed by on their way to the pasture. There was always fresh cow manure splattered about, green blobs with a crust on top, warmed by the sun. We trod right into them and watched the dark green mass squish between our toes. It felt warm and soft and friendly, comfortable. To clean off our feet we ran down to the river. The water was always cool, in constant motion. Tiny fishes darted off when someone disturbed their solar bath. And where the animals drank there was a swampy corner, its black mud furrowed through with hoof-prints. Near the warm puddles flies and dragonflies crouched on moist clods, beneath buzzing swarms of horseflies and bumblebees.

Oh, today it is too hot. The warm little pool emitted humid and oppressive noise. We children took our clothes off, piled them up on a tree stump, waded into the deeper water, paddled about a little. Someone started throwing slime-balls and the lightbulb went on in my head.

Let's play Negroes, I cried excitedly.

Oh yes! Immediately they were all on board. We dried ourselves off and covered our naked bodies with the dark mud, helped one another do our backs, smearing them good and thick, no holes allowed. Then we caked our faces and our hair too. No one could possibly recognize us. They would all think we were Moors. In this disguise we sneaked around the hayrack into the middle of the courtyard.

Uli, Dieter, and Georg were taking a cigarette break under the linden tree in the shadows. They were quasi-supervisors of the Polish workers.

Pssst! Pressing fingers to our lips, we slinked up to them with long feline strides. We were black, unrecognizable, and would give those three under the tree the shock of their lives.

They loafed around in the shadows, smoked, noticed nothing, heard nothing, looked up toward the sky, pointed in the opposite direction, where they must have discovered something remarkable.

Triumph was imminent. Within one second those three would be scared out of their wits.

Whoa! All three turned at once, each grabbing one of us.

Gotcha, said Dieter, putting a hold on me and heaving me high up into the air. I struggled and screamed, then started bawling. Everything had gone wrong. They were supposed to be scared. They held us squirming children in vises as they laughed themselves senseless.

Naturally a few curious bystanders came. Uli took a hose and peeled off our warm black skin with a cold shower. We were ashamed at the brown soup trickling down our thin bodies. Never had we been so naked and humiliated. I kicked and bit about me in rage like a maniac. Not the least bit funny. Where was my comforting mother? Oh, God, and we had left our clothes down at the river, an endless distance away.

The strident wailing attracted an even larger audience, laughing themselves sick and pointing fingers at us. All around us grinning Schadenfreude. What a hoot. The moment there was something to mock they were on the job. Unconcealed cruelty was an essential element of their joy, raw and hard, even when it came to children. As if pity had not yet been invented, this lust glowed constantly, like coal in the hearth, and ignited immediately with the tiniest piece of paper.

HOT CIGAR

Childhood winters, drunk with snow. High mountains and drifts along the fence. Yellow tracks crisscrossed the great white courtyard when the cow herd was led from one stall to the other like a fat snake. Big footprints crossed the yard behind the one-wheel track of the pushcart that carried oats for the horses. A thin bicycle track. Dog paw prints. Then a fresh snow laid itself white over everything so that the next morning telltale boot prints could inform the whole household that Umer had been visiting Justa.

We children sledded down from the hayrick driveway, swinging to a stop with a curving scrape of our heels. The big boys hung around in the cold and annoyed us little kids.

Peter said I should go get one of my father's cigars.

No, that's stealing, I said strictly. But they pressed me.

Go shoot one down, kid. They shoved me about, harassed me, until I reconsidered after all and provisionally promised—I did so want to be their favorite.

The cigars, carefully counted, slumbered in a humidor in Father's office, under the rolltop of his desk, beneath the telephone, near the courtyard window, on the right side, in the drawer, way at the back.

Go get it yourselves. I tormented them, feeling my power. Only I knew where the cigars were; only I could pass unhindered into the house.

The boys feared my father. I did too, to a certain extent. But today I played the overdog, thrilled to be the ringleader of so ticklish an operation.

I don't know if it will work, I said, stretching their desire like an elastic band.

Go fetch it, then we will play Amis with you, Louis flattered, quite close to my ear.

Play Amis, play Amis? Hmm, hmm, very tempting. Not that I had a clue what they meant by it, but the sound was thoroughly intriguing. Amis was what we called the American soldier friends we had been fishing with all summer long. "Thank you," we always said, "okay," "goodbye."

Allll right, I said, and hopped over on one leg to my friends Roserl and Lenerl.

Somewhat later I quietly opened the office door. The room was empty. Climbing onto a chair, I tugged the drawer, opened the humidor, grabbed a cigar, pushed it down my trouser leg until it met the elastic band above my boot, and ran outside.

Now we want to play Amis, I cried out, pointing to myself and my friends as I removed the cigar from its makeshift compartment.

The big boys beat their breasts: We are the Amis, you are the Ami-Schicksen. You sit in front on the sleds, we sit behind.

Important preparations were made. We girls received sticks of elderberry, their marrow dried to a white papery mass by the winter—our so-called Judenstrick cigarettes. Expectantly and excitedly we hopped from one leg to another, holding the twigs between our gloved fingers as we had seen the grownups do. We lit wooden matches behind our cupped hands and drew air through the shaft. The delight of forbidden fruit outweighed the dreadful taste and inevitable coughing.

Climbing aboard our sleds, we raced down the hill: Louis, Peter, and Xaver at the rear, we little girls in front. At the bottom we curved to a scraping stop where Xaver the "border officer" gesticulated with a stick in the air. Stop! he cried, his arms gesturing officiously. We had to climb down from the sleds and park them in a row.

Then came the great moment: the lighting of the stolen cigar. The boys inhaled, puffed, coughed heavily, and rolled in the snow, drunk with boyhood. We girls smoked our Judenstricks and watched.

Then we got bored and slightly nauseated. We wanted to toboggan some more. But it was not so simple, for now one had to show Louis one's imaginary passport—some random object from our pockets. One crossed the border, or not, entirely at his pleasure. The boys had the power, as the American occupying forces did over Germany. We girls thought this fitting and were thrilled. The game had its laws. Rules had to be obeyed, lest one be banished to a snowdrift as punishment and required to wait until one was released and permitted to drive again. Children love such protocols. The ancient game of lordship, as played on a farm in postwar Germany.

Time went by. We climbed back up with our sleds and raced back down, huffing little clouds into the cold air, our cheeks growing red. But the three cigar smokers, befuddled with tobacco, intoxicated with power, had rather over-reached themselves. One of them was already puking in the snow.

Their real trouble was just beginning. Far above us the portrait of my father suddenly loomed in the black hole of the granary door frame. I saw him instantly. Lame with fear, I could not take a step, nor make a sound. He calmly observed the scene. In his hand was the long training whip he applied so superbly to the Arab horses when he drove the carriage, gently grazing the back of the nearest two, slightly more forceful when they were sluggish going uphill.

Using matches near the haylofts was strictly forbidden, as everyone knew. Boys' smoking too, of course. My father was the only one who still had cigars like these from before the war. His ace in the hole. Counted out, sealed into the homogenous coolness of the humidor. Naturally he knew exactly what was going on, and I knew he knew everything. Slowly, step by step, he descended the hill. Only an illusory fragment of space and time still separated us.

By the time the boys heard the whistling swish of the whip, Louis's cap was already flying from his head. It was too late to run away. As fast as lightning my father had Xaver's sleeve in his grip, the whip in his other hand. The boys stepped backward and huddled together, eyes bulging with terror. Fritz's gaze held the little group like a magnet.

So, gentlemen. You smoke my cigars, you play with fire around the hayloft! His blue eagle eyes mustered the three criminals.

I'll show you! Dirty riffraff! he spat out in a cold rage.

He had already thought of the punishment. It had to fit the crime.

Tomorrow at four a.m. you are to appear in the pigsty. There the manure will quickly be rinsed from your brains, you wretched idiots. Step forward! Early manure shift. Every morning, before school. For a whole month! The threatening whip pummel drew closer to their red faces.

And woe betide you if you fail to appear! Then you will really get to know me!

Faced with the gigantic primal father, I felt sick to my stomach; but when he finally let go of Peter, I courageously took his hand. I wanted to position myself on his side, against the delinquents. Perhaps he would forget the cigar, and with this gesture I could remind him of the private feast we had just had at the table, of the Weisswürste with sweet mustard and the fresh buttered bread we had enjoyed a few hours earlier, when he even posed the astonishing question: Well, what do you want from Father Christmas this year? Did he remember?

And you? he said, bending down to me. The eyes behind his glasses did not blink; his gaze was fixed and attentive. I could not help thinking of the falcon we had watched as he devoured the chicken he had stolen and killed. Now he can have it, Father had said, laying his finger across my mouth to keep me quiet, so we could observe the wild creature at his bloody banquet. With this picture before my eyes, my thoughts drifted off, lingered with the bird, the scarlet feathers. How does he get them clean again? I racked my brains. Blood doesn't go away.

From the far distance the voice of eternal damnation blared further into my thoughts.

You left the drawer open and I followed your footprints in the snow, he continued in an uncharacteristically calm voice, openly revealing how he had found out. Was I meant to learn from this that the delinquent always gives himself away? Or that he should learn craftier cunning?

Hmm...still in the iron grip. Go now, take your sled, and off with you into the house! Take the brush and groom the dogs.

With that he let my hand drop. He had clenched it so firmly and bent it so far toward him that his ring had left a dent.

He turned around and went away.

The group stood frozen and silent, my father's voice still with us. Quite slowly our paralysis melted away. I took my sled. My father's whip had sketched a straight line in the snow next to his footprints, to his right. Slowly I followed the whip line, step by step, through the endless courtyard, past Pluto's doghouse, on past the dovecote.

Heaven and Hell

AS ONE TRAVELS THROUGH MEMORY, pictures suddenly take shape; behind them, without warning, a deeper cluster of emotion not readily processed by reason, fingering the brain like early rays of sun on the horizon, secreting strings of pearls, events thought lost but ever ready to break into the open as our personal history…

Once as I returned from a walk along a little river, I saw nearby a meadow surrounded by a very high fence. In one corner a herd of deer grazed quite peacefully: does, a single stag, and a few fawns. In another corner stood a tower with ladder stairs leading onto a platform. The tame animals, the fence, the tower: I had thought nothing further of them. Just a momentary snapshot. But this image forced itself upon me and suddenly pieced itself together: someone must climb onto the platform and shoot at the fenced-in, clueless wildlife. It was a shooting stand. Those who put it up had better hide it from others, for the cruelty of the setup was obvious. Suddenly a story jumped at me like a dog. A story of defenselessness, of being fenced in, and of utter horror.

Not long after the war's end, on an unforgettable day, Lenerl, Roserl, and I were playing on the road in front of the house. We had traced out seven boxes in the dry dirt. Seven days of the week. On the ground before us in the form of a crucifix lay the game. We were playing Heaven and Hell. First you drew lots. Then you had to toss the stone into one of the squares, hop on one leg from day to day to fetch your stone, and hop back, without allowing the other foot to touch the ground. If you got through the whole week on one leg, you went to heaven; when you lost your balance and your foot touched the sand, or you dropped the stone—Boy, are you dumb! —it was off to hell.

Look, look, cried Roserl, pointing into the shadows of the tree-lined avenue. Something was moving toward us, something strange, like an insect on the skin of the familiar landscape. Something multicolored, mobile, grew toward us, spread itself out, became more distinct, took shape, grew recognizable. A swaying crowd of people slowly approached, maybe sixty of them: heterogeneous, ponderous, almost soundless. Country folk in ethnic garb mixed in with others—brown-skinned ones with tousled black hair wearing red trousers and orange jackets. All of their clothes were ripped, often only shreds, hanging on their bony bodies. The group drew closer and closer, a whole that just barely held itself together.

We children, now holding onto each other in fear and curiosity, turned around and shouted into the courtyard: Come, come, look!

Everyone who heard us dropped what they were doing and came running. The farm community gathered into a coherent whole, forming a half-circle: horrified curiosity, curious horror, staring rigidly at the approaching strangers in their desiccated floral colors, the skin of their faces gaunt and gray like dusty paper. A faraway stare from gutted eyes. Who were they? Where were they coming from on this June day? Above shone the sun, warm and indifferent; between us and them, traced in the dust, the game of Heaven and Hell.

Dachau, breathed the young man who led them, almost inaudibly.

Oh god, oh god, oh mei, oh mei. Those in the back of the crowd craned their necks. So that was what it looked like, the thing one had heard about. Now everyone saw with their own eyes what their minds had not grasped nor been able to imagine.

My mother and my father came rushing onto the scene. With one glance: Make room, let them through! Fritz commanded.

Leaning on one another, the prisoners dragged themselves into our broad courtyard. The farmworkers ran here and there, exchanging barked orders. Bales of straw were quickly piled up under the roof outside the stables. Many sat down; others, exhausted, simply fell to the ground.

A magnetic field of rage, pity, and shame constantly buzzed around our farm: conflicting languages and qualities, characteristic differences, pride in things others thought nothing of, laughter where someone else took mortal offense, anger and drollery where others cried, pointed fingers of blame and shame. But confronted with this horror, we were unified. As the Slavic forced laborers interacted with the hungry prisoners, one felt a flicker of hope spreading across the courtyard.

Liberated from Dachau by the American army, they had landed here with us. They had simply headed eastward, toward the sunrise. Their homeland must lie somewhere in that direction: Serbia, Croatia, Bulgaria, Yugoslavia. The scene seemed more like a vision, or a stage set, or a film, a reality in which the seemingly impossible transpired. Now one saw in the flesh what one had heard, had been unable to believe, had pushed away to protect oneself, because such talk was—come on—it was insane. How could poor foreign farmers, gypsies, and country folk have ended up in Dachau? And why? What for?

The Aryan madness of Adolf Schicklgruber, foamed my father. The purest madness. He shook his fist against the absent criminal. Then, with his customary clarity, he organized the rescue operation. Provisional tents were put up.

First they have to eat, Mother said.

In the courtyard two fires were started up. My mother and Olga cooked porridge over one of them in a gigantic soup pot.

Many were too exhausted to eat, as they had eaten nothing but grass for months.

Days later, once their stomachs had become somewhat accustomed to food again, a few chickens went into the soup.

Over the other fire, in another great pot, boiled their all-too-colorful clothes. Lice and bugs tried to save themselves by running up the sleeves that protruded from the swirling hot water. Armed with a wooden spoon, Justa jabbed around until everything cloth-like drowned and the dead creatures swam in the soapy brew.

I am so glad it's not raining, said my mother, looking upward.

The refugees had to be deloused. Wordlessly, they formed a row. They leaned along the fabric wall, towels and bedspreads wrapped around their emaciated bodies. Their wraps reminded me of the pictures with the pyramids above my father's desk. But there, the people were bronzed and strong; an imaginary sun cast long shadows before them in the sand.

Thick clouds of dust hung in the tent. And while the delousing was in full swing, we children also had our turn. Oh, I hated the smell of DDT, which hung in the air like a swarm of wasps, thick and dangerous, refusing to be washed away, sucking on the skin like a tick, biting into the eyes. I waited with the rest, a towel across my shoulders.

But I don't have any lice! I protested. I don't!

Precaution, said Aunt Julia strictly. It could happen. And already my turn had come to be dusted.

Once I had taken a pair of scissors and quickly, before she could protest, cut off Roserl's braids right up behind her ears. Having the thickest hair, Roserl was always the first to bring lice home. That is why I had thought one ought to tackle the problem energetically. Roserl had run screaming to her house, pointing back at me, struggling for breath, unable to get a single sound out. Arriving at Mother Resi's, she had buried her face in her skirt. I had stood there, the braids in my hand, but no one had said anything, for I was Beatrix of the Osts and had my mother's soothing words: Oh, it'll grow back.

After the Serbs were deloused, they sat outside in front of the delousing tent and stared off into space, overcome by the incredible proximity of their salvation, the infinitesimal distance between certain death and new life, between the cabinet of horrors and the protection of this courtyard. They looked at the trees, watched the doves, the circling swallows, as if for the first time. They lifted their heads to the blue roof, took note of the gaping children, the soothing soup

steaming in the great pot, the farm dog, the bicycle, the bug diligently pushing its dust ball.

All this, here in our courtyard, seemed to burst the previous bounds of their imagination. Hours had flowed into days, days into weeks, months. The unimaginable horror that lay behind them was sketched on their faces. They stared incredulously. They studied, documented, engraved, probed, could scarcely believe it.

I helped my mother. I held bandages, passed the scissors and ointments, so she and Aunt Julia could dress their wounds. Alexandra ran and fetched alcohol and red iodine from the stables, where Umer used them to disinfect hooves.

Traversing the surreal ranks of the rescued, my mother was hope itself, touching a shoulder, holding a hand, stroking a head. Now you are safe, things will get better, she said, spooning soup into a bowl to feed an old woman. She could not share their suffering, but suffer she did, and through the strength within, her touch made those she touched strong. Once, a local miracle worker who healed diseases through the laying on of hands had told my mother: What my hands can do, yours can, too. Oddly, he himself sported a goiter on his throat, which distinguished him in the eyes of some, while awakening in others the question of why he couldn't rid himself of that growth.

For many days and nights, a fortnight perhaps, the Serbs lodged in the courtyard tents or on straw in the cow stalls. They sat around and took it all in like a foreign language or a new skill, the way children learning to walk first stumble along and have to hold on to something. They held on to a gesture, a word, a glance, the soup, the bandages, the warm blanket, sunrise. Their eyes followed a butterfly, higher, up to the cumulus clouds, back into the courtyard, to their new friends, their own hands.

Slowly a goodly heaven of clear blue hope expanded above the courtyard, with sympathy spread out beneath it like a carpet. Everyone in the house could measure their enormous luck by the misery standing before them. Rumors had naturally flown in already from every direction—mountains of valuables, clothing, skeletons—but this here in our courtyard was the reality. We saw it all; they did not need to speak.

Step by step, their bodies got a little stronger, their hearts lighter. Finally they decided the time had come to continue their journey east. Hand-drawn maps were rolled up, packets of food were wrapped in newspaper tied with yarn and thrown over their shoulders. At the farewell, some cried. One old man was very sick and weak. He sat on a straw sack, leaning on a cane, a gray braid dividing his back in two. Broad red trousers mended with colorful patches hung across his bony knees. My mother and father stood there with him.

He's not able to walk so far, my mother said, furrowing her brow.

Umer, come here, my father said. Talk to him, interpret for us.

The old man whispered something, looking up at my mother, his dark eyes watering and blinking, his lips trembling, his voice almost inaudible.

Umer nodded in agreement, touching the old man's shoulder.

Cannot walk with others, he said.

By now, many Serbs had already taken their leave. Some, on their way out, bent and kissed the old man. He shaded his brow with his hand and gazed after them.

We watched the last of them go. I could see their colorful clothes through the trees as they walked off down the winding road. Eastward.

My father decided we should keep the old man with us.

In the bee house was an empty room containing only the white linen coats and the masks hanging at the door for when the beekeeper and my mother tended the bees. An army cot was put at the window and the old man was laid on it, dull and flat.

With my hands I framed my eyes so I could look through the window and see the sick man in bed, my mother in the chair next to him, a candle burning between them. A warm strip of sun caressed my back for a moment. Then a cloud caught up with it and coolness returned. Near the three of us hummed the bees.

I was not allowed in for any reason, since the sick man had typhoid fever. My mother fed him; miraculously, her fearlessness made her immune to every disease. With her left hand she supported his head so he could better swallow. The old man could only eat one or two spoonfuls before he sank lifelessly back into his pillow. She talked to him. What did she say? Perhaps she murmured a magic formula to make him well. Or she sang. My mother held his hand. He was still; she was still.

My mother turned toward the window. Does she see me? I wondered. But she seemed to be looking further out: across the little stone wall, through the Königs' house, to the chapel, and on into the war.

The sick man's red shirt showed at his throat. His arm lay red across the gray wool blanket. The candle flickered. A white light played across my mother's neck, her hair, the blue of her blouse; it breathed across the man's face, then it went out. She rested her hand on his forehead. It must have been feverish, for she took a cloth, wrung it out over the bucket, laid it on the bushy brows, on his forehead, with her hand on top. She had done the same when I had fever and swollen tonsils. The fever, the cool cloth, my mother, the fairy books of Ernst Kreidolf.

Her sudden voice startled me.

Pluck flowers and bring them, she commanded through the crack in the door. And a vase.

Off I ran.

The next morning, my mother enshrouded the man's lifeless body in a linen cloth like a larva and laid the bouquet in his coffin, together with his bedclothes, spoon, and the plate he had eaten from.

Now they are going to lay him deep in the earth, I thought. There he will become a butterfly. No, first, a caterpillar.

The coffin was put onto the undertaker's cart.

Auf geht's! he cried, as the horse pulled the wagon away.

My mother stood there watching, her arms folded, lost in thought. She drew a deep breath. The wheels creaked in the gravel, the leafy boughs bent down to the dead man, until in the distance the avenue gate fell shut.

Adi wrenched herself away, went into the house, washed her hands slowly and thoroughly over the kitchen stone. The last scene had been played, the curtain had fallen; its fabric still swayed. Backstage was construction, moving, piling up, repainting. Now they all knew, the skeptics too, and the prettifiers, the know-it-alls.

The Taste of Salt

ELEVEN O'CLOCK, THE EMPTY HOUR. It is no longer one thing and not yet another. The day began before dawn, with the ants. As soon as it grew light, Justa already had her first round of chores behind her. Lugging hot water upstairs. Emptying the chamber pots.

In the upstairs hallway, in front of the Blue Room, General Brün and his son Peter stood waiting in their morning robes. Have you finally got this experience behind you, scolded the General impatiently through the wooden door. This eternal procedure!

Muffled splashing from within. Finally the door opened and a new shift began. Now it was the General and Peter who took their gentlemen's turn and Mrs. Brün who had to stay outside. She was still in her flannel robe. It was particularly embarrassing for her to be not yet impeccably dressed. If someone went by she apologized for her unpresentable exterior and went a little red, as if she were standing naked in the door frame with a huge love bite on her neck. The door opened again and Peter appeared, his wet hair combed close to his skull. Mrs. Brün made an unsuccessful attempt to force her way through the crack in the door.

I'm not done yet, Peter... the General's voice, from within.

With a polite sigh, Mrs. Brun gave in. Quarreling was not worth it.

Grandmother wrenched open the door to the corridor. Draft. Grandfather had been smoking and reading in bed. Now his fingers were frozen stiff from holding his book and pipe. This was how she got him out of the sack: she stopped it from being cozy. Marie-Louise's nagging did not much disturb him. That he could listen past. But the cold from the wide-open window…

Yes, I'm getting up, I'm getting up.

Theodor had kept his bachelor habits. Only a few oddball quirks, as he called them. A man needs them, otherwise he loses the individualism he needs to be a thinking man rather than a conformist machine.

When Grandfather was young he had a manservant, Alois, a strong, simple country soul, the middle son of a butcher dynasty. Little else was known about him. Why should I know more about him? Theodor would say. If he wants to tell me, he will. I know his name, and he likes his work.

Alois appeared in Grandfather's life and stayed on because Theodor liked him. This friendly fellow, with a perpetual grin across his broad and gentle face, swiftly and joyfully executed every task young Theodor was indifferent to, or could not be bothered with, or simply did not notice. So it was that Alois became part of Grandfather's life long before his marriage to Marie-Louise.

Marie-Louise tolerated Alois but was always eager to find fault with him.

The lazy lout, the good-for-nothing, she scolded. Didn't want to be responsible for the whole household, just for his master. Breakfast in bed, dressing, waxing boots, polishing silver cases, starching shirts. These male arrangements. She was insanely jealous of Alois. He was too free, too much of an individualist. She already had one free male spirit in her marriage. Now her manipulative character wanted and needed a more devout servant soul.

Minutes after my grandfather went off to fulfill his daily professorial duties, Alois picked up his hat and coat and fled the apartment. He sat on a park bench, fed pigeons, strolled in the park, or not—no one knew exactly where he was, just that he was not in the house with Grandmother. For him that prospect must have been unbearable, perhaps even dangerous. On his prowls he kept his eye on the clock, for shortly before my grandfather came home, Alois stepped across the threshold, at his service once again. Never once was he late.

One day a policeman knocked on my grandparents' door. He wanted to speak to Alois Schindhammer. Alois, shy and overwhelmed by the presence of such an authority and such unwanted attention, closed the kitchen door with a soft thud, then tiptoed to the chair and sat on its edge by the table, his hands resting on his knees, eyes downward. The policeman measured the kitchen with military steps, to intimidate Alois.

That, here, is your private affair, he said, pointing about the place, but do tell me a bit about your family, about the butcher shop, who has what to say, who buys the animals, who makes the sausages, who does the slaughtering. The policeman tapped the table with authoritarian finality.

The policeman wanted Alois to spill the beans on his brother Franz Schindhammer—in other words, on the whole Schindhammer dynasty, four family members altogether, with their butcher shop in the suburbs of Munich. Alois was the exception: he got sick just looking at meat, which is why he got into the manservant business in the first place.

My grandmother had both ears glued to the door. But the lips of Alois Schindhammer remained sealed. Supposedly horsemeat had been found in the Schindhammers' pork sausages. A sausage scandal. Surely even an outsider like Alois must have caught wind of it.

After that, Grandmother had something concrete to hold against Alois. She did not want a member of such a family in her husband's entourage.

That does it, she screamed. I do not want anything to do with someone like that.

And why not? Alois dared to say. For heaven's sake, I am a vegetarian! he added softly.

Yes, but that won't do you any good. It was you who brought the police into our house. What are the neighbors supposed to think?

Marie-Louise could tolerate a lot, she said, but no criminals beneath her roof. Her feelings displayed themselves with grand final gestures. Against her no one could make any headway, and Grandfather had given up trying.

I don't give a damn about the neighbors, said Grandfather, but it didn't do any good. Alois, reluctantly and with a sad smile on his face, slowly descended the stairs with his suitcase and canary cage.

Beneath our roof things were abuzz. Aunt Julia ran along the corridors in her wedge heels, click, clack, the shoes clattered, in counterpoint to the clanking of her bracelets. Even at this early morning hour the efficient Julia was dashing through the hallways, rationing the laundry soap and Justa's work time. The soap was produced in the kitchen, preserved in flake form in jars, and frugally dispensed.

Aunt Julia directed the progress of the cleaning like an orchestra, pursuing Justa through the rooms, testing bookcases and headboards with a sweep of her finger.

Look here, she said sternly, and showed Justa the gray residue.

Everything ran like clockwork. After all the beds were made, the chamber pots brought back, stowed away in the night cabinets, and various things swept, Julia ordered Justa into the washhouse across the way, where Mrs. Tafelmeier was already soaking the shirts. The collars had to be handled with particular attention, the cuffs, too, scraped up and down on the washboard.

Don't rip the buttons off, you stupid slattern! she scolded, when something hard clinked on tin.

With this efficiency she got further, but not far. Sometimes things went smoothly, sometimes not at all. Today the soap was stolen, a room locked from the inside; tomorrow Olga would not be able to take it anymore, and everything would have to be laboriously reorganized. Everyone had some ambition or other.

Once a month bread was baked. In the baking shed with its huge oven, the dough rose overnight in long wood troughs. Olga and Hilde formed oval loaves and carried them on a long-handled wooden shovel into the hot waiting maw of the oven. When fully baked, the loaves were piled up in the pantry on boards. This freshly baked sourdough bread was the most delicious imaginable, thickly smeared with butter that melted on the still-warm surface. After a while, when the bread was too hard to chew, the crispy crusts were dipped in liquid: soup, milk, meat drippings.

Lunchtime for the field workers. Olga made sandwiches. She cut large oval slices from the sourdough, laid them out in long rows, and deftly smeared pork fat across them. Then came a thick piece of blood sausage or liverwurst. The blood sausage came from the blood of the pigs, the liverwurst from their livers.

My mother had learned home economics, with all the tricks of the trade, at Arvedshof. This estate near Leipzig had been built by her grandfather, the prominent architect Arved Rossbach. Arved's socialistically inclined wife, Therese, had founded a women's school there in 1920. The school and the socialized housing experiment were one of the first to have bathrooms with toilets for the underprivileged. Therese Rossbach, with her communitarian heart, took in so-called fallen girls. Their children went to school on the estate. Therese made sure everyone made something of himself. The girls were raised to be efficient in the home, also in the hotel trade; the boys were sent into the military. Anything to keep them off the streets—anything but the church, was Therese's motto.

Grandmother Therese was Arved's second wife, several years older than her very wealthy, handsome husband. He had actually built the estate and the school with its communal housing for his first wife, who had been very beautiful but who died young. Grandmother Therese, with her passion and energy, took over. My mother told us the unimaginable story that this step-grandmother had had a facelift as early as 1922, to keep pace with the times and with the dream that had come true late in her life.

Therese and Arved also built themselves an alpine summer paradise: the Sonnenköpfl at Berchtesgaden on the Obersalzberg. A dreamlike country estate in the Bavarian style. There one spent the summer months in the fresh alpine air, drank goat's milk and washed one's face with it. When Adolf Hitler came to power, he confiscated the Sonnenköpfl, tore it down, and built his Nazi fortress in its place. Whenever the conversation turned to the Sonnenköpfl, my father fell into a rage. It made him ill that his wife's inheritance had been destroyed by the Nazis, and that they had got so close to his family. The thought alone incited his fury.

SAUSAGES

Once a month the butcher came. That day there was no washing. The washhouse became a slaughterhouse. There the butcher-magician transformed a giant pig into sausages and ham. My mother had to stand in the midst of it all and oversee the slaughtering. She wore a leather apron, splattered with bloodstains. Her excellent schooling in home economics had made Adi an expert on seasoning sausage meat, before it was stuffed into the sheep intestines and all sorts of delicious sausages tied off.

My father kept his distance, giving exact instructions from afar: Don't use too much marjoram, I can't stand it. I too did not look on, did not want to see anything or be anywhere near. I hated the smell and the screams of the pigs, who knew exactly what was happening to them. Aaw… I had played with some of them when they were piglets, ran after them, held them up, pressed them close to my ear, listened to their grunting, decorated their soft pink hooves with ribbons, driven them around in circles in the doll carriage to lull them to sleep.

All the knowledge about sausage production quickly sank into the abstract code system of my child brain. No sooner was the butcher gone but the slaughter was forgotten and the beloved sausages were piled three layers high between bread slices. I sat on the little wall, sharing a sausage sandwich with the König children. There was buzzing from the bee house. Sparrows multiplied beneath our swinging legs, around the breadcrumbs. Cuckoo, cuckoo, sang the cuckoo from afar. Under the trees hovered newly emerged mosquito swarms. Nothing was said. It tasted good.

Food was our currency. Everything was still rationed by the Americans. Horse feed, fabrics, shoe soles, even good conscience. Later, my schoolbooks, too, and cleaning fluids, medicines from the pharmacy—all was procured with food.

Since our needs went far beyond the American quotas, we secretly manufactured unofficial sausages, with Umer's help. The spicier ones from his Slavic homeland. Umer kept his mouth shut. Him you could trust.

It was decided: Georg, Dieter, and Umer would do the slaughtering at night, when everyone was asleep, many of them snoring deeply and loudly in moonshine intoxication. Away from the bustle of the farm, at the corner of the orchard where the old apple trees stood, in the hut where we normally grew plants, they went into production of spicy sausages. Then the treasure was smuggled into the icehouse. These delicacies were our ace in the hole: Depreziner and Hungarian salami.

PRIVILEGE

My father's kind of love. My father loved his land. His eyes caressed it with a lover's gaze. The world of critters amused him and filled his heart with tenderness. He knew about the smallest creatures. He knew ants kept mites in their cities, milking them like cows. Storks were married for life, wild geese too. And yet to us his love was almost indetectable, as with an unclear photo where you squint to sharpen the picture. He tolerated no physical tenderness, no smooching. That was my mother's department. I can only remember a sort of patting on my head, as if I were his hunting dog. Oh, but yes, his dry hand holding mine, that I remember. Warm, with a firm grip. He might take me with him to show me something, but—no kiss. I cannot remember a single kiss. And yet I knew his love.

Children know so much. They crank everything they see and experience through a usefulness machine, into a compost heap. Everything piles up and ferments, to become a nourishing bed for the plants of life. That's a country child's analogy, and I as a country child partook of what his love told me was a particular privilege.

The sacrament of privilege was celebrated at eleven o'clock, the empty hour, no longer one thing and not yet another. The tiled stove hummed in the large dining room. Beneath it dozed the dogs in their sleep niches. Our grandfather clock ticked. Tick, tock. Tick, tock. Otherwise only stillness, with an occasional noise from the courtyard or the corridor to interrupt the scratching of a knife cutting meat on a wooden plate.

My father had come to the table for his morning treat. My mother had prepared one of his favorite dishes, an hour before the others would arrive at table. A Fleischerl, as she called it. My father chewed in slow meditation. He was the privileged one. Everything you do not work for is privilege. No one disputed his right to it. Sometimes a piece of meat flew through the air and one of the dogs snapped it up.

I opened the door a crack, until my slender body fit through, and remained there, one foot poised on top of the other. Without turning his head, my father gestured me into the room with his finger.

Shut the door, he ordered.

I hopped up on the chair next to him and opened my mouth. Now I, too, was fed like a little bird with little pieces from his meat delicacy. Privileged? Only I was permitted inside the paternal seclusion. I was the smallest, the youngest, the straggler. The dearest? I never knew, would never find out.

Really, not a single other person dared penetrate Father's solitude. Only sometimes did my grandfather sit nearby, one with his armchair, part of the room itself, and of the silence, reading into his book. That Fritz sat at the table he noticed only when one of the dogs snapped at a snippet of meat that had almost landed on him.

Ah, there you are. Is it already that late? he would grumble, watching the dog chew for a little while, then probing his way back into his book without expecting an answer.

•

My mother loved nature. She talked to the trees. On Sunday walks she pointed admiringly at one group. All of us had to turn our heads, really study them, consider them through Mother's eyes, impress upon ourselves their age, their straight growth.

Majestic, don't you think, she said, pointing to a very old one standing next to the electrical shed, its door ajar, rotten leaves pressing in. One could see a swallow's nest sticking to the beams above. Her theory was that this tree flourished particularly well because of the energy wave pattern.

Here the river, otherwise wide and slow, was suddenly very deep. It swirled dark green with fish. Slow big ones, fast little ones. Just after that the water was forced into a narrow pass, shooting through beneath a bridge covered with slippery green moss, then falling about six meters into the depths. There you couldn't hear yourself speak. As we leaned on the bridge, my mother pointed to the gigantic weeping willow farther below, past the waterfall, where the river was itself again, wide and slow, drawing the branches along in the water.

Majestic! she shouted again, pointing at the willow to nods of agreement.

HORSEFLIES

Sometimes, on particularly hot summer days, we drove to a lake where Uli and the others could really swim. On its bank were wooden planks for sunbathing, and a wooden tower to jump from. And girls. The three lads, Uli, Dieter, and Georg, climbed onto a motorcycle with a sidecar they had gerrymandered together in their spare time. Off they went, the carriage following at a distance.

My father always had a reason to stay home. I don't swim. I'm needed here. Leaning on the door frame, looking mistrustfully at the weather, his forehead clouded with worried furrows, he took a few puffs on his Virginia cigar and watched us go. Perhaps he wanted to be alone for once.

After an hour's journey on country roads we saw water glimmering through the trees. Finally we had arrived. The horses, freed from the carriage, were tied firmly beneath a shadowy tree. Cool blue shadow cloth lay across their gray dotted coats. My mother spread the checkered tablecloth on the grass for the picnic later on. Now there was awkward dressing and undressing underneath clothes. Anton held a bathrobe up to screen Aunt Julia; behind it she transformed herself into a pinup with a two-piece bathing suit. Mine and Alexandra's were made of wool. When they were drenched they got very heavy and drooped down between our legs. And they itched. Mine was red-and-white striped, a hand-me-down from Anita.

My mother could not swim, so Georg and Dieter had invented water wings for her: a damask pillowcase, with two seams through the middle of each half, left and right. Dieter got the pillow wet, and Georg pulled the fabric apart and blew air into the wings. As long as it was wet the air stayed in the pillow.

My mother lay on its center and paddled off, like a swan, into the lake, toward the water lilies. In horror I saw her drifting farther and farther away.

Mummy, Mummy, come back! I shrieked. Come back, come back! I was worried about her, did not trust the invention.

The lads had just left us and crossed the lake, disappeared to the wooden tower, to the wooden planks in the hot sun, across which the girls draped themselves. There I could see them bobbing up and down amidst the summer crowd. They had long since forgotten the swan—and me.

Dragonflies whirred around my mother. Relaxed and happy, she peered into the sky mirrored in the dark brown moor water, paddled out a little farther, enjoyed the water on her skin, the sun on her back, the solitude. Now it all belonged to her, and she thought about nothing at all.

On one of these jaunts my mother, Aunt Julia, Alexandra, and I sat near the horses, on the checkered cloth, eating our sandwiches, drinking our lemonade, and sunbathing. This time Anton had not come along. He was on one of his mysterious journeys, which were always vaguely defined or passed over in silence. The horses swatted the tedious horseflies with their tails, snorting and stomping. A nervous disquiet spread beneath the tree. Sometimes a horsefly landed on our naked skin. Whack, dead.

If only someone were puffing on a cigarette, my mother wished. But no one was smoking. Aunt Julia had forgotten her cigarettes.

Out across the far-off fields the landscape vibrated. In the sky the cumulus clouds gnarled themselves into an afternoon storm. The picnic would not last much longer; soon we would have to break it up.

Aunt Julia's eyes wandered off to the patch of bad weather. Aaah, she groaned.

Tears were already welling up and running down her face, her lips quivering, her voice smaller than a sigh.

It is all over, she moaned.

What is over?

He is gone.

Why? Who, for God's sake? my mother wanted to know.

Aunt Julia merely gestured.

Ah, I thought so. She bent over to Aunt Julia, touching her shoulder. Hm— my poor darling. Where did he go?

Aunt Julia shook her head. She did not know.

He lied to us. To me, too, she said. She could scarcely speak.

He lied?…no, it can't be…actually, on second thought I can well imagine it.

The truth quickly dawned on my mother. She moved closer, holding out a napkin for Julia to blow her nose.

I kept silent, staring at the women with curiosity and disbelief. I understood none of this drama. The steely Aunt Julia was crying. I felt small spurts of tenderness, some kind of love for her warming my heart as never before. I wanted to help her.

Who is lying to you? I asked.

Really, it is none of your business, said Aunt Julia flatly but strictly, already her old self again, as if she had realized showing weakness is an unforgivable mistake. One must always be strong; otherwise people tread on you.

Alexandra had laid her head on her mother's lap and looked angrily at me. Even my mother was looking away into the distance for an answer, a remedy for tragedy, perhaps. These three had sealed a pact. I was now on the outside.

I stood up and in doing so managed to spill a glass of lemonade onto the cloth.

Ah, you idiot, it's just like you—klutz! said Alexandra, tapping around with her napkin.

I thought: I had better go over to the horses, to help them to get rid of the horseflies. I fanned the flies away from their eyes, but as soon as they lifted off, they landed on other eyelids. A huge specimen of horsefly hummed around me. I watched it settling on Tamara's hindquarters. Whack! I hit her flank. Horsefly dead, Tamara startled. Perking up her ears, she strained at the restraint. I jumped aside. Up went Tamara on her hind legs. Tumult and outcry. Before I knew what was happening, the beast had wrenched itself free and was making for the forest. Alexandra and Aunt Julia, crying just moments earlier, jumped all over me.

You have to stick your nose into everything! You always have to be the center of attention! You spoiled brat! Yes, brat!

But, but, but I only wanted…I unsuccessfully interjected.

It was as if they had found a sliver of reality on which to unload some of their grief; and where better to unload it than on the object of jealousy?

My mother, busy with the broken reins and more concerned about the dark clouds, said calmingly: Tamara will be back, let's get our things together. She was looking at the storm, at the free, happily grazing horse by the trees, and pondering the task at hand.

•

Anton returned to tell my father why he had lied, to spell out the whole misery of his life. Returned also so Aunt Julia could say he was an honorable man after all, in spite of everything.

In reality Anton already had a family of his own. They had been torn apart in the chaos of war and the topsy-turvy aftermath. Then for some time he was not sure whether he would ever find them again, nor whether they were even alive.

This was completely plausible given the general confusion of postwar Germany. Just as marbles silently disappear beneath the sofa, past one's foot, into the twilight, behind the curtain, family members disappeared into obscure hiding places, climbed onto wrong trains, landed in opposite directions; children were parted from maternal hands; wrong doors opened into interminable investigations, judicial hearings with no passports, no identity, until finally a thread of fate reached out a hand. Finally! It could take years.

After the war, Anton first had to hide from the Americans until things quieted down. He could finally confess to Fritz Ost that he had been with the SS. The Nuremberg Tribunal had made it possible for him to be denazified. And with unbelievable luck he had found his family, wife and child.

Now everything became clearer. That was why he was always going into the city, to the reunion centers. There he studied lists of names and nameless lists of children who did not know their names, reduced to interchangeable notes on a piece of paper: perhaps three years old, blue eyes, curly blonde hair. There he listened in on the endless radio litanies for the deracinated. There, in these offices, he found hope. Anonymously he fished in the pond of the other anonymities, and hoped. On the farm he hid all that behind the mask of good manners he dared not lift from his Nazi past.

Now I understood the tears. Alexandra had no new father, Julia no husband.

Don't give me that stupid look! Quit staring, you cow! Alexandra shouted. I had everything and she had nothing. She had always clung to the hope that things would once again become fantastic, much better and more beautiful than here on the farm, in the country. No, the way it once was. She could still remember it all quite precisely, even the lighting in the staircase. For her and Aunt Julia the future was firmly bound up with Anton.

He'll get us out of here. That had been a fact. It was just a matter of time. Anton had been one of those knights of hope. But now they were waiting in uncertainty, and it was raining.

Nazi?!! said my father sarcastically. We can count ourselves lucky they didn't find you here among us.

After these tumultuous revelations Anton left us on his bicycle, with a cardboard suitcase laced up on the back. In shock, and because there was nothing more to be done, we wished him the best and waved after him, waved until he and his bicycle disappeared through the eye of the needle at the end of the tree-lined avenue. His secret stayed behind with us as gossip. Aunt Julia dried her tears. For her it was a hard blow—yet another—but what could she do?

In any case, he looked fabulous, she said once the pain had abated, her gaze scanning the far misty horizon as she sighed. Then she went back to her work, but without the interruptions from her mirror, no longer the seductress with the hopeful future distancing her from our predictability. Grandmother no longer cleared her throat to spit out sharp remarks; her thoughts had fallen into line with those of the rest of us.

I liked Aunt Julia much more after this, for sometimes she stood still, leaned somewhere and cried over her lot in life, and Alexandra, and lost love. It came at her like a mosquito bite, suddenly, without notice. Now even I could comfort her, so much gentler had she become. My mother laid an arm around her and pressed her to her bosom. Then Aunt Julia smiled, and that suited her well.

I Bit My Tongue

I REMEMBER WHERE THE GYPSIES LIVED. Right along the airport road, on the eastern edge of Munich. There stood their wagons, in colorful disarray, blind to the usual order of things that surrounded their patch of land.

They were always ready to go on the road at short notice. This was how they had survived the persecution, and how they returned from hiding in desolate mountain corners, in the no-man's-land between borders. With the swift minds and agility of road warriors they took up where they had left off, attending to their various mobile businesses: sharpening knives and scissors door to door, welding pots and pans, or, like Buchs, trading horses.

And I still remember how the Arabians came to us. A wagon careened through the tree-lined avenue. Two gray-and-whites in front, two more running along behind. Again it was Buchs the gypsy, the horse trader, Father's friend, from whom we had already bought Bella. A wild black mane of hair, broad grin, silver tooth, rings on his fingers, even an earring in his right earlobe, which he believed would help him see better. The old farmer next door had a ring like that in his ear, too.

Coming to a halt, Buchs jumped down from the carriage. By way of introduction he led the horses forward one by one. The usual trade protocol: Stand still. Look into their mouths. Go in a circle. Touch the flanks, admire the breast, appraise the back.

Superb. My father was thrilled. Many hours later, after interminable negotiations, there was finally a handshake to seal the deal. Fritz had fallen in love, and bought all four.

My father could never tell apart the three mares, Aurora, Tamara, and Pusta. Like an affectionate Musselman with his harem, he loved them all equally. Their temperament he would study later. That was the fun part. And having taken the stallion Janosch, too, he could sometimes drive four-in-hand...

Buchs came visiting more often, with his family, for the horse trading was largely barter, produce in exchange for horses; money was secondary. Eula Buchs peeped out from beneath the wagon cover, then one by one a dozen children came springing down. Their black onyx eyes, sparkling beneath dark tufts of hair, their red cheeks, painted on by the weather, and their runny noses. They were all stuffed into grubby grown-up jackets, with trousers rolled up high, clothes too big or too small, shoes cut open in front or in back. From one shoe peered a bunch of hay instead of a warm sock. The girls wore wide little skirts, draped cloths, old woolens, with an occasional cap on their raven hair, or a red ribbon around it.

The colorful gang could scarcely be held in check; it forced its way in through the door, shoving, jostling. Once inside they clung to the wall, or the door, and gaped. Slowly the ball of gypsy yarn unraveled itself in the strange surroundings. Like butter in a hot pan they melted apart and grew impudent. Then they had to be drummed back together, so nothing was smashed and nothing went missing. If they ate in the house, Justa counted the spoons at the beginning and end of the meal.

Olga took a firm Russian stand in front of the vitrine: Where has key gone? Was just here.

Olga and Justa were altogether opposed to letting them in the house at all. Gypsies steal like ravens. My grandmother thought so, too. But my father liked Buchs and found the little band highly amusing.

Buchs, in my house nothing gets pilfered. Agreed? Yes, agreed. Handshake. Grin.

Eula Buchs said nothing.

Wherever she went, Eula Buchs took center stage; her dark glance sized up the room silently and earnestly, strategically investigating the weak points of the strange environment. She would prop her arms on her hips, a sergeant laying down the order of battle. You don't mess with me stood written on her handsome old face.

I looked on from a certain distance, given the uncontrollable power of lice.

THE TOAD

One day my mother and I took the carriage with two of the Arabians into the village to buy sugar and flour in Mrs. Hagenreiner's store. The store smelled of everything and nothing. The odors were melted down into a compact mass and had crept into the flour, the sugar, the washing powder, the margarine, and stayed there for days, long after they had been stored. The sugar smelled of washing powder. That in turn you could taste in the margarine. The all-purpose flour stank of gasoline, pudding powder reeked of mothballs, the ersatz coffee smelled like ammonia. The store was the only one for miles around, and it was a gold mine.

People on the farm had become accustomed to the Americans, their gigantic cars, the noisy motors of their Jeeps. The four Arabs, by contrast, could not get used to anything new. Everything that moved, every motor vehicle, gave them a start. Their nervous systems were tensed like the electric wires that weaved from pole to pole across the countryside. Genetic electricity hummed in their aristocratic blood and made them oversensitive. Paper shreds in the road: ears perked, snorting. Motor rumbling from the camouflage-colored military vehicles: high on their rear legs, teetering back. Highest alert.

Though the horses wore blinders and could only see right in front of them, everything was an occasion to run off. Perhaps it made them still more mistrustful not to know what was taking place outside their visual field. They rolled their beautiful black long-lidded eyes in fear, in constant alarm; perked up their ears, forward, backward, forward, backward, started stomping with their front hooves, and crowded one another aside.

On the way home the back of the carriage was packed full with the delicacies we had procured. The road, which in many places was almost a meter higher than the surrounding land, scarcely left room to yield on either side should another coach come from the opposite direction. We jogged pleasantly along. Suddenly my mother's Argus eyes discovered something crossing the road in the distance. It was small, unimportant, just a point in the flat panorama. But my mother saw it.

Her body shot forward. Her attention flew far out ahead of the trotting horses, farther into the distance they vacuumed up with each of their steps. Farther still! She squinted, forced everything to a narrow point.

Do you see that?

No, I shook my head.

When I sat in the carriage I always looked for any obstacle that could disturb the nervous horses, hoping to simplify it for them, discover it first, investigate its possible dangers. As we drew nearer I, too, saw something small creeping along the street. Ah, one of Mother's beloved toads.

She brought the horses to a halt just before the spot where the creature was crossing the road. Brrrr... She climbed down and while shortening the reins she comfortingly addressed the horses—Ho, ho, ho, good, good, good—bent down to the toad, and shooed it away from their hooves, away from the wheels of the carriage.

You enchanting little person, come, hop, hup, hup, hup, a little faster. It has golden eyes, she called up to me. Pure gold. Now go, hup, hup!

Yes, yes... I didn't care what my mother said. I was not so interested in toads, and was much too scared that the horses could take off. They were already shoving the carriage and snorting, on the verge of one of the predictable hysterical outbursts I feared so much.

My mother was still with the toad. She did not see the warning signals, the perked ears: up, down, up, down, forward, backward. She was not disturbed by the shoving, nor did she see the approaching dust cloud.

The horses tugged at the reins, tapped their hooves, reared, shoved the carriage backward.

Mummy, Mummiii!

My mother gave the toad a last nudge down the bank.

A giant army truck stopped abruptly in front of us. My mother jumped up on the carriage, tautened the reins; the horses stomped nervously.

A black fellow had left the truck and was coming toward us with a broad grin, gesturing wildly with his arms. The animals snorted, pricked up their ears, and with a sudden lurch the entire chaise twisted off to the side, teetered, and rushed backward, crashing down the embankment. We flew from our seats.

Aurora and Tamara went galloping off, with the carriage stumbling along behind on its side. A short distance, then the shaft broke and the reins ruptured, flying in all directions. Freed from their burden, the team galloped away across the field toward a fence of trees. Away, away, from the black man, from the clanking of the truck, just away.

Though I was quickly back on my feet, I was bawling.

Did you hurt yourself? My mother lifted her head, smeared with soil, from a potato furrow.

I bit my tongue, I cried. Now I tasted the blood and the pain. The purchases from the Hagenreiner store lay strewn everywhere, shredded paper bags, sugar and flour. I bawled even more.

My mother hoisted herself to her feet. Amidst all the tumult she suddenly broke into peals of laughter and pointed to a small, self-propelling blob. Sprinkled with flour, ready for the frying pan, it left behind a fine, thick dust outline with every hop. The toad.

Several GIs came running down the embankment to help my mother up. Others looked around to see what else could be rescued. The shattered carriage was loaded onto the back of the truck. The two horses, standing farther out in the field, now watching the accident as if they had nothing to do with it, offered no resistance as they were led homeward.

Mother and I clambered up onto the truck, beside the dark-skinned GI. Between sobs I was fed little pieces of chocolate. The sugar and flour remained behind, absorbed by the moist soil. Fun for ants. I did not know which was sadder: the fall from the coach, which had already been sweetened with chocolate and forgotten along with the bitten tongue, or the loss of the good things that were so hard to get. Particularly sugar. My mother had promised to make caramel bonbons.

I wiped my face and examined her white blouse with the embroidered sleeves, torn all the way down the back. This blouse was my mother's favorite, the Bulgarian blouse from a visit to Aunt Frenzi. My mother had visited her and Uncle Methodi there in 1920, after the First World War, at the end of an adventure through the Balkans in a Mercedes.

Oh, well, we can stitch it back together, she said. Otherwise we are both fine. That's what matters.

I craved endless repetitions of this Balkan story. Uncle Methodi had invited Adi on a wild tour. From Berlin to Sofia in a Mercedes-Benz complete with armed chauffeur. In Bulgaria Uncle Methodi was a famous biologist; in Berlin, ambassador of the Bulgarian monarchy. My mother told of gravel roads, snow-covered passes, then the path resuming across rivers without bridges; she spoke of robbers descending on them, of breaking camp each night, of overnight stays in bug-infested dives. She was enraptured by Uncle Methodi's charm, his winning ways. The simple mountain dwellers thought they had the king himself on their hands. They knew him only from pictures. And no one had ever seen such a car firsthand.

When we arrived home and sat down to dinner, my mother told of our ill-fated adventure and ill-advisedly entrusted Fritz with the story of the toad.

My father's brows darkened. His forehead wrinkled. He exploded.

Brilliant! Typical! Just like you! Rescue a toad! RESCUE A TOAD!? He shook his head angrily. Just what had he expected from a wife who came into the house with a snake coiled around her arm to check whether the book said it was poisonous. No, he could not remain in his seat. He jumped up and stormed chaotically up and down the room. Back to the table. He shook his head in disbelief. There was disconcerted ladling of soup as the assembled company fell silent.

My mother sighed. Her gaze wandered through the window. Outside stood a tree. Aha, a tree, and what sort might it be? A horse chestnut. Castanea sativa? A majestic tree. We planted it. She smiled, lifted her eyebrows; for a moment she looked around the table, like a startled child.

We are healthy, that's the main thing.

She, the artist of life, recovered quickly from her embarrassment. My father, by contrast, went on knitting at his anger a while longer.

Intelligence and Tenderness

WHERE DOES SCENT COME FROM? I wanted to know.

Easter Sunday. Family walk. Grandfather Theodor came along, too. At first we held hands, he and I. Then his pace became too slow for me, and I rushed off, leaving him behind. He waved, stopped, and looked on; looked, waved, slowly turned around, and strolled back, getting smaller and smaller, until the hedges slid in front of him.

My father talked with the young people about their future, when everything would be better again.

So, what do you actually want to do? he probed.

The lads had no idea. They were preoccupied with their cigarettes. Father's direct gaze and the impatience in his voice made them a little nervous.

Father's habit was to walk the entire grounds. He stuck his cane into the earth, took a step forward: the cane, the leg, down onto the ground. Step, lift up, set down. In precise rhythm, interrupted only when an object impinged on his sense of order. Like a golfer, he used the cane to deal the obstacle a blow: Out of the way, don't interrupt my rhythm. Or the cane would whistle through the air, underlining a word, a thought, explaining the life cycle of the dragonfly, naming a print in the mud.

My father was a well-regarded breeder and farmer. Wagons with pyramids of cabbage heads rolled into the city to the sauerkraut factory. There were fields upon fields, as far as the eye could see: potato greens, sugar beets, four sorts of grain, corn, and beans. There was dairy farming, pig breeding, sheep herding, fishing.

He held our workers and the foreigners in check with a kind of military order. But even so there was always something tragic or dangerous happening. Quarrels had to be smoothed out. Picture my father addressing two bloodstained brawlers. That much German they could understand, and they knew, too, that his sharp tone of voice meant he would brook no disobedience. Rough characters had to be restrained by several men, or locked up, until the moonshine had evaporated.

For the moment Dieter and Georg were working for him, keeping everything going, keeping a sharp eye on the Slavs and all the others on the farm. That they assured him. Dieter ran the pig-breeding operation: several hundred swine, a gigantic responsibility. He was quite thrilled with the pigs' cleverness. Soon they recognized his step. When he entered the sty, they screamed and squealed, trying to climb onto a bucket or scamper up on the wood planks to look out over the perch. They stuck their snouts over the rim and grunted at him. Never in his wildest dreams would Dieter have imagined that after his fine schooling he would be in charge of a pigsty. But in two weeks' time he reported quite proudly that a sow had had a litter fifteen strong, and that owing to his care not one of them had died. My father patted him on the shoulder in recognition.

Uli had quickly fled the farm and gone away to study brewing; Father was too authoritarian for him. Uli's war injury had healed, but his arm still hung weakly at his side. Traces of the trauma would always remain. When he came to visit I always had to get used to him all over again, for my crowded childhood days stole their way between us, and he seemed more grown up every time.

Sometimes my father lightened up, forgot himself a little, and sometimes he could relax and laugh, cracking jokes. Then he immediately became the center of attention and could bowl people over with his charm. They would have done anything for him, just for the sake of his gaiety, to hold on to it. At such moments my mother was overjoyed, but with her encouraging D'You See, Fritzl, Easy Does It, Too, she achieved exactly the opposite. He withdrew into his strict order. There he felt more secure, for if one were simply unselfconscious and overly glad, things could easily go off the rails. He did not trust fortune, did not trust himself. He could become dead serious in an instant, unapproachably strict and often mad with rage.

One day Dieter summoned us to gather round in the pigsty, where lived the giant boar August. Dieter had trained him in his free time at night, teaching him to take a fall. My father stood seriously and expectantly among us.

August dead! ordered Dieter. August lifted himself up, slowly at first, his curly tail dancing. With a friendly grunt he left his corner swamp of straw and mud and moved toward the waiting group. He lifted his head and grinned.

Dieter repeated: August dead!

Suddenly, with a lithe twist, August threw his weight onto the floor and, after struggling with indecision, stretched his four legs into the air, away from his pink underbelly. For a moment he held this position and seemed to be smiling; then, with unexpected smoothness, he swung his weight back onto his slender legs with their dainty feet. He looked around him in the ring, grunted and nudged Dieter with his snout to get his reward: nuts, greens, and an apple.

We applauded, laughed, and clapped: Bravo, bravo, August!

My father was so amused that from then on guests were often led into the stinking pigsty, to see August and his circus act.

On the walking path my mother made the children aware of the little balls and knots that deer and hares had left behind on the forest floor. She wrinkled her nose and said, sniffing, I think I smell the Easter Bunny. Right—we will soon find something.

Scarcely had she said it but there was an egg in the grass, a bunny portrait painted on it in watercolors. And there, by the tree stump, two eggs: one red, one blue. We children were ablaze with excitement, collecting the treasures in our baskets, naturally sensing something Easterish behind every bush and tree trunk.

Look up here—I saw something running!

We looked up, and in the fork of a branch sat another, a wondrous egg. Quickly one of us clambered up into the tree. Broken eggs had to be eaten immediately, and scarcely had one turned one's head but another bunny was running by across the meadow.

Didn't you see it?

The strollers strayed off in various directions, splitting into groups. The young men started telling stories. After being around my father for a while, they and their tongues loosened up. Georg talked about his parents, whom no one knew, who had totally disappeared, whom he would perhaps find, or perhaps never. My grandfather listened out for them on the radio, the missing persons service. No luck.

My father took Georg in particular under his wing and gave him words of advice: For the moment you will go on working for me. Then you will study journalism, then you can become a reporter.

Really? Do you think so?

When it came to other people my father always had plans for the future. For himself he perhaps had dreams, but without a future. He was always the oldest, with the thoughts and fears of a man who already had too many lives behind him not to be cautious. He seemed to see through everything, to have already arrived at the other shore. However seemingly firm the stone beneath his shoe, it was about to sink into the mud. The bicyclist far in the lead had already crashed into the wheels of the carriage ahead, was already in the hospital with a fractured skull. Sometimes the lads played Fritz Ost Predictions and laughed themselves sick. The bicyclist dies, the widow cannot pay the bill, she lands on the street with seven children, whom the farm takes in, cares for, clothes...

On the way home, close by the farm, we children tumbled across a meadow, throwing hard-boiled eggs over the electrical wires. It was an Easter custom. Whoever sent their egg sailing farthest through the air without bursting it in the grass was the winner.

I leaned up against the hayrick wall, warmed by the Easter sun, sniffed the skin on my arm, and watched the boys going wild.

SCENT

When we children were summoned to go berry picking in the woods we were ecstatic with joy. We carried small buckets with us, searching for blueberries in the forest, beyond the meadows, toward the black lace of distant pines. In even rows, stiff and orderly columns sustained the needle roof. The soft ground yielded to our feet. Moss crept across stones and old stumps, covering every moist niche. It was gloomy in there. The trunks of the trees fled upward like the pillars of a Gothic cathedral. Through a window, swords of light pierced the darkness. This was the German wood whence sprang the fairy tales. If one entered the soft duskiness, one saw a hare tearing off, heard the screech of a bird, the treetops moved by the wind, the call of the cuckoo. Then the elves, too, were not far off, nor the hunchbacked witch, the warlock, the giant Rübezahl, dwarves, the good fairies, all moving noiselessly through the Arcadian corridors.

We reached a clearing, an irregularity in the regimented order, covered with low hedge underbrush. This was what we were looking for: blueberries! We went into a crouch and plucked into our buckets. When we tired of gathering all the berries, we stretched ourselves out on the soft carpet, played hide and seek, ate some of our harvest.

My mother and Mrs. Tafelmeier were more diligent and very nimble; their buckets were soon full. They crouched in the blueberry patch, bending the bush aside with one hand while the other deftly stripped the berries from the stalk. My mother had the same touch with chickens when she lifted their hindquarters up by the feathers to see whether they were sitting on eggs. Mrs. Tafelmeier followed suit—lift-pluck-lift-pluck—but a little ways off, so she did not wander into Frau Ost's territory.

Psst, keep it down, exhorted my mother, or someone will hear us. We did not want to give away the location of our happy hunting ground. The forest was open for all to gather berries, mushrooms, and twigs, and we didn't want to compete with strangers.

There. A bough snapped. There. Again. We froze and listened. My mother straightened up and peered concernedly. Nothing. Must have been a deer. There. Again the snapping of branches.

Let's quickly finish these bushes. Children, stay with us, quite close, ordered my mother.

Suddenly—we all saw him at the same time—a figure crept through the undergrowth. Even at a distance we could see he was pushing a bicycle. His rucksack hung on his shoulders like a hunchback. The man had seen us, too. He leaned his bicycle against a tree trunk and came slowly toward us.

Mrs. Tafelmeier whispered: I don't like this guy. C'mon, let's get out of here.

In the postwar chaos many uprooted people were wandering about the countryside. Madmen, too. Hiding in lofts and woods, outside the law, they slipped through the net and floated along.

Quickly we packed everything up, full buckets and empty ones. My mother took my hand; Mrs. Tafelmeier, the twins' hands. With brisk steps we hastened from the clearing toward the meadow, which flashed green through the dark trees up ahead.

My mother turned around. Funny, the guy has vanished, she said. As if he had been a ghost.

Once we got to the sunlit meadow we could take a deep breath and feel safe again.

That's enough for today. Mushrooms we can look for another time.

All this suspicious trash sneakin' around, Mrs. Tafelmeier spat. D'ja hear about the murderer runnin' loose around here? He slits his victims up the middle. All women...

Please, not in front of the children. My mother restrained the Tafelmeier woman from further elucidating the horror story. She was just getting going and wanted to provide even more bloodthirsty details. But the farm with its red brick roofs and dovecote was already greeting us across the fishpond. We children wrestled ourselves free of the women's grips.

Sometimes we gathered raspberries, blackberries, and wild strawberries. The raspberries, shaped like gentle finger-caps, were red and full to bursting with their sweet blood. The black-purple juice of the robust blackberries bit into the cloth, permeated skin and teeth. Then came the perfumed strawberries with their bitter bite.

Mummy, where does scent come from? I asked over and over, but no one seemed to know. The fragrances of the berries, so different, sweet, yet unrelated—who knew?

Mother's fragrance was the Chanel No. 5 my father brought back during his wartime leave. From Bordeaux, she said proudly. Your father was stationed there before they shipped him off to Africa. She looked at me cheerily; the little smile at the corners of her mouth did not reveal her thoughts. She always took great joy in small things, noticed tender changes, like fragrances, that she shared with her Fritz, nuanced observations extending across all imaginable areas. Perhaps that was what bound them together: that this pessimist, who often shouted so loudly, would rather have been quite different, and that she knew about it.

Looking for mushrooms was a science, and strenuous, because you had to pay very close attention. Many mushrooms were poisonous, some even deadly. A single poisonous mushroom spoiled a whole meal. Every summer you heard about mushroom fatalities, whole families poisoned by a single bad mushroom. But finding them was fun: beneath trees, next to certain bushes, at the edge of the forest toward the meadow. There was a big hurrah when someone discovered king boletus mushrooms. They tasted the best, sauteed in butter.

After slogging for miles on these excursions, we were always exhausted. Either our arms and legs were all scratched up by the thorny raspberry bushes, or a child had stumbled over a tree stump and cut her knee open. The mosquitoes were voracious, and if your luck was bad you got nabbed by a wasp: your hand would swell up, or your foot would no longer fit into your shoe. Exhausted from the heat, sweaty and thirsty, we hauled ourselves home like Saint George after the struggle with the dragon. But it had been superb even so, and I always wanted to be part of it.

•

Where does scent come from? I wanted to know.

Out back, across the meadows by the carp ponds, it was as if noise and quiet had become one. The tweeting of the birds, the conversation of the frogs. The raging waterfall. In the arena of the heat, bee buzzing competing with the humming of bugs. The loud bumblebees torpedoing blossom chalices. Lemon moths, the Admiral butterfly with the big round scarecrow eyes on its coat, all dancing rhythmically with nothing on their minds but swinging, fluttering, twisting upward, tumbling downward. We children lay in the grass and watched the free-time air game, sniffed the earth, and listened.

At the edge of the ponds hundreds of tiny frogs leapt into the air, sticking to our bare legs and skirts.

That is carp food, my father instructed us. It makes them thick and fat.

Birds swarmed across the meadow and hurled themselves into the grass to feast.

Storks had built their disorderly nest on the roof of a hayrick. When they returned from their winter lodgings, one could count on spring coming soon. By the same token, winter was not far off when their airy house stood empty one morning. On lucky days one could observe how they queued up along the river-bank and patiently fished for the larger frogs or trout. The delicacy lurched down their throats and disappeared in their breastbones.

MY GARDEN

Where does scent come from? I wanted to know.

In the garden the paths were covered with black coal slag. It did not blacken one's feet, but it was hard, and jagged, almost impossible to traverse barefoot. The garden was as big as a nursery, with rows of tomatoes, carrots, red beets, every vegetable imaginable. Strawberries and bushes of red, black, and white currants strewed the walkways. My mother created an elegant rock garden with prickly cactus and mosses, evergreen, foxglove. The shade plants and bleeding heart grew in the twilight next to the tea pavilion, bed upon bed: bee food, bird fodder.

Mother planted one bed with poppies. Their seeds were for cakes. When the blossoms withered, the papery petals, pink and red, sailed from their pods; by then an oval jar had filled up with seeds and we children sat on the hard, sharp gravel in the sun, sucking the black seeds from their seed cabins.

I was given my own miniature garden where I could plant what I wanted. This was supposed to teach me patience. But I could not wait. Each week my stately gardens had to be reordered anew. Here there were too many roses; over there the forget-me-nots were too dense; I wanted to shift the columbine into the center; the dahlias had to move closer to the corner. Thus I was continually busy uprooting and reanimating my plants.

When my tomatoes took too long to redden, I thought the problem was not enough sun in my garden. I harvested them all at once and spread them out on the black garden path. This way they could ripen more quickly in the sun while I watched, turning and sniffing them. In my impatience I smeared honey on leaves. Bees, do come along, visit my flowers first, I pleaded, hoping the whole garden would hurry up.

With a spade I attacked the earth, trying to dig a deep hole for the peony bush. Already drenched with sweat, my braids unraveled. My mother came walking by.

Are you maltreating your poor garden again?

She tried to help but I did not let her. I had to deal with it myself. It was my design, my creation. Firmly resolved, I forcefully drove the spade into the earth and jumped on it, but nothing moved, not an inch, beneath my unweighty weight.

Deeper! I screamed.

My mother could no longer look on. She took the spade from my hand, thrust it deep into the earth, reinforced it with her foot, heaved it up, flipped it over, and repeated the cycle, until the hole was big enough to sink the peony bush into.

But now you must let the poor plant grow in peace, she exhorted.

Yes, yes, sure, I promised, and seemed contented. For the moment. My critical eye drew up the balance of my overall structure, my architectonic secretion. For now I was too exhausted, but there already lurked in a corner of my creative existence the destructive impulse to tear down what had just been erected.

All our dogs were beloved and led a superbly spoiled existence. Cats were not allowed inside. There was milk for them in the stables but they had to look after themselves. They lurked in the meadow for mice, caught bugs and butterflies and birds, occasionally cracked larvae or an egg. They were wild and ran away if one wanted to pet them. We called them all Mitzi.

My father loved his scientific seed and potato breeding; also the beasts of the field. Above all, he adored his fine Arabians, and he always had his personal little Schnauzer at his side.

My mother's heart encompassed all animals and plants. It was this shared love that soldered them together, more than their possessions and us children. They were both experts, knew the Latin names, and sometimes they competed. Juglaus alba? Walnut. Black currant was called Rubus occidentalis, Tilia americana the linden tree, Betula alba the birch, and so on. They could not always agree on who was right.

Almost everything, my dear Adi, can be processed into alcohol, said my father. Everything has its spirit content.

Yes, naturally, she answered, growing quite earnest. She had not got his joke.

The plants are part of creation, links in the chain of existence; without them things would look grim, she said, and looked out pensively across the garden.

My father gave me a terrarium, green with glass walls, a fine wire mesh for a roof, and a ring in the middle to lift the lid. I hopped through the house, beside myself with joy. Now I can raise crickets, raise crickets, raise crickets.

To get me started he took me along to a meadow. There was singing and buzzing and chirping around us, birds shrieking, a nightingale trilling somewhere.

Pssst, said my father amidst all the noise. We went into a crouch, kept still, and listened. Quite close to us, chirping. Kirrr, kirrr.

Down onto the ground—where is that tone coming from? Crickets always sit quite close to the hole where they live, whispered my father.

Aha, there was a little hole, and next to it, a cricket. Father held the spade up and plunged it into the earth right at the entrance. Swiftly, precisely, faster than the cricket could retreat. It tried to, but the entrance was blocked with the metal gate. Quickly I held my hand over it, and it was caught. It squiggled inside the dark room of my closed hand: a tiny organism in panic. Straightway I lifted the lid of the green glass palace and dropped it in. Then we fetched a little piece of the meadow where it had just been chirping, roots and all, and lowered it into the terrarium.

Before long many crickets had been given lodging in my miniature world. There it was again: a tender gesture from my father, whom everyone so feared. He had taken me by the hand, out to the meadow, and made me a present of attention.

I put the cage next to my bed, up above on the windowsill, and fed the crickets with mealworms, which were plentiful in the flour barrel up in the attic. And sometimes it rained, real showers from the watering can.

In the winter the terrarium was packed off to the living room, where there was a tile oven like the one in the dining room. The idea was for the crickets to be better off than they would have been outdoors. In the bedroom it was almost as cold as it was outside. Overnight a world of ice grew on the windowpanes. Ferns and flowers, crystal cliffs and glass trees took shape. The world outside had disappeared; it had fled to the windows. Is there still something out there? Is Nothingness out there now? What does Nothingness look like? I lay in bed, motionless beneath the mountain of down.

Later that morning a corner thawed, and quite slowly my ice landscape began to portray itself once again outside, just as it had been before, secure and familiar. Nothingness had been only a specter, a mare in the night.

In a bowl on my washing table sat a pitcher. In the mornings a thin layer of ice covered the surface of the water. From afar came my father's voice. One heard him energetically striding down the corridor, banging his first on each door and shouting: Six o'clock! Get up!

I stayed in the warm bed, since the room was so cold that you could see your breath. I did not get up until Justa used hot water to thaw the ice in the pitcher. I washed my face and neck a little and brushed my teeth. Enough. I took my cold clothes, slipped back under the bedcovers into the warmth, and laboriously got dressed.

Layers of clothing. Undershirt, flannel with holes, scratchy pullover, undies, woolen long johns, cotton stockings, over them woolen knee socks. Pants with elastic ankle bands, skirt on top. Thus layered, I roamed the icy house. My grandparents wore wristlets, woolen scarves, and wool vests, often patched. My grandfather often burned a hole in his clothes when he cleaned his pipe too early and blew the embers on himself instead of outward, or put his still-glowing pipe into his pocket. Then there was trouble with Marie-Louise.

VIIP

One day Georg came running into the house from the hayfield with a little doe on his arm. It was still tiny, just born. A tiny perfect female, its little heart pounding with fear. They had almost killed her with the mower as they cut the grass near the ponds. Her ear was bleeding. A little piece was missing.

At first she was kept in the office and fed with a bottle. Slowly she got used to people, stopped jumping in fright when someone entered the room. She grew tame and ate from one's hand. After a long search for a fitting name she was dubbed Viip, after the sound of her cry.

Viip roamed freely through the house, then in the garden, then in the courtyard. She knew nothing of danger, nor was she afraid of the dogs. Viip came into the house with the tak, tak, tak of her dainty hooves, sniffed about, went to the tea cart, licked up a little of the coffee dregs, the milk in the cups. Then she looked for a niche, folded her long legs, sank into an oval form. Balls of grass rolled up her throat were conscientiously ruminated and digested. When she got tired her head sank next to her, her eyes closed, and she slumbered.

As moths flutter through a window, confused by a downpour, hang on to a wardrobe, mistake it for a tree, separate from it in the dusk, flee into the pleats of a curtain, deposit their eggs in the twilight of window blinds, live out their days in an unused room—so the doe shared its exotic existence with us, adapting itself to the circumstances. The carpet her moss. The satin armchair her piece of forest floor. The garden her delicious meadow, humans her foxes, hares, hedgehogs, geese; each of us a subspecies she learned to differentiate by scent.

Viip never got clean. You could find her little droppings strewn all over the house. Little lakes, too. She had something stuck-up about her, like a prima donna. And she was mysterious. She came and went as she pleased. Sometimes one heard her longing cry, not in the house but in the courtyard outside. She did not look at us but through us, past us, into the distance, as if through a glass bead curtain. She was not afraid, just somewhat timid. She knew nothing of danger. People, dogs, it was all the same to her. She strolled past our hair-trigger dog Pluto, sniffing at his bowl. Pluto just looked up; he was trained to attack males and strangers. Viip was impassive, like a Buddhist monk resting within himself.

It was comical to behold how she irritated the dogs in the house. Viip had discovered the cave beneath the tiled stove and kept it occupied for hours on end. There was nothing left for the dogs but to make do with the space in front of the entrance. Over and over one of them stood up and looked to see whether the shameless wild thing was still making itself at home in his house. Then he lay down again, yawned, stared, and after many deep sighs went back to sleep.

My father sat in his armchair and watched the doe, his head swaying: her shining black eyes, this perfect, gorgeous creature. He melted, forgot himself a little, whistled a few bars, walked around the doe. Splendid, he said, pulling a cookie from his pocket.

Another one of Fritz's loves. Loads of hay traveled into Munich; the circus animals had to be fed. Corn, oats, potatoes, and often meat, too.

I heard my parents quarreling over it when the office door was ajar.

Yet again! A sack of carrots. Carrots! scolded my mother. They have simply vanished!

How? My father made an astonished face.

You know how. Smuggled in to your circus. Fritz, we need them so urgently for our people!

The elephants like carrots too now and then, he grinned.

You're crazy with your circus critters.

My father was pleased with himself, looked about in amusement, let my mother rant.

Hay would be plenty! she said.

Not for training, he said whimsically. For once he was not proper, and enjoyed it.

Step rrRight Up

WE COUNTRY CHILDREN had no diversions other than the spectacle of the farm and a little music from the radio. The hit parade. Sometimes. Otherwise it was just the news, or Grandfather's missing persons service. You had to shape your days yourself.

When work let out, the laborers crouched at their doors. The men smoked, striking a manly pose; hands in their trouser pockets, they boasted, palavered coarsely, and cracked jokes. The women stared or knitted, and gossiped. On Sundays they dressed up. Some went to church, others fishing. In the afternoon they ate cake or the like.

Right after the war there were no cinemas in small villages like ours. When cinema eventually returned it was something quite special, quite an undertaking, an expedition with a horse-drawn wagon, or on bicycles. Even more exotic were the visits occasioned by news of a merry-go-round, a Ferris wheel, or a shooting gallery in some village not too far away. The odor of burnt fat on a sausage rotisserie would greet us from afar as we approached the beer tent with its little banners. Inside sat the beer corpses of tomorrow, staring vacantly into space, tightly clutching their steins. These were the illiterates of joy, who never moved, not even from their beer to the port-a-potty with the little heart in the door: they just let it run down the shafts of their walking sticks, right where they sat.

Once we children had discovered the carousel, no one could hold us back. You were whirled up and around in a circle, over and over again. You could see everything, from a bird's-eye view: hats, bald heads, a room through a window, two people kissing up against the tent wall—by the next pass the melee had swallowed them—a dog mounting a bitch, babies in carriages, a breast in the cleavage of a blouse. Then the carousel slowed down, and the chains across the seats folded into an umbrella. The tickling in your stomach ebbed away, and the carousel came to a standstill.

Do it again! I would shout. Do it again!

One glorious, unforgettable day we jammed into the carriage. Alexandra and I sat on our mothers' laps. We drove to the station, then by train into the city. There we climbed onto the tram. It squeezed its way through the shattered precincts: mounds of debris, freestanding house frames with boarded-up windows, then a row of chestnut trees, and finally a big meadow. In the middle of this meadow, a circus tent with a banner waving from its peak. Krone, I read on the banner; next to it, embroidered in gold, was a crown. Hurraah! There stood the circus tent.

We pressed forward through the crowd of spectators. I blindly held someone's hand, gaping with astonishment. A completely new world of wonder spread out before me, a wondrous dream offering itself. An elephant from the Thousand and One Nights stood before the tent and waved us in with his trunk. Enthroned on his shoulders was a beautiful woman, fanning herself with her gloved hand. For a moment her face lost its queenly rigidity and lit up as she glimpsed my father. He took off his hat, bowed. Honored, Madame. The horns had started blaring. Tah-tah-reh-teh-teh.

We shoved our way through the archway, on into the arena. I had never seen such a great mass of people. It pushed and pressed, it screamed and tossed and gestured and grabbed. A man turned a hurdy-gurdy and a song pushed forward from its pipes. Far above, skylights in the tent ceiling threw a golden ring into the center. A clown seated us in the first row with grandiloquent gestures. We sat and stared.

Fritz put his arm across Adi's shoulders. She took off her brown Parisian hat and slipped it over the pocketbook on her lap.

Yes, this is the circus, he said, to make it clear once again, and because he was so glad, he whispered: Here farting is permitted. After everyone laughed, he looked contentedly about, making a face, as if it were he who had organized the entire hurly-burly and the anticipated acts, for us alone.

Anita sniffed the arena air—was that the smell of lions? Bears? The piercing reek betrayed the presence of a carnivore. She knew!

Goats, I whispered.

Nonsense, they eat grass.

But they smell pungent.

Pssst!

For this special occasion Anita had been allowed to free herself from boarding school. Her long thick black braids lined up down her back. She was almost grown up, her skin light brown—olive, like my father's. I, by contrast, was fair-skinned, like my mother, but without her black hair, and because my hair was already light, my mother dreamed a blonde dream. To conjure forth a bright shining effect on my head, my hair was rinsed with chamomile and I was sat down in the sun to dry. There I sat on the balcony in the sunshine, watched over by Justa, until it became boring for her too and we went inside to use the hair dryer.

Anita had taken her seat to Father's left. He bent over and listened to her. When it came to animals they were agreed. They whispered, gestured, traded. Animals lived by rules laid down by nature. That was purely scientific, outside the emotional arena with the pain, disappointments, and broken promises that exacerbated the reticence and shyness the two of them shared.

So as not to miss anything, Anita fixed her gaze on the blazing lights of the central ring, looking away only occasionally to trade connoisseurs' observations with my father. She leaned at the edge of her chair, bending into the action, her cheeks red with excitement.

I, on the other hand, was so excited that I squirmed left, right, stood up, sat down again, tugged my cap over my forehead, put my coat on, then took it right back off. I wanted to see everything, wanted to know who else was sitting with us in the tent. Perhaps I knew someone in the audience I could wave to, or call over to join us.

There! Trumpet blasts from somewhere high above. The red curtain flew open.

Look, here they come! cried my father, thrilled.

A group of horses burst into the sawdust circle. Trapp, trapp, trapp, they plodded in mincing paces, necks bent, along the rim. In twos, in threes, one after another. In the center stood a man in uniform with a trainer's whip. Sometimes he let them race off, sometimes he drew them back in.

Look at that—the one on the left hurt his leg. Sembach got him back on his feet. Lame, get it? My father knew that.

Pegasus flew past, blew silver dust from his nostrils. As light as air, he whirled off across the cloud floor, circled, returned with black flashing eyes. Golden dust sprinkled into my lap. Drumroll. We clapped. All five horses reared up on their hind legs. With white draped across their haunches, bundles of feathers between their ears, they gave a well-behaved bow. Mr. Sembach pointed with his whip in our direction. My father tapped his temple in greeting.

The curtain still fluttered. Anita looked up at our father admiringly. I did, too. He knew everything, knew everyone; like that of a magician, his vision extended from the farm to the tent, from our horses to these.

A lady in a tutu made a dog twirl a ball on the end of his nose. The ball danced, fast, faster still, until the dog was so pleased with his own act that he barked for joy. It all went by much too quickly. Suddenly everyone was staring up into the cupola. Again, a drumroll. A man in a golden tricot hurled himself down at us, swift as an arrow. Cries of fear shot through the audience; it held its breath, but there it was: just short of the golden dust he jerked himself back to safety. Relieved exhalation. There! Two more acrobats hurtled downward and my stomach with them. I had to cling to my mother. A clown in gigantic shoes waddled into the ring of light, blowing on his whistle; then another and yet another somersaulted out from the curtain folds, doing their preliminary flips with birdlike weightlessness. I sat at the edge of my chair in taut excitement.

How did that water squirt from his hat? Unbelievable. And the streamers from his ears? The rabbit from the top hat? The doves from under his robe? The acrobats stacked themselves into a tower, with a child acrobat, smaller than me, sitting up on top on a little chair.

That takes practice, mused my mother with a serious face.

A tiny person danced tiptoe on a round wood floor as a boy swept out roller-skate circles at top speed.

Those are the skates I want so badly! Look, Mami, he went and got the roller skates! I was on the verge of tears; after all, it was I who had managed to find out where the only ones in town could be had.

Pssst! hissed Anita.

Drumroll, kettledrums, trumpets, teh-teh-reh-teh-teh: the elephants.

Step rrright up, step rrright up, shouted the barker. A queenly lady sat in state atop one of the wise beasts as he swayed and swung, waltzing around the ring. Stars fluttered from her hair, a mooncalf bowed deeply in greeting. The golden wand in her hand glittered, beckoned me to come along. The elephant smiled across to me. On roller skates I circled the bright ring of lights. I was the elephant queen. I wore the diadem of light. I caught the acrobat in flight. I sang the song and everyone listened.

In the streetcar home I keeled over from all the magic and fell into a deep sleep.

•

The storks came, announcing spring.

Viip was now a grownup deer. She wandered in the forest, sometimes staying out of sight for days at a time. With each passing day her horizon expanded and familiar people became stranger to her. Every day she took a leap further away, stepping deeper into the tall grass, into the undergrowth, disappearing in the blue beneath the pines. Foxes, hares, pheasants, hedgehogs lived out there and stole through the mottled green. They were now her comrades, their scent identical with their cry. Proprietors of meadows. Hoteliers of the forest patch they ran through. No one in the house could tell whether she would get used to life in the wild and survive the dangers.

Then one summer day one of the workers recognized Viip at the ponds. He could tell by the notch in her ear. With her were two fawns. The children and I ran and called her name, imitating her cry: Viiiiiip! Viiiiip!

There she stood on the embankment near the river, at the verge of the great freedom. She pricked up her ears toward the sound. I stretched out my hand, with a piece of sugar on it. Viip stuck out her neck toward me; her ears went up, down, up, down as she hesitantly approached me step by step. She sniffed at the sugar, at my hand, and snorted. Her two fawns stayed off to the side, little toy deer. I dared one more careful step. Then, in a fraction of a second, Viip remembered her wildness, remembered what drew her further and further away every day, even though for many months humans had been the only ones she knew. She stamped her hoof, made a quick turn, let out a cry, and tore off toward the forest, her children in tow. She lifted off on all fours into a high arc, vanishing in the summer grass; resurfaced; sprang once more, and they were gone.

Never again would Viip come so close. Now and then someone stumbled across her and called after her, but the only sign of recognition was her frightened gaze, the up and down of her ears.

Viiip! I screamed as I threw myself into the grass, tears flowing down my cheeks.

God

RELIGION, THE OPIUM OF THE PEOPLE, my father quoted from Karl Marx. Ours was an irreligious household. Catholic Bavaria had grown close to my mother's heart because of its Baroque churches and art. Otherwise my parents were atheists and left everyone in peace with their beliefs. The tone of the household was liberal where religion was concerned. There was no grace before meals. No priest came to visit. One went into churches to admire the art. Bavaria was Baroque, joyous; the north, all Gothic severity. God and the Church came up only in historical contexts. We were cultivated bourgeois, culture our religion.

Cultivated was a word my parents frequently used. A cultivated man. A cultivated household. Cultivated language. One behaved in a cultivated manner, or uncultivated—how revolting! Cultivated hands, cultivated table, cultivated dining, one even had cultivated thoughts and...other thoughts. Then there were the Philistines: culture was all the same to them. And the culture vultures: they exaggerated.

Our household was cultivated. My maternal grandfather's pictures, Venetian glass, carpets from Africa, Jugendstil furnishings mingled with Baroque, a Piranesi collection, the "Carceri," a Rembrandt engraving, a portrait by Ingres, scattered here and there. We ate from Nymphenburg porcelain. The poppy design was by Grandfather Max, the fish porcelain by his friend Gradl. On special occasions we used our fine Meissen and silver cutlery. In the kitchen there was earthenware and tin dishes for the servants. This distinction was also part of our culture.

Nature too was invited into our cultivated house as decorous decor. In the corridor hung stuffed deer and stag heads with horns. A wild boar with his tusks gave a hostile stare down from the stairway. A whole stuffed peacock hung over the tiled stove in the den, a colorful woodpecker on a branch next to it. In a glass case on the vitrine stood a kingfisher with real preserved fish in his beak, and behind him a dried swamp landscape. We used ladles with silver leaves mounted on horn handles, salad implements with boar's teeth grips.

And books. Mainly heirlooms and gifts. Photo albums from Mother's childhood in Venice. Black and white, already a little mildewed. Italian art gems: Titian, Tintoretto, Canaletto. Volumes of Goya, editions of Breughel the Elder and the Younger. Comparative studies of the Wiesenheim altar and the Baroque Wieskirche. You also found reference books on mad King Ludwig, his castle on the Herrenchiemsee, Neuschwanstein, and all the rest. All that was called cultivated and was read thoroughly by my mother.

Way up at the top of the bookcase, not so easy to get to, leaned the moderns, the less easily comprehensible contributors to our twentieth century. Georg Grosz, Kandinsky, Münter, Blaue Reiter, Otto Dix, Kokoschka. The Impressionists and Expressionists, a Feininger, too, had somehow stumbled into their midst, but no Picasso. He was considered a charlatan. At best his Blue Period... No Henry Moore, no—please! Better Gainsborough, something quite fine.

My father read the newspaper, or technical agricultural literature for continued education. Now and then a biography in between. But his real preference was travel journals, mainly about Africa, to which he could append his own experiences: the rosy morning light, a silk cloth across the desert sands, a caravan on the horizon, the blue of a turban, dew on the horses' coats like confectioner's sugar, Agadir, Tunis, Casablanca. He described the people there, their brown skin, their high, slender form, as phenomenally beautiful. Exotics one could not fathom, merely observe from a distance. They were mysterious. One did not criticize them, simply let them be, which was hard to do with one's own compatriots.

Africa was his continent. He had already been there once in a previous life, he joked. I could sit and listen for hours when my father lost himself in the desert, ducked into the twilight of a bazaar, negotiated with carpet dealers, sat on the floor eating spicy foods with his fingers.

My mother had her Italy, my father his Africa. Their storytelling merged inseparably with myths and fairy tales. The stories became experiences; events drawn from life melted into the pages of books.

When I was small, my mother recited a disquieting nighttime poem to end the day:

Kätzchen läuft die Trepp' hinan,	*Kitten runs up the stairs,*
Hat ein rotes Jäckchen an,	*Has a little red coat on,*
Messerchen an der Seite.	*His little knife at his side.*
Wo willst du denn hinreiten?	*So where do you want to ride?*
Ich will reiten in	*I want to ride to*
Bullemanns Haus,	*Bullemann's house*
Will holen eine fette, fette Maus,	*To fetch a fat and juicy mouse*
Will machen Wurst	*To make it into*
und Schincken draus,	*sausage and ham*
Und ein Bisschen trinken	*And drink a little bit*
Von dem süssen Mäuseblut.	*Of the sweet mousie blood.*
Schmeckt dem Kätzchen	*Tastes just great*
gar so gut.	*to kittens.*
Quik, quik, quik,	*Quick, quick, quick,*
willst du mit?	*want to come along?*

It was always the same poem, and although it was exciting, repetition gave it a comforting effect. At the end I would send out good wishes for everyone in the house, the dogs, too. In another evening song God stood at the foot of the bed and watched over my sleep.

In wintertime, along with ice and snow and the Christmas tree, Baby Jesus came into the house. Under the heavily decorated tree an ox, an ass, three kings, Mary, Joseph, and little Jesus met on real straw in a miniature moss hut hand-molded from colored wax by the artist of the family, my maternal grandfather Max. The little group was always in danger of melting or being buried beneath the dripping wax of the Christmas tree candles.

If yellow beeswax from the candles had trickled on the Christ child, it had to be liberated right away with a toothpick and tweezers, and the candle clipped onto another branch. The king's gift of myrrh drowned under the wax, a tower of unnoticed drops built up on the cow's back. The wax family had to be continually rescued from a waxy death, reshaped and molded anew. It was as much a part of the Christmas festivities as baking cookies, as the scents: roast goose, pine sap, dried apples mingled with something rotten, and mulled wine with cinnamon.

Wild cursing abounded on the farm among the workers. Cross crucifix, Lord God Sacrament! Cursed shit! A whip cracked across a pair of oxen that refused to budge, or something else that failed to do its duty right away—always a reason for loud cursing. Beni, the chief cattleman, could not even begin his day without his litany of curses.

Beni was a huge man with a hunchback, like the Hunchback of Notre Dame. He dragged his right leg along with him sideways, with a pained air. One heard him coming long before his wild forelock appeared. The red rising in his face, he hauled the big metal milk canisters on his back from the cow stalls to the wagon. A warning growl rolled from his throat. Once he arrived at the wagon he turned around and let the canister fall onto the flatbed with a loud bang, rolled it into position, spit into his hands, and, relieved of his burden, proceeded cursing back to the cow stalls. Cross crucifix, Lord God Sacrament! And another repetition, until thirty or more milk canisters were loaded. My mother said he was frightfully good-natured, stressing the word "frightful," for although she found him good-natured, this quality was hard to discern. He really did look terrifying.

When I leafed through the Goya book and found the picture of Zeus eating his son, I always had to think of the childless Beni.

Saint Nicholas came down from God's Heaven on the evening of December sixth. Alexandra, Peter, and I had been sitting on the bench by the stove and waiting for him since twilight. He was supposed to come from the moor, on a sleigh with bells. With him, in a pedagogical capacity, was his sidekick Krampus, who carried the sack and the birch rod, and acted like a wild animal, louder and more fearsome every time, or so it seemed to me. Children who were disobedient during the year were shoved into this sack and hauled far away. Krampus was the climactic terror, which one awaited with a morbid fervor from late autumn on, as the days grew shorter. Krampus did not peep out from the pages of a book. No, he was reality, like arctic weather, like the fog over the moor, the potato fires, the pressed cabbage heads, the cool moon, the remains of moth wings between the winter windowpanes.

There we sat on the bench by the warm stove. Under the bench slept the dogs. They made little noises, and their legs twitched when they ran after something in their sleep. But tonight I had no time to watch them dreaming. I racked my brain for every conceivable piece of misbehavior Saint Nicholas could dredge up. Nothing occurred to me, so I merely recalled last year's terror and rummaged in my head for a conciliatory song or a poem. Fear had made my head feel like an empty snail house: complicated, with thoughts intertwined, spiraling upward into a closed capsule. The grownups looked over at us, grinning.

Uli: I know someone who is exceptionally quiet tonight.

What of it? I dared quickly say.

Then we heard tinkling bells and clanking chains at the door, and the terror began. The dogs burst forth from beneath the oven, howling and barking as if they were after a hare.

That must be Krampus, said the grownups unnecessarily.

I clung to Peter on one side, to Alexandra's hand on the other. The grownups sat or stood around in the room, smoking and grinning. My mother gave me a cheerful wave. But even she was powerless against what was about to burst in upon us any moment now. She could not protect me from Saint Nicholas. No one could deter this primal force. Wishing he would stay away this year, impossible. Nicholas came without asking, without being invited. My mother could not disinvite him. This was one guest the grownups used against us children. The nearer it got to Christmastime, the more often they threatened to expose misbehavior to Saint Nicholas.

Sometimes my mother silently relinquished her power, smiled, and withdrew. Despite this I felt protected. My mother was like a river cliff with water playing around it. A colorful bird sat down on this particular stone, ignoring all the others; or a society of similar butterflies landed and drank. When she gave in she was just being yin, merely releasing the terrain, leaning back to observe. Unnecessary resistance was a waste of energy. Had she insisted, she would have lost her power. Adi always has the upper hand, my father would say. But with Nicholas there was no upper hand.

In they crashed: Saint Nicholas, dressed like a magnified dwarf out of Snow White; Krampus, in a torn dark something or other, a fur across his back, his face blackened with coal, his chains rattling. We children, frightened, silent as flowers, powerless—another one of those words that says everything—stared at the play that was put on for our benefit yet solely to frighten us. Paradoxically, it was only amusing and laughable for the older audience. Then Saint Nicholas ceremoniously opened his great book and read from it our long-forgotten naughty acts. First Peter's, then Alexandra's, then mine. Plus a few good deeds on the side. Finally, thank God, after we had promised him to better ourselves next year, Alexandra and I were released. We were allowed to sit down, and each of us got a bag of sweets—from Olga, from our kitchen, flashed through my head.

The saint passed his hand across our hair once more and gave us a pat on the cheek, telling us to smile and look friendly. Everything had gone just fine. And next year—his voice swelled—you have already promised… A threatening finger. Alexandra always smiled anyway, even when she was highly disconcerted. People like you better with a friendly face, Aunt Julia had drilled into her head. I, on the other hand, could manage only a forced smile while I was recovering from my fright. The hostile members of the audience puffed on their cigarettes, scarcely able to contain their laughter.

Saint Nicholas stroked Peter's hair. But Peter, what do I see here?

The holy man was quite astounded. Something else must have sprung from the pages of his great book.

Yes, I had almost forgotten about that.

You were disobedient to your poor mother.

You didn't brush your teeth.

You left the chicken coop open.

You kicked the dog.

You—you dropped a crystal bowl on the floor!

His voice reached a crescendo, and his eyes rolled in their crevices above the white cotton beard. Krampus cracked his birch rod across the floor. I winced and Alexandra's grin froze as Peter dissolved onto the floor.

So swiftly that one could scarcely follow it, Krampus slipped his sack over the head of the trembling Peter, threw him across his shoulder, and stormed out the door with his squirming bundle. None of the grownups said anything. I was appalled. No one protested, not even Peter's mother. Auntie Brün seemed to be in cahoots with Krampus. As contentedly as if nothing had happened, or because he had now caused enough trouble, the holy Saint Nicholas clapped the book shut with a loud bang, gestured goodbye to the grownups, shook a threatening forefinger in the direction of Alexandra and me, and disappeared through the doorway, leaving behind a mood of general festivity, laughing and joking as punch was passed around.

Moments later, Peter slid back through the door into the room with no visible alteration other than red ears and red cheeks. I could relax, swing my legs and prod the dog a little, unwrap my sweets, slowly become myself again. Even think again. Hmm: why does Saint Nicholas wear the same ring as Georg? I looked around the room and chewed on a cookie. It had gone well.

Alexandra laughed with relief. Her politeness and docility always made a good impression on the grownups, yet with me she was often domineering, sometimes to the point of torture. She was some years older and many things came easier to her, like bicycling, which Aunt Julia had taught us.

Alexandra would race into the avenue on the bike, come to a slightly wobbly stop, turn, and pedal toward her, growing larger and larger, coming triumphantly to a perfect standstill. Then it was my turn. Since I was smaller I had to stand in the giant machine. To keep me balanced, Aunt Julia had to run alongside. Out of breath, she gave the bicycle a push. I panicked. Feeling suddenly abandoned, suspended too high above the ground, I pedaled a few meters farther, then just let go. The metal monstrosity careened to the side: a crash, a terrible pain somewhere in my arm or leg, and I was tumbling through a dark blue undertow.

As I opened my eyes, Aunt Julia's furrowed brow hovered above my face.

You fainted.

I had no idea where I had been. My head sat in a yellow fog. My knee was bleeding. Thick drops ran onto the gravel.

That looks like a concussion to me, she said expertly, and carried me to the house.

That shit bicycle.

My mother took care of the bloody knee and my spiritual condition. I was confined to bed and forbidden to move. Yellow iodine was daubed on all the wounds and a cool cloth laid on my forehead.

You really got it, said Alexandra, skipping rope now on the left leg, now on the right.

You're not allowed to skip rope in the house, I reminded her, weakened from my fall and the compulsory immobility.

You're the only one dumb enough to knock things over, not me, she answered impudently. She thwacked the rope on the feather coverlet, pushed the doll off the chair onto the floor, and hopped out of the sickroom.

Grandfather had been listening to the missing persons news on the radio for hours, sometimes jotting down a name. Thousands of parents were looking for children lost in the war, men for their wives, and so forth. Oh, the senseless war.

I heard my grandfather's footsteps coming up the stairs.

Would you please sing me a soldier song? I begged through the open door.

Yes, I'll sing you something. Then I'll lie down for my afternoon nap.

He sat down on the bed and sang:

Ich hatt' einen Kameraden	*I had a comrade*
Einen besseren findst du nicht.	*A better one you won't find.*
Die Kugel kam geflogen—	*The bullet came a-flying—*
Gilt sie mir oder gilt sie dir?	*Is it for me or is it for you?*
Sie hat ihn weggerissen—	*It tore him from this world—*
Ich hab' es leiden müssen,	*I had to endure it,*
Als wär's ein Stück von mir.	*As if it were a piece of me.*

My grandfather gently stroked my head.

Don't have to cry, that's just how life is. I've known three wars: '80, '14, and Hitler's war.

I stopped crying, since this required strenuous thought.

White rain pounded the courtyard gravel. I lay in bed, and my mother read from the books of Ernst Kreidolf. Bugs danced with butterflies, a pale moth wove a crown from pollen for a larva. Caterpillars got drunk on the nectar of a rose, fireflies lit a nocturnal dance of luna moths, and I got well.

•

After Saint Nicholas had disappeared and everyone had sat down to dinner, Georg too came into the room and sat down at the table. I took his hand and carefully studied his ring, to be quite certain.

How come you are wearing Nicholas's ring, the exact same…

Well, because I am so well behaved, then you get this ring. Only when you are very good, he said so loudly that Uli laughed, then quickly held his hand over Anita's mouth. She had been just about to say something.

You were not good at all, I blared. You and Dieter blew up the tiled stove.

The three of us looked across the table to my father, who spooned his soup as if he were not listening.

No, it's not true, whispered Georg.

Oh, yes it is, I said, again quite loudly. Papi almost threw you two out.

Psst, sshh, they implored in a whisper.

I know you had a bomb hidden in the stove, I blared on, watching my father's reaction from the corner of my eye.

Shut your mouth and eat, he said. And I did.

I knew exactly what had happened. Uli, Dieter, and Georg had distilled amateur vodka from potatoes, filled beer bottles with it, and secretly hidden the bottles in the warming compartment in the middle of the tiled stove.

The explosion happened the day their friend Axel came to visit. Because it was cold outside, he made a fire to warm up the room and waited for his friends' return. Suddenly, with a spectacular bang, hell broke loose. The liquor in the bottles had exploded. It sounded like flak from the war they had just put behind them, still ringing in everyone's ears.

My father had responded with one of his own supernovae: you cursed idiots, he raged, no one can get a moment's peace in this madhouse!

VICAR MOSER

In wintertime, when the cold crept through the house like an untamed animal, I got up at six o'clock, as all children did. Before school they had to go to chapel, and so I too walked the four kilometers on foot with the other farm children, the Catholics; or when we were lucky, the milk wagon gave us a lift.

God was Catholic. Strict and vindictive. Almighty and omnipresent. God sees everything you do, thundered the Catholic priest from the pulpit. He knows what every one of you is thinking. There are no secrets. The fear of God's almighty, wrathful omnipresence gave teachers boundless power. This exerted a great fascination on me, as I was not accustomed to such a tone at home. Soon I knew the whole litany by heart, and the Lord's Prayer, the Hail Mary, all the important church holidays. I was thrilled with the drama of the Church, the play acted out at the altar, befuddled with incense. I kneeled on the hard benches, leaned on the edge of my pew, and found Vicar Moser's strictness appropriate. Early rising was fully compensated by the solemn carnival.

There you have it, you idiots—even though she is not a real Christian! Vicar Moser praised me when I rattled off a Hail Mary at a fast clip. He boxed Roserl's ears resoundingly for her ignorance.

I wanted so badly not to be different from the others. I wanted to belong among the farm children, to be one of them, to be part of the colorful Baroque church with its bells. I wanted to belong to the fragrant incense, to the damning saints, to their implacable God, who resided in the cool church with his twelve apostles, six on each side, along the rows of pews. From up above he let Heaven descend to the church dome; there angels played by the dozens in the clouds with roses and lambs. On one side stood Mary's altar, like the one in the little chapel at home, just grander, with a sternly staring Virgin. The Christ Child was not naked, he was swaddled in a sky-blue plaster cloth. Mary had a host of angels with her, who must surely have been allowed to play with Jesus when no one was looking. I was drawn to the sense of order, the strictness, the majesty. It was so exotic, so different from my family.

A few of the boys I knew became acolytes. Then they belonged to Vicar Moser and his holy circumstances, to which the girls had no access. Mary and Mary Magdalene seemed to be the only women in God's house. All other figures were men and boys. Keep God's house clean, thundered Vicar Moser from the pulpit. Naturally I reflected: So that is why he has two women there, to clean up after we have all gone.

Sometimes my mother had no time to accompany us on our way to school, even though the radio had warned of a murderer running loose in the woods, or it was foggy and we children were afraid. Then the neighbor lady walked part of the way with us.

C'mon, ain't nobody there, she said amiably, gathering us children about her and leading us through the high pines, thick and dark, interrupted here and there by a thicket of Christmas trees. But we would not be entirely convinced, since when they passed by there was rustling in the green confusion.

Suddenly a deer sprang up, ran across the road just in front of us, and on to the next thicket. The forest was fearsome, not least because of the fairy tales we had grown up with, and the way the grownups held us in check. Don't you dare… they would say, waving a threatening forefinger. You will be dragged into the forest, where the Forest Schratz and his people live. They love the flesh of unruly children.

I told my mother, but she just laughed, which did not exactly defuse the threat. There remained only one small glimmer of hope: perhaps I was excluded from the curse. Perhaps. Possibly. Under certain circumstances. But I was never quite sure. The others, my friends, the workers' children, they were quite sure. Their mothers dealt not in laughter but in threats: You don't cut it out, I'm takin' you into the forest, they'll eat you alive.

Our neighbor's wife, whom we children loved so very much, had given birth to a little boy. In Vicar Moser's eyes birth was a sin, proof of a sex act committed within Catholic Bavaria. She had to be forgiven for her apparent transgression. A monetary contribution was also required, and during the period preceding her absolution by Vicar Moser, she had to enter the church through a side door.

When she attained forgiveness, she and her children once again entered the church through the main portal. Beaming, she carried little Ferdl bundled on her arm. Ferdl awakened, yawned, stretched, looked around the cold overflowing nave. The air was so chilly that you could see your breath almost all year round. A bell interrupted the frozen stillness. It was sounding for holy communion. Frightened, Ferdl started to bawl, so loudly that it resounded from the cold high walls, from the dome with the laughing cherubs who rode on clouds, played with lambs, hovered high above, up to the ceiling. Then the pandemonium of the bells topped it all off, and Ferdl shrieked even louder.

The small chapel on the estate was dedicated to the Mother of God. There she was enthroned in the middle of the altar. She was about my height, with her baby Jesus on her arm. I was enchanted with the long yellow hair cascading down her back, with her blue gaze.

This Maria possessed a box full of raiments that were supposed to be rotated in accordance with the church holidays. But no one bothered, so instead she became my ultimate doll. I clambered up onto the altar, lifted her from the floor with all my strength, liberated her from her stiff silk dress, and began a thorough investigation of everything that emerged underneath. Fabric arms filled with sawdust, likewise the legs, indeed the whole body. Her head, hands, and feet were made of porcelain.

I changed the doll's clothes, wove her braids, and parked her somewhere in the chapel. As the fancy struck me, I laid the stiff Maria on a bench, strewed flowers around her, and covered her nondetachable Jesus with them.

Sometimes I invited Mrs. Tafelmeier and my mother, commanding them to fold their hands, kneel, sink their eyes, just like at a real service. Then, imitating Vicar Mosar, I fired off the commandments I knew so well. I felt something resembling the power of Vicar Moser, and his whole sermon made sense.

Mrs. Tafelmeier told my mother Vicar Moser's cook was expecting a child. No one knew who the father was. Oh, really? my mother marveled discreetly, arching her brows. With this Tafelmeier one could only hold brief conversations, otherwise she glommed on, and the interaction took on epic proportions.

Often after school we children went through the cemetery instead of detouring around it. The cemetery was the other place where God reigned. On one side of the mortuary lived Heddi, the daughter of the mortician; on the other side, behind a glass door, the dead were laid out in their coffins, their hollow faces framed in beds of flower petals. They looked as if they were just sleeping there in their Sunday finery.

Heddi—her nickname was Gottesackerfliege, God's harvest fly—had only one eye. The other was an empty shell covered by the eyelid. It must have been an accident; the poor mortician had no money for a glass eye. When her father was away Heddi waved us into the mortuary. The empty eye looked at us; the other had wandered sideways, fearing the sudden return of her angry father.

One after another we slipped inside and contemplated the corpses.

She's real white 'cuz she was still a virgin, Heddi explained.

A pale man in a suit slept between white lilies in a black enameled coffin. A white rosary enwrapped his folded hands. Next to him in a matte box slept a little girl. Her forehead was covered with a violet wreath.

She done fell outta the window, Heddi instructed us children, right on her haid. That's whah they done covered her.

The dress was white and much too large. It lay loosely on her body and was tucked in at the feet. A bunch of forget-me-nots withered in her waxen hands.

A sacred shiver ran through me, courtesy of God and his almighty presence, not to mention fear of the gravedigger. But the adventure was worth it. The forbidden entry into the cold house. The arched space, the white marble floor, where even a whisper caused an echo; the scent of something one did not understand; the sickly sweet fragrance of the flowers; the bluish light from above; the fear that lifted one's hair like a stiff breeze. And if one looked back at the entrance door, one saw standing there, small and thin, Gottesackerfliege as policeman.

Once the mortician caught us emerging from his mortuary. He dropped what he was carrying, ran at us, managed to catch Xaver by the ear and would not let go until he had dragged him out of the cemetery, giving him one last twist of the earlobe and a resounding box on the cheek, screaming: Get lost, you dirty lot! Ah'll rip out yer ears, I'll beat ya to a pulp!

We ran away at top speed, but really one had imagined far worse.

During recess we children hung around in the schoolyard and ate our sandwiches. Mine were gigantic and fat, filled with delicious sausage slices, or with ham.

With these delicacies one could strike good bargains. There were hundreds of saints' pictures circulating around the schoolyard. Many children collected and traded saints that hovered on clouds or were crucified on trees. Jesus with Mary. The Trinity. Jesus with a lamb. Jesus as a boy in the temple. All of them had halos around their heads, even Joseph, who always stood next to an ox and ass, somewhat removed from holy Mary and her child, as if he did not quite belong. The pictures had lace frames or were embossed, strewn with silver frost, silk plissé curls at the corners. Semitransparent cellophane allowed only an unclear view of the picture, maintaining the suspense for a time.

Most people were still very poor from the war years and in need of the simplest things. But naturally the church business was booming. Typical, commented my father when I spread out my sacred pictures on the table. I checked for duplicates, and took my time observing the most wonderful of them, with particularly lavish ornamentation and shrill colors accentuating the holy scenes dusted with gold glitter.

Then one day the church was locked up for a whole week. Vicar Moser was nowhere to be found. No one had noticed anything out of the ordinary. It was rumored that his superior had sent him into the Bavarian Forest. The vicarage cook, Zenzi, had given birth to a little girl. The child had the red locks of the vicar, and his blue eyes. One glance sufficed: the resemblance was obvious, the act of generation undeniable. What was to become of Zenzi? The curly red bastard meant no one wanted to give her a job. Aunt Esther from the neighboring castle took on the role of Saint Jude. When she heard about Zenzi's predicament, she said gaily: Catholic bad conscience likes to work. Glad to do both a good and a useful deed, she summoned Zenzi to her house.

After the scandal I no longer wanted to go to church. The play was dead without its star, Vicar Moser. The collection of saints' pictures had also been wrapped up with all that magic. I gave them to Lenerl and Roserl. Only occasionally did I still visit the doll Maria in the farm chapel, played a little bit with her hair, dressed and undressed her. But it was not the same.

ORANGES

Frau Hagenreiner's shop was now carrying something new, exciting, and quite special: oranges. Each orange was wrapped in a fine sheet of silk paper with an exotic image: a faraway landscape, a volcano, the face of a negress with a turban, a Moor laughing out at you with his big white teeth, perhaps a palm tree with a red sun.

Thus began a new adventure with educational value. Procuring an album and some glue, I nestled the delicate little sheets of paper with the greatest care between the pages of a heavy book and weighted it down to smooth them out. Grandfather gave me a pair of tweezers and helped order the collection. Because of his trembling hands he was only allowed to look, not touch, since the fragile sheets ripped so easily.

My mother had to make sure she always bought different kinds of oranges, from different exotic countries. At my insistence she telephoned Frau Hagenreiner. Had she received a new delivery? Did the papers have faces? Palm, sun, mountain?

Now I could swing deals with the wrapping papers as I had with the saints' pictures. I hauled the album along to school and traded, at first collecting whatever was around, then going at it systematically, the way Grandfather had shown me: by country, by color, seeking a pink or yellow background to the romantic paintings that told of the great distances at which the oranges grew. Portugal, Spain, Sicily, Turkey—they were all so far away, so unattainable. What must the oranges not have experienced before they arrived in boxes at Hagenreiner's shop, individually laid in wood shavings? I collected with growing passion, as a zoologist does butterfly varieties, discovering a boundless and eternally novel world of silk paper wrappings.

When it came to this passion Grandfather and I understood one another especially well. He had collected all his life, boxes in particular, made of porcelain, ivory, silver, wood. After the war, in my grandparents' apartment in Munich, I was allowed to view his collection under his supervision. Home from the war, there it lay once again, unpacked, in vitrines, under glass in display tables, spread out on velvet. It had been well hidden, squirreled away.

These Marie-Louise could not get at, he said; she couldn't squander them.

His erotic boxes lay hidden in a locked drawer. At my insistence he turned the key, fumbled around in the drawer, and pulled out the most innocuous of the silver boxes: Leda and the swan. On its delicately painted enamel lid, Leda reclined on a cushion, the swan poised above her.

Leda had a tame swan, he chattered amiably.

In the house? was my practical question.

Yes, of course. Tame, in the house.

As my questions piled up, my grandfather noticed his mistake and withdrew into his hardness of hearing.

Now let's put 'er back where she b'longs. Otherwise Marie-Louise will scold us.

That was it. Drawer closed, key turned.

And my mother? She collected plants for her garden, exchanged seeds with the neighbor, another infatuated flower lady. She raised small seedlings inside in the warmth of the greenhouse and transplanted them to the garden in spring.

When she was visiting a private garden and spotted a plant she did not yet have, she would squat down, act as if she had lost something, give a lightning-fast jerk, tug out a sample complete with root, stick it in her purse, soil and all, and feign innocence—as thieves are wont to do. In the same spirit she made Umer drive her to the Botanical Gardens in the city. They were still partly in ruins and had not yet reopened. Because she was the only visitor, they let her stroll unsupervised through the shattered glass houses. When she resurfaced from this excursion she looked very broad and heavy, and walked more slowly than usual toward the carriage. Umer carefully had to help her first out of her coat and then out of her jacket. Every pocket was crammed full of cuttings, roots and soil.

Mother and Grandfather were the only collectors I had around me. There was nothing to collect then, anyway; one was busy procuring the necessities. People had become much more hard-boiled. Spartan virtues had grafted well onto certain traditional aspects of the national character: refusal to be a prig, determination to stay in for the duration.

These characteristics came in handy when we had to procure important equipment from across the big water reservoir. Whenever our carriage pulled up the steep curving path to the reservoir rim, fishermen were sitting at the water's edge as if they had sat there all their lives, watching their lines expectantly. Anita's boarding school was also across the reservoir. On journeys to and from school she rode out in front on her Bella, with the rest of us sitting in the coach behind. Because the narrow gravel road that ran obliquely across the reservoir had only a few spindly bushes and wind-bent trees growing along the sides, this trip with our highly nervous, easily startled horses was dreadfully dangerous, miles from the calm and friendly atmosphere of orange-wrapper trading.

Ominous clouds might roll in from the west. A hailstorm could sweep in quickly, bringing hail of ice as large as eggs.

There—a barn in the field. Down the embankment we rolled, toward the saving roof. On his box Umer valiantly grasped the reins as the horses began performing like tango dancers, rocking the coach back and forth. My mother pried open the door. The storm howled. Lightning bolts chased the thunder. We were truly entangled in the elements; everyone was dripping wet and shivering. My mother with her presence of mind had no time for self-pity or any sort of whining. She was courageous and practical and fearless—when all was said and done, one of the goddesses.

Goddesses

AT A CERTAIN TIME, in a single moment perhaps, in childhood, you make a discovery from which you profit in a way that stamps you, molds you forever. You are not pushed into it. No one says: Take a detailed look at this, or This you must imprint on your mind. The grownups rank it as unworthy of notice, or overlook it. Or they think: the child is still too much a child. Suddenly there it is, in the midst of the game, between the dolls and the worry whether the hamster has eaten, or whether the crickets need worms again. It incorporates everything, has an unforgettable odor, feels like the first time, looks like nothing before; and with it is a voice, a word, a sentence—vanilla.

One day Evelyn visited the estate, in an American car. Was she driving or was she chauffeured? Was the driver an American, an officer, young and good-looking? Was he her fiancé? Her father? I did not remember. There was no need to. She might have been the daughter of a painter, a friend of Fritz and Adi, but it was irrelevant. She was just there, slipping up through a crack in the pavement of childhood.

At the first glance I knew: that was who I wanted to be. Black hair piled up jauntily into a little tower. Eyebrows arched like swallows' wings over dark eyes. Lips painted red, as red as Mother's—no, redder. Red nails, too.

Evelyn and her tide of white pearls bent down and gave me a kiss on the cheek. Ah...fell from my lips. A new perfume hung in the room—the silk dress with the shoulder pads, the high heels, the stockings with seams, the hand holding a cigarette, the tilt of her head as she listened, her glance. When she burst out laughing, her dark hair leaning down toward her shoulder, I saw the red half-moon in her mouth, the gleaming strand of teeth. I gathered it all up, sucked it in, drank my fill, and would never forget her.

My father told a funny story, politely killing his cigar—it stinks too much, he said—and secured himself a place next to Evelyn. He was in a great mood and stayed that way. As if transformed, he cast a twinkling gaze around the table. My mother found this infectious; a little intoxicated with the memory of her Fritz, when she was as young as Evelyn, her jet-black hair parted in the middle like raven wings, and he was not yet so wounded, so forgetful, not yet etched with too many unbearable events.

Aaaah, today Evelyn was our guest. We were sitting at the festive table in animated conversation. The boys had their hair moist, combed back, as if they had just come up from underwater: red ears, fresh shirts. The fragrance of soap lingered beneath the lampshade. All this because of Evelyn. She was the patron saint of good breeding. She had brought wine, a rarity. All eyes converged on the American boyfriend. People nodded. Aaaah. My father smacked his lips. Delicious! General Brün saluted across the table as each of us got a taste of wine.

I elbowed my way next to Evelyn on the bench, smoothed my skirt, and stared at her. The wine glass, the hand on its shaft. A fly landed on her red thumbnail. The hand left the tablecloth, levitated up to her ear, played with her earring. Light gleamed in the cutlery. The Watzmann landscape stretched out across the wall behind her chair; across the foreground leaned Evelyn, between shadow and skin, fuzz on her upper lip, next to her the American boyfriend.

I was Evelyn, leaning at the vitrine in high pumps, a cigarette between my fingers.

My father: Today you look enchanting.

Thank you. I lit his cigar. Anything else?

He bowed. Would you like to play the piano with me?

Right away we were at the keyboard, our fingers hurrying across the keys, a song springing from the heart of the instrument as a rainbow kissed the edge of the field.

The hand on the glass moved, said something.

My fork was stuck in the gap between my front teeth. Anita nudged me. Wake up, eat! The clinking of silverware returned, along with the loud voice of my father, laughter in every direction, and my mother's happy face at the end of the table, reddened as if by a kiss.

My grandfather leaned back in his chair, half closed his eyes, and let Marie-Louise's annoying fingers wipe a spot from his vest.

The Brüns sat tightly packed next to Peter. A miniature clan of military correctness. They ate more politely than the others and nodded thankfully across the table like birds. Mrs. Brün's eyes wandered about, to the platter with the roast goose, to the mound of potatoes with onion rings on top, to the purple cabbage. She stroked the wrinkles from the white collar of her blouse. Her hand wandered downward from button to button, accompanied the blouse into her skirt. Her visual field expanded upward to the lamp with the pigskin shade, over to the mahogany vitrine behind my mother's chair, toward the shadows on the carpet. What was she looking for? For all the things she had to leave behind? For independence? Peace? For the good old days that sat locked up in the glass case of the past?

Aunt Julia's eyes made the rounds, finally resting on Alexandra. A pyramid of loss was growing here at the table. The Osts were so far in the black, she so far in the red. She had lost so much. It was still too fresh; time had not yet granted her the consolation of distance. She still gnawed at the war, and also at the people who had taken her in. No one had had any choice. In her time of need she had remembered the distant relatives of her departed husband. Country bumpkins, she thought, looking down on us. They know the stimulating pulse of a great city only by hearsay.

Sometimes she could not contain herself. Well—in our house only the servants drank beer. Or, correcting us: nightshirts are called "pajamas," morning coats "negligees." Before dinner there were "cocktails." The down pillow was called "plumeau." My mother's informality she mistook for naivete.

The family for its part was agreed that Julia had married far above her station. We saw through to her insecurity. She was obliged to be thankful, but because she was acting out of duty rather than inclination, she exaggerated her industriousness and was somewhat dissatisfied.

It is dreadful when you always have to say thank you, she said to my astounded mother.

Why, for heaven's sake? I am glad I can help you.

Julia, you are a true Catholic, my father sometimes jested in a moment of oblique mockery.

She would go red. Ach, you and your cynicism. What have I done wrong now?

No, no, not wrong. Much too right.

•

Evelyn's father, the portraitist Erich Hirt, was going to paint my mother in exchange for food. Mr. Hirt said Adi reminded him of Anselm Feuerbach's Nana. But he had to promise Fritz to paint her as she really was, not as the character of his fantasy.

My mother was used to sitting for art. Her father, Max Rossbach, who belonged to the Munich School, had often deftly painted her as a child, with a pug on her arm, leaning on a rock, in the foreground of an alpine picture with hints of Expressionism. He was a man of modest stature, well fixed, married to Grandmother Ännchen, who also came from a family of artists. A pair of doves. He was called Pülli, she Blüschen: pullover and blouse.

Yes, the Italian element. That came from the Italian winters, my mother laughed. It rubs off.

That was around the turn of the century, up to the First World War. They would pack gigantic trunks full with clothes and her father's paints and climb onto the train: Father Max, Mother Ännchen, Brother Adalbert, and she, little Adelheid, followed by their servant Elli and the pugs.

An alpine adventure awaited them. The train chugged upward, past villages and waving shepherds, into grand panoramas and unsuspected abysses, their hearts full of anticipation as they roared toward a foreign land. White-gloved attendants scurried through the coach, juggling pastries on a tray for their distinguished clientele.

Back then there was still the emperor. His portrait, one of the first mass-market products, was impossible to forget since it peered out at you from everything you touched: pillows, porcelain plates, the handle of a walking stick, the lids of pipes, shoehorns, cutlery, vases, cups, money.

These early travels to Italy, in an era when only a few ever left home, imprinted on my mother her sense of adventure and her gusto for the wider world. They whetted her curiosity and schooled her eye for the beauty of foreign cultures. There were people, pictures, climates, statues, buildings, foods—to sample, wonder at, read about, soak up. School was less important. It was the school of life that gave you a real education. Her father, Max, was the driven entrepreneur, her mother, Ännchen, more tender, glad when they had arrived in Venice and a certain quiet set in.

I knew Grandfather Pülli only from a handful of jolly, unforgettable visits. At the table he could conjure up anything imaginable from behind his napkin. He was an impassioned teller of tall tales who once insisted he had seen a panther slinking across the street in the early light of dawn. The animal revolutionary front must have liberated the zoo, cast open the doors and gates...It was just the beginning... He also had a tailor in one of his parallel universes who had sent him a bill that ran: Unbukld genlman's Trusers, Stiffnd up under lady's skirt.

Like Grandfather Theodor, Grandfather Pülli did not need to earn a living; he could devote himself entirely to painting. The landscapes in our house, in the hallways, over the beds, all came from his brush strokes. Now and then he made

designs for the Bayerische Königliche Manufaktur, to keep a finger in. He had designed the fine Nymphenburg poppy china. He was friends with Lehnbach and Lehmbruch and Riemerschmidt. The latter had also built his house, where the writers and artists of the Simplizissimus came and went, along with his other friend, Ernst Kreidolf, who had written and illustrated my favorite children's books.

Right at the start of the First World War, when my mother was twelve, her beloved brother fell in battle. Her mother, Ännchen, went to pieces, in the true sense of the word, like a pitcher that can no longer be glued back together—too many pieces are missing. Adi's wonderful childhood was extinguished like the flame of a candle. There were no more trips to Italy; her father retreated into his atelier and forgot the tall tales, the magic tricks; the rose arch at the garden gate withered; Mother Ännchen fell ill; but within Adi, as if to spite fate, grew a strong and joyful tree of life, and a feline tenacity.

It was also tenacity and zest that gathered us all again and again around the table at the farm. It meant nothing that one person was in a mood, or that the other had suffered a loss; it was immaterial who was cross with whom, or what else there was to carp about. We were alive. Life. Tomorrow? Who could tell? Yesterday? Escaped it by the skin of our teeth.

Around the table with Evelyn, my father's excitement infected everyone. Loud—louder—chatting and laughing. Chomping, conversation about food, tall tales, wisecracks, rumors, and malicious gloating all gathered into a bouquet of sounds and smells. The war was not yet often mentioned; no anecdotes had yet been woven around it. It still sat like an evil monkey on their backs. As unemployed actors style their past roles into trailblazing performances, so one preferred to speak of earlier times, how superb everything had been. Magnified by narration, the past stretched upward, outward, lengthwise, became heroic, brave, elegant, even princely.

General Brün said to Evelyn's American: How do you do? How do you like German food? Fine, thanks, he answered, adding a few more rushing words. It sounded like the speech of the GIs from the riverbank, very different from Brünian English. When the American laughed, General Brün laughed, too, much too loud, pretending he understood everything. Yet none of us spoke English as well as he. Some at the table could answer only with a thin smile.

Understanding is everything, said the General, lifting his glass.

Cheers, Grandfather announced, and drank to his own health.

Do say something to our guest, my father said to Anton. He was still with us then. You speak quite nice English, too.

Anton, hemmed in by table and bench, lifted himself halfway to his feet. With a short friendly nod, his hand suspended in the air like a parachute, he warned us not to expect anything from him.

Evelyn passed around the bowl of dumplings. Who wants some more?

Georg, Dieter, and Uli stared perplexedly at Evelyn. She was only a year or two older than they, but already so self-assured. The boys, having only recently escaped from the limited world of the Hitler Youth and the hellish detour into war, had never experienced anything as exotic as Evelyn, least of all right here at the table, close enough to touch.

My grandmother contemplated Evelyn with ice-blue judgment, eyeing her quiet companion, the wine. She was keeping her opinion to herself, she whispered.

That's a good idea, Mama.

Before dinner my mother had gone into the kitchen to supervise Olga's preparations. Her gaze darted across the pots. She dipped a spoon into hot water and drew twists and curves in a fresh lump of butter until her magical hand gave form to a thick rose, with leaves on both sides, surrounded by a symmetrical pattern. That's enough, she said. Pausing to give me a kiss, she cut open a cucumber, took a handful of the soft seed interior, and rubbed it across her face. For refreshment, she said. After a few minutes she rinsed away the cucumber slime with fresh cold water and daubed a little linseed oil across her face. One of her cosmetic recipes from the forests and meadows.

After dinner, much later than usual, when I finally had to go to bed, absolutely had to, could no longer stonewall, when I had cleaned my plate in slow motion, when the hissing against me had become intolerable, I stormed out of the room, Mirza trotting behind me.

Later, as I was lying in bed, scarcely able to hold back my tears, I heard it coming up the stairs: the unknown footstep. A fairy, a good, beautiful, sweet-smelling fairy sat down on my bed, took my hand, and started to sing. A magical light bathed the pillow. Up from the blouse into her mouth ran the thread of her voice, woven into the web of a song. Buttercup. Her red-fingernailed hand rested on the back of a reptile. A moth hovered over Venice behind glass. A blue teddy bear drifted into the blurred picture. A bird listened in, its beak hanging open in the heat. With the red kiss of an elective affinity began the alphabet of a woman's life.

•

The portrait. Originally it was supposed to be a double portrait.

Double portrait? What rubbish, my father said. Then one person dies and the portrait just makes the absence more conspicuous. Two separate portraits are better. Then you can always take me off the wall. I'm not going to be in the picture, he once again made clear.

Nonetheless we arranged to get to Munich for the sketches. A visit to Evelyn and her father. My mother was to find her way to the artist's atelier.

Finally it was time. Father was even more nervous than usual, because of his wife's unpunctuality. Today we would be taking the train from the village into the city. Fritz had already been waiting quite a while out front, with every hair in place, the horses at the carriage, Umer already sitting up on the box, I behind him in the blue coat, with a red hat pulled down over my braids. My shoes pinched. They were inherited from Anita. But we were off to town, and that was wonderfully exciting. This time, once we were in the city, I could surely pressure them into buying me the roller skates. The skates stood waiting for me on a piece of red velvet in the window of a hut, amid the ruins, right near Evelyn's father's house.

Oh, God, a new memory caught up with the old: the roller skate artist from the circus, whizzing through the tent! I became quiet and pensive. And hopeless. There was no way the skates were still sitting on the velvet.

Up above, next to me, were baskets piled high with fresh vegetables from the garden, meat in covered porcelain containers, sausages and ham, also some tobacco for the painter. It was always like this when we went to town.

Fritz, in the green wool coat with the possum collar, his checked cap and visor correctly seated on his bald crown, marched back and forth between the house and the carriage, whistling impatiently. Adi stuck her head out the upstairs window and waved gaily, still in her slip, her hair still down: Call the station! Just five minutes more!

My father trudged up the stairs to his office, to the telephone on the wall, and had the operator connect him with the train station. He shouted into the receiver: My wife is running a little late today. What? Yes, late. Five minutes, is that all right? As he dropped the receiver onto its hook, there she was, running down the stairs, still buttoning her blouse, a hairpin between her teeth, up onto the coach, and off we went to the station.

ESTHER AND GITTA

The beloved aunts Esther and Gitta came visiting in their carriage. They needed a change of pace; the roof was falling in on them. Their moated castle was full up with Americans and fourteen Schnauzers, from the same dog family as our Lexi. Each aunt held one under her arm.

I could not remember their husbands any better than I could Evelyn's American friend. But I could remember that with these two, elegance entered the house: tailored tweed suits, pumps with ankle straps, felt hats, rooster feathers, crocodile purses, compacts with red mouths enameled on the lids, a leopard muff and cap, a shoulder fox with head and bite. There was much laughter, and gossip slipped from red lips: It really happened, cross my heart!

Since the end of the war, Aunt Gitta had lived in the city again. She had to earn a living somehow, so she kept her head above water by writing novels. Romantic pulp is what she called her scribbling. My parents were not allowed to read it. No, please don't! That would be excruciating.

To make ends meet, she rented one of the rooms in her apartment to a certain Herr Worzig, an opera singer by profession, who was waiting for his chance, his big role, his big break. Strangely enough, he never sang at home, perhaps to avoid disturbing her. He must have been going somewhere like the English Garden to rehearse. No matter, one did not need to know everything about a tenant.

One fine day two policemen rang Aunt Gitta's bell and pressured their way into the vestibule. They wanted to see Herr Worzig's room.

Hmm, I don't have a key.

Then we'll just have to break in, Ma'am.

Great lightning—the room was chockablock full! The wardrobe, the table, the chairs, the sofa—every surface was packed, heaped up, piled high with watches, bracelets, boxes, cases, purses, brassieres, lace panties, every conceivable object of desire small enough to disappear easily under a coat or into a pocket. What a shock—Herr Worzig a pickpocket, cunning and hard-boiled! Aunt Gitta had to rein herself in, to avoid falling into the arms of the policeman in a fit of laughter.

We've got him, he's in custody at the police station. We're sorry about all this, Ma'am.

The perfect Herr Worzig had always paid his rent on time, never made a sound, was thoroughly courteous, took Aunt Gitta's dog for walks, cleaned his room himself. Tidy, fussy, quiet: in short, a dream tenant. Nor would she easily forget his useful connections to the American PX. Now and then there had been whiskey or cigarettes or coffee or the cognac she loved so much. When you think it through, apart from the shock, things were still going fine and could have been a lot worse. He had stolen nothing at all from Aunt Gitta, and she would have kept him on, even as a thief, as a character for a novel.

Like my mother, Aunt Gitta knew the art of life. Her humor got everyone listening, ready to burst out laughing.

All these goddesses, with their glamorous gestures and exotic perfumes, visited our house, our nature sanctuary, as if I had summoned them. Each of them gave me an inexplicable sensation of déjà vu.

Elegance—a word like a sigh. I was so drawn to it, was never too young for it, understood it, could decipher it; it was my ABC before I even started school.

A Parcel of Land

THE NOVELTY TRAVELED IN A COVERED WAGON up the tree-lined avenue into the courtyard.

They were expected. It had to be the Balts. A tall young man jumped down, two more men, then a slender young woman, the dark daub of her eyes one immediately noticed. Her conspicuously red hair one simply absorbed as part of the overall impression. Dogs peered out from beneath the canopy.

My parents greeted the visitors heartily. My father kissed the woman's hand. Somehow he knew about their fate.

They were to get a piece of land, ten acres, just before the moor. There they were to settle in and begin a new life, running a garden business.

Everyone went into the house and sat down at the dining room table to get to know one another better over strong coffee. The talk was of the past, with a tap at the door of the future, too.

The dainty personage was a princess, Larissa; the tall man, Mikhail, had been her riding instructor; and their two friends, refugees. A tale of escape unfolded. Though the Russians were already quite close, they had still been able to bury her father on his own land; he had died of a broken heart. Then they had to get moving. Their property had been immeasurably opulent, as large as a piece of Bavaria. Their life there went up in smoke, a Baltic dream.

God, they are brave, my father said, thrilled with their zest. The other household members who had lost everything could only agree.

On their estate in the Baltic the grain was loaded directly from the fields onto boxcars and brought to the next town, so immense was the harvest. Where they came from, the land stretched out endlessly, epically, a Chekhov story. In the icy winters the days and nights flowed into one; horse sleighs galloped through the endless white; white breath settled on brows and beards, on fur caps and fur blankets, veiling faces. The howling of wolves. In summertime, birch woods trembled above the landscape.

For the nights Goddess Lucina offered invitations; boots illuminated by the invisible northern sun danced to the balalaika. The Eastern Sea beat coldly against the chalk cliffs. Liveried servants bowed as they opened the gates. Retired officers taught boys fencing. Her mother had maidservants. The princess had piano lessons, studied languages. Naturally she had never worked. Mikhail had taught her riding. He had also saved her life, had simply ripped her away from her father's grave at the last minute and hidden her in the covered wagon.

•

My mother often took me along when we visited the Balts at the edge of our fields. More history, stories, anecdotes filled the four walls of a hut, the first shelter they cobbled together. We brought along everything we could do without. Mattresses. Shoes. Dresses. Soap. Broom. Food. Sometimes, behind Grandmother's back, a pouch of coffee.

The princess worked in the fields like a day laborer, her trousers tucked into men's boots, a blue cloth holding back her red curls. She waved, came running to greet us, and laughingly showed us the newest improvements: walls made of stacked-up peat, a staircase up to the second floor. On one side cement walls were already clambering upward. Ground floor, second floor, a kitchen, a room next to it with a warming oven.

Out in the fields she looked like any other female laborer—only at a cursory glance. Then she gave herself away. With her slender body bent like a juggler's, she carried the unaccustomed burdens deftly on her shoulder, or in front of her in the basket. She joked and laughed herself into strength, permitted not a single dark thought into her being. The Baltic "rrr" rolled through her speech as if she had started to purr.

Their diligence steadily enriched their lives. Larissa's horse had a foal. My parents gave them a cow for milk, eggs from which they hatched chicks, and a little pig that also reproduced. They cultivated whole rows of vegetables, every imaginable foodstuff from the wilderness, from the reed grass, from the undergrowth whose tendrils no longer crept upward into entanglement.

One day the telephone rang.

Listen, frrrriends, we'rrre getting marrrried, Mikhail and I, the voice purred. Come to lunch on Saturrrday. A celebrrration. Mussst all come. Whole house. Won't that be too many? No, no, not at all.

On wooden benches, planks stretched between rocks, we sat and feasted. There was pork roast with sauerkraut, beer to go with it, and roast lamb with blue cabbage and dumplings.

Larissa wore her mother's wedding dress, a filigree silhouette of white fragrance. Cascades of tulle lay on the grass, her red hair, her cloak. She could not afford matching shoes. She lifted her skirt: laughing, she showed me her boots, the same ones she wore every day to work in the fields. She took my hand and twirled me around:

Widele, wedele,	*Inside out, upside down,*
Hinter dem Städele	*Out behind the town*
Hält der Bettelmann	*The beggar is having*
Hochzeit	*his wedding feast*

She sang and laughed gaily. Over there on a bench someone played an accordion, someone blew on a comb. More beer had to be drunk to get everyone dancing.

Mikhail, in a white shirt to highlight his suntanned skin, his trousers tucked into his boots, with a freshly cut mop of hair, danced a Cossack dance. That, Olga should have seen!

Yes, that was exactly how I too wanted to marry. A dress like that. With this music that pulls at you, as if it were yearning. We applauded. The accordion bound us all in a single wish. Larisssa and Mikhail danced the wedding dance of the Baltic Sea.

They were the last that came to us, the Baltic settlers, and they stayed.

Twenty years later I went past a flower shop in Munich. Through the open door I heard laughter. What was that? I was startled. So familiar, so close to the bone; where did it come from? I stood still. Again the laughter from the flower shop flew through the open door, between bouquets of roses, jasmine, and tulips, evoking a summer day from my childhood. A shabby unfinished house, a horse tied to a pole. A dog sleeping in the sun. I was balancing around on my bicycle. To my right a gigantic tongue of roses, and in the middle of them Larissa's red hair. She lifted her head and waved, the eyes two dark daubs. And there it was again, that contagious laughter.

I stepped into the shop. Yes, there she stood: the face, the hair. She looked up momentarily from her work.

What can I do forrr you? she purred, looking back down at the wrapping.

Frau Jakubassa? It's me, Beatrix.

Larissa came slowly out from behind the counter. Across her face spread first recognition, then joy. She held her hand out near her breast to recall my childhood height.

Yes, little Beatrix, there you are.

We simply stood across from one another, quite quietly, and looked at one another. Beatrix had grown up, Larissa grown older. What did she think of when she recognized me? Something lost, perhaps? Something won?

Yes, your father saved our lives. How is the old pessimist? And your horse-crazy sister? Yes, we've become a quite respectable nursery. I have thought so often of your father. He was so particular about his horses. She laughed again, intoxicatingly. He never let them graze the sour pastures. Not good enough for them, you know. Why did he ever sell the place? He was so rooted there, his whole heart... I loved him, tell him that. I owe him my—this life I have now.

She reached across the bouquet, pulled me over, and kissed me on the forehead. That was our reunion, between the garlands and flower arrangements, in our new, other lives.

Part Three

I have observed that the butterflies are dying out. Or are they only seen by children?

—Karl Kraus

Espionage

SOMEONE OR OTHER was always loitering around at the gate, at the little bridge, at the chapel, under the last trees on the avenue, watching people come and go on their bicycles or by coach or car. The latter was always a sensation, since there were not yet many civilian autos, more military vehicles, or gerrymandered contraptions like the Holzgasser.

One day a Volkswagen drove slowly through the gate with a man in civilian dress at the wheel. It came to a stop in the middle of the courtyard by the linden tree. We already knew it had to be a stranger who did not know the lay of the land. His eyes were casting about before he even came to a stop. He climbed out slowly, somewhat hesitantly, and stood still by his car. He wore a long raincoat belted at the waist, his hat pressed deeply into his forehead.

My father watched through the office window. Georg, go on out there and have a look.

Do you know Olga? the stranger immediately asked Georg, without greeting him.

Georg shrugged his shoulders as if he did not understand, beckoning the man to come along.

In the office the visitor buried his hands deep in his pockets and pretended not to understand German.

I Russian, no German.

Well, if you can't speak, we can't have a conversation. My father shrugged his shoulders.

Olga Vlatinova interpreter, the Russian impudently ordered.

Hah…I'm afraid that won't work. You'll have to bring your own interpreter.

The stranger gestured for Georg to leave the office.

Georg, you stay, my father ordered, and called Dieter in, too.

The three stared expectantly at the stranger. After a moment's hesitation he took off his hat and sat down. Now there were four of them, waiting. The stranger's face was freshly shaven, his lips thin, his nose short and strong with wide nostrils. His eyebrows lay heavily above his eyelids. He pulled a tin case from his breast pocket and pensively began rolling a cigarette. Everyone relaxed. George offered his Marlboros around. That must have been the trigger.

After a deep drag the visitor noisily pushed the smoke through his nose and spoke in fluent German, without the slightest accent.

I have found out that Olga Vlatinova lives with you. Probably for more than a year already. Right? He smiled. I have to speak to her. As he said this he wiped from his brow a little rivulet of sweat that threatened to give him away.

We are not giving out any information about the people on our farm if you refuse to give me any information about yourself. Who are you? my father demanded.

The stranger drew a folded note from his suit pocket, a meaningless identity card, and let Herr Ost inspect it.

Now my father was getting curious, and dangled some bait.

Olga lived here, yes. She was our cook, from June 1943 until four weeks ago. The man wrote this down.

Actually, by now she must already have arrived in Russia.

Nothing Russia, shot from the stranger's mouth. If she is not here anymore she is in Berlin. That is 100 percent guaranteed. Who else lived here? He tried to intimidate my father. Do you know Vladimir Pzukoff? Was he here? Did he visit Olga? As he said this he bored his eyes into his adversary's.

No, we were not about to give out any more information, and now he would have to leave. Since we did not want to be sucked into any opaque adventures, there was nothing more to say.

After he had rolled himself another cigarette—quite slowly, concentrating, as if rolling would improve the situation—the man thanked them briefly, put on his hat, tapped on the brim, marched through the door, climbed into his machine, and disappeared down the avenue.

The rumors flew like paper planes. Now the hunches could no longer be suppressed. Everyone had something to chip in. Olga had gone into the city with Anton Reznick several times on her day off, "to visit a girlfriend." He for his part went about his dubious business in the city. Who was this "girlfriend"? Why did Olga almost always go with Anton? Were they in it together? Was his family story a fabrication? Words, words, all meaningless if he were a double agent. It could just as well have been the other way around: she ratted on him, the SS officer. Or he could have been an informant. Did they share the same handler? Had anyone seen them speaking with one another? Now one suddenly recalled scenes, some invented, some not, one could no longer keep it entirely straight: Olga with Anton, whispering, then darting apart. Was she concealing something beneath her apron? But what? Hunches and fantasies played blindman's bluff. Olga, a spy? It would certainly explain her reserve. She had no love affairs on the farm, no "fiancé."

Olga's behavior around the Americans was also very suspicious in hindsight. Was she hiding from them? Or from someone else? Who was this Vladimir Pzukoff? Had something beyond Nazi membership forced Anton into hiding? Had he really done worse than just deceive poor Aunt Julia? Had he simply bided his time here among us? In hindsight he, too, had acted very conspicuous-inconspicuous.

The scales fell from our sleepwalker eyes, and we set about deciphering the mystery of our willfully banal companions. That Olga had worked for Mother Russia became established fact. Anton eventually, too. And Umer? Probably Umer too had been part of the ring.

No, surely not Umer. I'd bet my life on it.

I wouldn't speak too quickly if I were you.

Umer was no spy. But the winged imagination of the women hoped the contrary, even though his conspicuous elegance was inconsistent with the profession of espionage. Umer would have fit better in a postwar movie. Yes, but Olga—her definitely. Her cunning, her outrage at the randy Uncle Erwin. Had she not played her role outstandingly? And Anton with his good manners certainly must have had plenty going on beneath that SS cap.

·

Truths, hunches, and pure gossip, like the fog hovering above the moor, spreading out across the edge of the field, forever visible. Olga sat in the sidecar while

Anton drove. He had borrowed the motorcycle for the day from Dieter and Georg. Olga wore the flower print dress and a kerchief bound around her red hair. She looked just like a cook going shopping, tossing on the knit jacket with cherries embroidered on the breast. Whether she looked forward to her day off one could not see. She was always the same. Nothing gave her away. Not a gesture, not the tone of her voice, not a glance.

When they arrived in the village, Anton stopped at the train station. Olga disappeared inside without looking back.

The ladies' room door opened again. A woman emerged in a gray suit, high-heeled shoes, and seamed stockings, with her hair done up in a chignon, her hat with its jaunty brim pulled down over her brow, and her lips painted red. She no longer resembled Olga, certainly not the Olga who stood daily in the steam of the kitchen. She went through the terminal and put a packet into a locker, withdrew the key, dropped it into a black leather pocketbook, and checked her watch, comparing it with the clock in the waiting room. One could hear a train steaming in from the distance. Olga was now Anna von Protik.

Once the train arrived in the city she made her way through the crowd in the station; paths had been shoveled through the rubble. Anna walked quickly, her eyes inconspicuously counting the pillars in front of the bombed-out portal. She positioned herself at the third pillar to the left and looked to her right. After a five-minute wait she joined the queue pressing forward.

From the other side of the melee emerged Anton. He, too, no longer wore the shabby remainder of his uniform. He had draped a coat over it, wound a scarf around his neck, added a shirt and tie, and slipped a brown hat over his black hair and horn-rimmed glasses.

For a split second they touched. No glance, no body language revealed that Anna, pressed on ahead by the crowd, was now carrying a briefcase. She looked much like any other woman, and she had not met anyone, not received anything.

She hurried along the street, through an underpass, up the stairs again on the other side, approached a house, and rang the bell. An invisible hand opened the door; silently she stepped through and it closed. Inside she sat down at a desk, opened the briefcase, took out several written documents, and set about decoding them.

Much later that evening, Olga sat once again on a bench in the village, under a lantern, in front of the train station. Her hair fell onto her shoulders as usual. She wore the familiar flower print dress and the woolen jacket with the cherries embroidered on the breast. There was an old purse on her lap and socks with flat work shoes on her bare legs. The noise of a motorcycle made her turn her head only a little. Silently she climbed on.

Half an hour later Anton and Olga rolled into the courtyard. Pluto did not bark; he greeted them. The house was already still. Aunt Julia was looking out from an upstairs window. Olga did not look up, just went over to the stable and up the stairs to her room.

That is how it could have been.

Tales of Parting

EVEN MY GRANDMOTHER was helping in the kitchen this afternoon. Why must they all go away at once? she scolded. Nothing is in its place! Time was when the help was grateful…

Grandmother had a gift for playing with atmospheric dynamite to provoke malicious glee. She could also be nice, but really only after she had been particularly disgusting to someone. Her character was shameless.

Olga hated it when my grandmother came into the kitchen and tossed a handful of salt into the soup without even bothering to taste it first. Chort vozmi! The devil take it! she cursed disapprovingly. T'fu chort! To hell with it! From her expression, and from the way she stood in front of the oven, her feet planted broadly on the tile floor, one could see she despised my grandmother from the depths of her heart. Soup good, henh?! She planted her hands on her hips, raised her eyebrows.

Grandmother: There wasn't enough salt!

Olga: You try nothing, Missy.

You don't call me Missy! She instantly whacked the back of Olga's hand with the wooden ladle. Where will this all lead?!

To heaven, I said impudently.

But now Olga went on strike. Physical punishment crossed the line. She fell back into a chair and blew on her knuckles.

Don't be so maudlin, set the table.

Olga did not move. The kitchen, the all-important nexus of food, often became a war zone when diplomacy collapsed amid the heat, the ever-boiling water, the hissing of fat, the rattling of the oven rings. My mother had to be summoned to discharge the overloaded atmosphere. She tried the wordless approach, patting Olga on the shoulder and simply ignoring her mother-in-law.

But the next morning Olga, who forgot nothing, got her revenge. Olga had used more water than usual for her morning cleanup. This maneuver was guaranteed to leave drowned cockroaches floating throughout the kitchen; moreover, Olga knew she could set her watch by the moment the coffee-addicted Grandmother poked her head in the door.

The door did indeed open at the exact minute predicted, sloshing aside the water with the insect carcasses, creating ripples Grandmother could not bear to wade through in her felt slippers.

Olga sat grinning on her chair, cheerily sipping her morning coffee, which Grandmother was dying for. What a pity; Marie-Louise would just have to wait until the floor was dry.

Then came the news that Olga and Justa would be leaving. Soon, very soon. One had known it but not wanted to believe it. And one day the time arrived for the first parting.

Several boxes stood before the house, tied with red yarn, from which everything imaginable had been knitted: gloves, scarves, socks. It was the beginning of the end of an era. Despite our longing to return to normality, we had become so accustomed to turmoil that it had grown difficult precisely to imagine what it was we were longing for.

My mother gave Olga and Justa each a glass of honey and a piece of ham. Then all three of them had a cry. I clung at each of our old friends' bodies in turn. Kitchen odor, sweat, unwashed hair, country smells, body musk—my beloved Olga, my beloved Justa.

When Justa did her waxing she would kneel down on the parquet floor with her skirt hiked up so high that you could see the preserve-jar elastic bands holding her cotton stockings above the knee. When she was done she let me sit on the heavy polisher for a ride through the rooms. The smell of wax and Justa's rather sharp body odor combined in an unforgettable fragrance. There was not much bathing then. Deodorants did not exist. All humans smelled intensely like themselves—their skin, their sweat, their sex.

The plucking of geese and chickens in Olga's kitchen was another of my delights. She would dip the animal in boiling hot water and clamp it between her thighs. A bucket stood below. The feathers were easily plucked from the cadaver, then the hindquarters were slit open and all the innards scooped out. When it was time to stuff the spiced liver filling into the opening, I was allowed to hold the two rear cheeks apart.

Later, when I was grown up, I could quite simply cook. I had watched so often, through the whole hungry postwar period, that I automatically learned many clever recipes. That was my cooking school. I was a cheeky devil anyway.

Oooh, Justa, I cried, don't go away! Don't go!

She is irresponsible, like a child, my mother had said. Often it was I who watched out for her, not vice versa; and yet Justa was my dearest friend, my soul, my real sister. What a school I had gone through with her. Justa was magical. She needed secrets, or life would bore her. And she kept her mouth shut. Cut off arm, nothing out from me, she would say. I too had to learn this, small as I was, because Justa threatened me: I strangle when you say. That sounded credible. It carried some weight.

Together we had torn out the roosters' feathers in their sleep and gathered poisonous mushrooms in the forest: she wanted them to kill Anna Maria, her enemy, who had also been making eyes at Umer. In the end nothing came of it, for Anna Maria left us before she could be murdered. Justa and I had sat together in a tree while Aunt Julia and Anton were kissing beneath us. As dumb luck would have it, my mother called us just then, and we were exposed. Justa thought this a great pity, since who knew what else might have happened under that tree. Justa had shown me her pubic hair and strictly forbidden me ever to mention to a single soul that she never wore undies. Cross your heart.

My first parting. Now my heart had two halves. In one dwelt the knowledge of transience, that everything can change. That there is a death in parting. In the other half curiosity awakened about novelty, new loves. I sensed already that everything repeats itself, gets replaced; that only the form alters.

Why are you going away? Why?

I have to go home, I have to find family.

Justa stared into nothingness, not looking at the boxes, nor at the flowered summer dress, the runny nylons. Her limp and lifeless hand lay in the arch of her hat. The rooster feathers in its band trembled. I looked up at Justa, at the flood of tears welling over the rim of her eyes.

You're crying, too, so stay with us.

Aaah, she moaned, and tapped around for her things. She found her dress, her shoes, her jacket, stowed it all away in the box, pushed the feather hat in on top.

Doesn't matter, she said.

What? I said.

No, nothing matter, no money, no… Her voice drowned in sobs.

But now you're going home?

Oh you little… you are stupid. She pressed me to her, so firmly that it hurt.

Justa wanted to look like the aunts, Esther and Gitta, with their hats and their elegance. She imagined, when she no longer needed to work, she would paint her nails red, eat cake, go for walks.

But Aunt Gitta works, I reminded her. She writes novels. And Aunt Esther breeds Schnauzers.

Only fun, nothing work. Justa shook her head, tugged vehemently at the red band around the rim of the box, stopped to blow her nose, and stared once again into nothingness.

I never really got to the bottom of Justa's character. That too was part of her magic. Nothing was clear and simple. There was always something lurking in the background, something unexpected, a situation that complicated the situation. One never got the whole story. She kept a firm grip on it, whatever it was, like at the circus, where you never knew where the rabbit came from or how he got into the hat.

Justa and I shared a great secret, which had cost me plenty of agonizing. One day Justa had taken me along to the chicken coop down by the apple garden. On her arm hung the basket for collecting eggs. As we approached the trees, we saw through the leaves that Jim was on my swing: Jim, the American who always fished in my father's ponds. As he saw us, he slipped down with a grin, hoisted me up, sat me on the swing, and gave me a push with his dark hand. I flew up and away, into the blue, past the leaves, high and higher.

As we walked home, with something in our basket—I no longer remember what—Justa suddenly turned toward me with a vehement look. I had never seen her like this. Her eyes squeezed together, her cheeks flushed, her soft mouth a tiny hole, she grabbed me painfully hard by the chin, bent my face upward, leaned over me so we were almost touching—I could smell her breath—looked me straight in the eye, and shouted something at me that I was never to tell anyone.

You understanding? I did not really get it, but I remained silent, holding back my frightened tears and merely nodding anxiously up at her. I had heard the individual words but could not grasp them. This often happened with Justa. Since she was shy with the other adults, she used me to get rid of many unsaid things. Once again she had got something off her chest by transferring the burden to me. I thought I would drop dead were I to betray a single word. Since I feared and loved Justa, I concealed her threats in a fold of this love and forgot them. It was dreadful and glorious at the same time.

But now, out front, in the final moments, I finally let go and clung to my mother, sobbing.

My father patted Justa on her petite shoulder. He knew her all too well.

You use this opportunity to travel directly home, you don't get off the train, and above all you don't get mixed up with strangers. Do you hear?!

Yes, I hear.

Justa's devoted love for my father had transformed itself into naked fear.

Olga looked out into the courtyard and said goodbye, looking over toward the linden tree in the middle, toward the dove tower. A cock pigeon waddled high above along the sill; a dove lifted off and sailed down. Olga looked over toward the house where the Slavs lived. One of them was sitting on the stoop chewing on a straw. What was she thinking, being the only one here from Russia?

Olga, please stay! my mother had urged, taking her rough hand.

Can no. She shook her head.

Don't be so stupid, you have it good here, better than at home.

This triggered an avalanche of longing for the homeland.

You knowing nothing, she gulped. Her country was the only one that called the homeland "Mother." You saying Germany like is table, no heart. Rossiya "moya rodina." Then she sobbed still more, as if she would never be able to stop.

Despite her pride Olga had often cried. She thought of her village in Russia, the birch woods, the little dachas, her music. It was harder and harder to bear. There was nothing like the homeland. Perhaps it was less the homeland itself, more the language, the sharing. The war had taken her by surprise and she had not been able to return. Beyond this no one knew much. Don't ask, don't tell. We on this safe island are just a momentary shelter for the stranded, was my father's motto.

Over her years on the farm homesickness had turned her hut into a manor, rewritten her drunkard father as tender and caring. That she had been chased out of the house made her desperation and longing to return all the more urgent. In the beginning, happy to have found a roof over her head, she had revealed to us what she later no longer wished to believe.

Often she sat in the kitchen, stared into space, for an hour, two hours. It was almost unbearable to see how sorrow lay upon her like lead. At some point she would pull herself together and go slowly and sluggishly about her work, like an automaton. On such days the food was inedible. Sadness had made Olga mindless.

Lousy grub. My father pushed his plate away. My mother grew impatient and scolded her. But it was no use. Sometime the next morning she was her old self again.

Someone finally said out loud at dinner: Everyone who goes back gets liquidated—the Russians are a cruel people. Everyone nodded in unison. My mother pleaded with Olga at length: I can't bear to watch you rushing off to your own misery. At least wait until it is safer! But Olga was homesick and believed neither my mother nor the other Germans, who knew nothing.

No, no, not know Russian people.

Uli stood before her, feet planted firmly apart. I know them, the Russians. And he did know what he was talking about, from the war, from Murmansk. He and Dieter were the only ones entitled to talk.

They will shoot you as a spy.

No, no, no, Olga shook her head, lifted her forehead haughtily, stood on tiptoe, and looked him in the eye. I going away, Russia big heart. I must, she whispered, as if to herself.

Uli went into a real rage, went at her, shaking his forefinger right in her face. This is about the political order, not the national soul! At the border you will be a number. A number! Mark my words!

No, no, I no number, I have passport, I Olga Vlatinova. Nothing number spy! She beat her breast, leaned defiantly toward him, grabbed his arm. Ya, Russkaya. Nothing foreigner, she hissed proudly, her face red.

They're pulling your chain! You will remember me, Olga. Uli imitated a revolver with his hand, pulling the trigger at his temple. Bang!

Nyet, nyet! She shook her head emphatically. Three brothers. I three brothers. Are soldier. Ya nazyvayu ikh imena, i oni menya otpuskayut. I'll mention their names and they'll let me go.

There she stood facing a skeptical wall of humanity, yet she could not be restrained. She proudly jutted out her jaw, her fists firmly planted at her hips. How much of this was spite, and how much true conviction and longing, was hard to tell. One could neither look inside her nor understand her. Uli drew a deep breath, then rested his hand on her shoulder. Well, then, good luck, he said resignedly, shaking his head. She had to go back. Had to go home to her Russia.

I writing you then, she promised. Defiance still stood on her brow, but a weak smile flitted across her face.

The flower Olga blossomed in Dostoevsky's garden, between the pages of the *Brothers Karamazov*, casting her roots through the chapters and epic paragraphs: heavy heart, heart and heaviness. If she cut her finger, she cried, I dying. But for dear little Mother Russia she would endure any pain.

My mother had taught Olga reading and writing, at least the essentials. In the kitchen hung a blackboard for menus.

Olga read loudly and slowly: P - o - t - a - t - o.

Plural, ordered my mother.

Potatoes, said Olga correctly and grinned.

Write it down.

Olga wrote, peering at the singular.

Then my mother took the chalk and wrote on the left side, in a column:

> *Potato*
> *Chicken*
> *Feather*
> *Plate*
> *House*
> *Pot*
> *Cat*

Write the plural next to each one, she ordered, and left the kitchen.

Yes, I do, said Olga.

Later, next to the singular, stood:

Potatoes

Chickenes

Featheres

Platees

Housees

Potes

Cates

Table talk: She'll learn it all right. –Dumb as a post. –No, no, she's a Slav, the Slavs have a gift for languages. Think of Aunt Frenzi, she speaks seven languages. –But she's your relative. –What of it? –We're Indo-Germanic. –Everything is random. Her husband, Methodi, he speaks five, too. –Now there is a Slav, a Bulgarian. –And an ambassador. –Well, exceptions prove the rule. –Olga is clever. Cunning, more like. –She's no Indo-German, said the General, bending into his plate, lifting his hand as if in greeting. Let's make that much clear. –That's not open to debate. – Yes it is, 'cause she has a hard time. –Well, then, why don't you learn Russian, said Uli. –Russian is bloody difficult. The General admitted defeat and silently ladled on. –Offense, defense, said Uli brazenly, shoving Georg with his elbow. –In any case, Justa is dumber, if you like, said my father. –Although she comes from Yugoslavia, said Mrs. Brün. She doesn't want to learn anything but American. You are my sunshine. Everyone laughed. –Doesn't matter. In any event, Olga cooks superbly, said Father. And because he was in a good mood, he looked across to his wife: You're the one who taught her.

The day of parting. Everyone stood around the horses and the coach. Umer was already sitting up on the box. It was time. Olga and Justa clambered up onto the carriage and sat next to him. The cases and everything else were piled up in the back. Blind from crying, beside myself with sorrow, I fell backward across Pluto, who was so fierce that he was chained up all day and roamed freely only at night. Everyone froze with horror—Oh God! But I was so sad and confused that I grabbed Pluto by his thick coat and bit into his pelt. Oddly, he just growled, rolled over on his side, and paid me no further attention.

Handkerchiefs fluttered in the breeze as the horses pulled away. White doves gamboled as the wheels creaked. Scarcely were they off through the gate but some were already turning back toward the house.

I was to forget them and later remember them again, together with the curious detail that as they departed my grandfather had just turned off his missing persons broadcast at the letter K.

Aunt Julia and Alexandra stayed a while longer with us, until Julia met and soon thereafter married the owner of a hotel in the foothills of the Alps. We did visit her there once, I remember. Years had vanished, I was a teenager by then. When we arrived in the village, Aunt Julia stood before the stately house, beneath the balcony bursting with geraniums. She greeted us, my father, my mother, and me, with outstretched arms. A triumphant smile lit up her superb cheekbones as she gestured us inside. She looked fuller in the Bavarian dirndl, which suited her perfectly, as did the cozy room with the green tile stove, the tables decked in white linens, topped with bouquets of flowers. "I have made it" stood written on her proud face, although she had pictured it quite differently.

When Alexandra came into the room to greet us, I felt a rush of warmth. For a droplet of time, there was Goldachhof, and we were children. But that vanished quickly into the wall of words about her scholarly accomplishments. She had to run off quickly. And for years the only impression that remained was her long legs in heels, her reluctance to speak to me.

•

In the eyes of Fritz Ost General Brün was "the military idiot." He had a hard time among us, being unfit for the practical business of farming: from a fine family, to the uniform born, in short, useless for anything but war. Naturally he did not want pity, and doing nothing at all was not an option, so he always made himself uselessly useful. Mostly without being asked, for he felt it degraded him—he was accustomed to giving the orders—he would undertake something unnecessary: water the already watered window boxes, use brown shoe polish instead of leather oil for the saddles—Anita's gray riding trousers were forever brownish on the backside. When the bitch Mirza was locked up, whining in heat, he let her scamper off through the open door. After a few weeks came the discovery that she had successfully mated with Pluto: five black-and-white bastards hung at her nipples. Now there was nothing for it but to give them away.

On top of all this my father would offer him the painful reminder: One thing is certain, you are definitely not going back into the military. We will not be having German armed forces again anytime soon. Not while you are still fit for service, my dear General.

Auntie Brün, by contrast, always had something to do. If only from the perpetual gratitude she felt, she ran industriously through the house, upstairs, downstairs, dusting, mending, stirring, ironing, and making friendly. She feared my father a little and was not quite sure what to make of him: on the one hand too strict, on the other humorous and tender. If he entered the room, she leapt from her seat and ran out, as if she had just remembered some uncompleted task. You can always find something useful to do, she said, slipping through the crack into the neutral hallway.

But then the Brün family got lucky after all. General Brün was determined to get back on his feet somehow. Something had to be done. For him it was awful to be so dependent. And so one day he came back from the city with a sales position in coffee machines. The machines were a sort of rectangular box you pressed between your knees before turning the crank on top. As soon as you heard the beans crunching, the strong odor of coffee forced its way out of the little drawer beneath. Thank God, a solution, modest as it was. At least a beginning.

It was not long thereafter that the brave Brüns too moved off the farm. Mrs. Brün sewed one more wardrobe for my doll, then the time had come. Peter was thoroughly glad to move away with them. Finally. The farmworkers had often mocked Peter: what could you do, he was simply a Saupreuss, poor guy. To amuse himself, Beni had grabbed Peter, set him atop the bull, and led him around in the courtyard while the workers whistled and laughed. What a hoot. Peter bawled, screaming for his mother. No one helped him down. That was just part of the rural rough-and-tumble: giving someone a real fright. One did not get involved.

Peter had been my hero, having fled through the flames from a big house into a real air raid shelter, not under the bridge among the rats as we did on the farm. Peter's survival story became one of my fairy tales and heroic sagas. Grown tall, with straw blond hair, he was my Siegfried. But now he was leaving me. I swallowed emptily into my throat. Tears tried to well up, and my upper lip trembled. There it was again, the death of parting. Peter himself wanted to leave us, leave me. A new life! Indifferently a cloud dog sailed across the courtyard.

You must become a teacher, I heard my father say to Peter as he tousled Peter's straw hair. That is a good career for you. Why? Because Peter was such a good boy.

My God, those good people. That will be a difficult beginning. My mother nodded. And let us hear from you! Okay?

But of course, we'll stay in contact.

Everyone owed everyone else so many thanks: the Brüns for the roof over their heads, the Osts for the rescue of their son.

And after the Brüns it was Umer who stood before me one day in his long military coat with its high collar and worn sleeves, lifted me up, and pressed me firmly to his bosom.

You little baby Beatrix. You be good.

Will you visit us sometime?

Yes, of course I will be coming. He had set me back down on the ground and gone into a crouch. And then, when I come back and you have grown up, maybe you will like horses and I will teach you to ride. Okay?

He turned to my mother, took her hands, and bent over them with much too long a kiss. Then he bowed before my father. Both had to smile. They held one another's hands a little while longer, looking into one another's eyes. And then something unusual happened, something exotic, not typically German. Modest. Tender. Something never there before. No... Umer kissed my father on his right cheek. And for a moment the whole room held its breath.

A new coachman had to be hired and naturally there were none as elegant as Umer, none so loyal, so dapper. No one came close. Mother lifted her eyebrows. Ah, Umer, there will never be another one like him. He had a monument in her heart. And then came the gossip and speculations again.

Umer's elegance and its consequences. Umer wore a checked peaked cap, a hand-me-down from Father; his trousers were always tucked into his boots. He looked like a Cossack. But then he paired his trousers with the English tweed jacket with patched elbows. That gave him English flair. There was always an ascot inside his collar. The English cap sat sometimes in the middle, sometimes right, sometimes left, jauntily above his ear, as his mood dictated. When he was feeling serious, it sat low on his forehead, competing with the big hook nose. My mother thought he looked fiery, with eyes like lightning bolts. She admired his jaunty moustache, or more familiarly: his whiskers. My father: don't exaggerate. Umer's hands were elegant, she rhapsodized. He also had leather gloves for driving. When it was cold, the long military coat covered the entire Umer.

The women of the house, those at the table and those who visited, found Umer sharp, dapper, and elegant; the prevailing mood had it he looked like a spy. –What drivel. No spy looks like that, much too conspicuous, my father

255

soberingly. –But he speaks very good German. –Sure, he comes from Hungary, they speak everything. –Can he speak Russian, too? interjected the General, raising his brow. –Rubbish. I have never yet seen him conversing with Olga, my father said, dismissively. –That's precisely why he is suspicious, said the General. A spy who creeps in among us, of all people, when everyone knows us. –Impossible. Who knows us, anyway? After all, there is nothing left, everything is bombed away.

The women were not convinced. Did not want to be convinced. Were a little in love with the spy. Because Umer was so reserved, the spy story spun its web. Finally Father sat him down for a talk.

Are you? Yes or no?

Either Umer was amused, or he was sly, or he really had been one.

Herr Ost, it's 1946. The war is lost. What difference does it make?

Umer remained mysterious, polite, and elegant. My father would naturally have been all too glad to know the exact truth.

And then the time came for Grandmother to turn on the pressure. She had to get away, back into the city. She could not bear rural life any longer. The bombed-out houses, the heaps of rubble in the streets, the wide, unobstructed panorama across the misery of war, the smashing of the city's trademark cathedral—none of that disturbed her; her rebellion was against the diminution of her power by my mother's authority. Did my grandfather want to go? He had long since resigned himself to her and said nothing, merely gesticulated through the air with his hand and pretended to be deaf and dumb. Now Marie-Louise whirled through the house, busily moving out. Theodor moved with her, silent, like the beautiful furniture that went back with them.

What most conspicuously disappeared along with my grandmother was restlessness, sniffing about, incessant bustling up and down stairs, criticism of everything and everyone. Also the wailing about the good old days, long vanished into the past, when she still swept along the boulevard with one of her gigantic flower events on her head; or glided along the street, decked out with feathers, her Cul de Paris under her skirt, her corset above it. Ah, that cut quite a figure. Children, you have no idea! A waist of only fifty-two centimeters. Fifty-two centimeters! she cried in thrilled remembrance, demonstrating it between her thumb and middle finger.

No one really liked her. She was impossible to like and did not care. She had no feeling for friendship and love, merely used up everyone's congeniality as fire does hydrogen. When she stepped into the room the gaiety clicked off as if with a light switch; the pillow next to her changed color; dogs crept into their hiding places; my crickets stopped chirping; my mother left the room and lost herself in the garden; my father was nowhere to be found; repose became strenuous. So her absence was palpable. The breeze blew more lightly. There was no more nagging, no tyrannizing. Things lay comfortably strewn about, remaining where one had left them, waiting to be found.

A story made the rounds that doubled everyone up with laughter. My grandmother, in black silk, took the five-year-old Uli with her to the zoo. Everything had to be in proper order. They bought a dark blue Bleyle sailor suit with a cap, on the rim of which stood: S.M. Tirpitz. Grandmother, with flower hat overflowing, glided between the cages of the wild beasts, holding her handkerchief to her nose. Such a stench. She was constantly aware of herself: of the hat, the dress, the posture, the well-mannered boy next to her.

Ah, the elephants. She let Uli buy a bread roll to feed the adorable pachyderm. The elephant's trunk made a perfunctory examination of the offering and was just about to suck in the roll when suddenly he stopped in midair, came to his senses, and swung right, probing: Ha, what have we here?! The flower hat lifted off, spirited away by a magical hand; the ribbon beneath Grandmother's chin, buttoned at her throat just a moment earlier, ripped loose. A helpless cry, and the hat with ornaments and feathers vanished disrespected into the elephant's mouth.

Ah, my grandfather, he was the soul of goodness, and everyone loved him. The dogs lounged around his chair, dozed in the blue of the warm afternoon. His placid thoughts caressed the cat's fur. Animal semper amicus hominis. He ran his trembling hand across my head. His breakfast egg clung to his beard. Just leave it. When it doesn't want to hang any longer it will fall of its own accord. Sometimes, admittedly seldom, when my grandmother was absent, he announced his opinion, took part in discussions; but as soon as she reappeared he clammed up. Closed his eyes for a moment, like blinds. Darkening, silence, silencium. Don't fight against the wind, it is stronger than you.

Everyone felt the loss of my grandfather, I most of all, like a scar that always reminded me of him.

The measured step on the singing planks; the soft opening of the door; the friendly smile; the handsome old hand resting on the dog's head as he read; his watery gaze wandering through the room, enfolding everything in kindly thoughts; the lyric singsong about the soldier; the philosophical observations about death and the eternal sameness of the world.

My father, who loved so secretively, felt it, too. Yes, Theodor was a wonderful presence, and so immensely clever.

•

The grandparents' house stood, with holes here and there, to be sure, but otherwise intact, on an undemolished block. Now and then we traveled into town to bring food from the farm. These visits were brief, for we had to be back before dark; horses do not like to travel in the moonlight.

At the edge of the city a stable took charge of the team of horses and we climbed onto the tram. The streetcar smelled of cold smoke. We sat down on the wooden benches with the picnic baskets and boxes on our laps. The conductor went around snipping tickets, calling out the name of each upcoming stop: Maxweberplatz—Mauerkircherstrasse.

During the trip through the destroyed city I saw people bent over the heaps of rubble, searching for anything useful, sorting the still usable bricks and other objects from the rubbish. Every few minutes the driver stepped angrily on the bell to shoo people off the tracks. If a heap of rubble lay on the tracks he rang even harder, and there was fumbling in and out of the streetcar until the obstacle had been pushed aside and one could travel once again.

There they stood, the gleaners, with kerchiefs over their hair, knotted at their necks. Knitted wristbands peeped from their men's jackets. Their stockings were rolled down below their knee-length skirts. Boots. Here in the city they were called the rubble women. They stood around in groups, squatted on upended buckets, or formed a chain to toss the bricks along. They bent over to heave heavy stones into carts, and poked about in pleats of debris.

Charred walls looked out at us through window holes in the devastated houses. Apartment interiors became exteriors. A picture hung on a papered wall by a bared stairway leading up to the memory of an etage. Many now lived cooped up in the rooms of the houses that were still intact. Stovepipes bored randomly through walls; cardboard was nailed across smashed-in windows. Burnt pieces of furniture and carbonized trees littered the streets. A flag protruded like a tattered old petticoat through the gaping maw of a backyard fence smashed through by a giant's fist. It was as if a ball had fallen into my delicate doll kingdom: everything scattered, crammed together, with the heights brought low and the layers beneath tossed willy-nilly to the top.

The city did not care what its name was, which ground it stood on, which country; nor into what river the garbage flowed, nor where the dead lay buried beneath the debris. The sky, too, pulled its grimaces indifferently above the nameless. Fungus spores flew about, settled down indifferently on stoops. Birds swarmed indifferently above the trash heap. Bees hummed, butterflies fluttered; rats gnawed indifferently on meat; squirrels nested in cupboards. Indifferently the rain pounded into houses, and silent snow fell from an indifferent cloud. A division of ants descended upon a child's grave, indifferently.

At home in his own place, buried in his thoughts, Grandfather once again belonged solely to his books, no longer to me. On these visits he was shy and silent and needed a long while to warm to me. By the time he finally wanted to sing something, we had to depart. Then he gave me a gentle kiss, held my hand for a long moment in his soft dry fingers. When my hand slipped from his, he cleared his throat: Ah, that comes from smoking. He laboriously shifted his chair, took my hand once more, and looked about the room. After all the preparations he began in a wobbly voice.

This's from th'Arabic. Translat'd it for you:

DER KALIF	THE CALIPH
Einst hab' ich die Kamele	Once I grazed the camels
meines Vaters geweidet,	of my father,
Meine Ruhestatt war	My resting place was
das weite Feld,	the wide-open field,
Und mein Gedecke	And my coverlet
das Himmelszelt.	the celestial tent.
Bis mich der Gläubigen	Until the voice of the faithful
Stimme rief,	called me,
Ihr Herrscher zu werden	To become their master
und Kalif.	and caliph.
Da machte ich auf	There, on the powerful path
mächtiger Siegesbahn	of victory
Die grössten Reiche	I made the greatest realms
mir Untertan,	my subjects,
Und bin nun so hoch	And have ascended
gestiegen hier,	so far here
Das keiner steht zwischen	That no one stands between
Gott und mir.	God and me.

Nun fühle ich erhoben durch   Now, exalted by
Allahs Hand   Allah's hand,
Mich kleiner als dort,   I feel myself smaller
wo ich niedrig stand.   than when I stood low.

My grandfather held my hand one more moment, as if he were holding fast to life itself. Upheaval was already all around us. The others were standing impatiently at the door, Grandmother tapping her shoe impatiently.

I had grown beyond little Beatrix and had discovered a new kind of life. Grandfather was in search of the perfect death.

Grandfather died in his bed at age ninety-two, when I was twelve. Grandmother survived him another fifteen years. She moved into an old people's home. Though already well into her eighties, she continued to set great store by her appearance. She had to be the most elegant. When one visited her one always heard which of the gentlemen was currently courting her, and why the boyfriend from the last visit was no longer to be seen. That boyfriend was now with the woman from the third floor, so he was history as far as she was concerned. As she rattled on she forgot she had just taken a pep pill, and took another, with the consequence that she would not let her visitor leave, asserted that he had just arrived, the clock was running hours ahead, he should have a piece of cake, and another. She was on a coffee rush, had taken too many tablets, and could no longer stop jabbering. One night she finally managed to poison herself, and died. A diminutive, crinkled shell, with burnt yellow locks, she finally lay still, no longer dangerous, amidst Theodor's wonderful royal furniture.

Predictions

THAT DAMNED MOB, that riffraff, fulminated my father. Yet again fate had vindicated his predictions.

Often there was fighting at night in the workers' house across the way, so loud that I awoke to find Anita had already thrown the window open to listen. Psssst, she hissed, when I asked sleepy questions. There it was again, the quarreling that pricked up everyone's ears, that no one could evade, that fired our interest the same way as the announcement on the radio, the sensational news that made everyone freeze in mid-work: The war is over, the Americans have marched in. Everyone had been jubilant, going wild, embracing one another in uncertain elation, making comments, throwing their hats up in the air, lighting cigarettes, clapping their hands.

So, now you have all heard it, called my father. Get going. Back to work.

He had seen that coming, too.

More cacophony from across the way: the echo of feet stomping down a stairway. Someone screamed something in Slavic. I recognized the voice of Svelva, then the voice of Janosch, her father, who had looked so sad since his wife's recent death. It sounded like cursing. The next voice belonged to Josef, father of Svelva's little daughter, Miriam.

Doors flew open and shut. More screaming raced through the night, carried by the breeze through the linden tree branches like enraged barking. The mercy of distance permitted only incomprehensible scraps of words through the window. Yugoslavian. Prokleta kurvo…prokleta nevaljavice…sta hoces? You damned whore, you good-for-nothing, what do you want? Sudden stillness. Then more trampling, and a door slamming.

None of the Slavs ever mingled with our workers. Svelva, though she must have been young and was the only one I ever really approached, seemed old to me. Her hand sometimes felt heavy when she rested it on my head with a vague smile, and with her little girl she was very strict.

To my father they were lowlifes. One heard the screaming and knew about the drunkenness. One could not come to a real understanding with them. First X would brawl with Y, then with Z in every possible combination. Then suddenly some quite quiet fellow who had always kept out of it would get mixed up in a card game and lose his cool in a booze-up. Or it was about some woman whom two men both wanted, or had, at the same time.

The high-strung Slavs felt foreign, uprooted; their days on the farm were numbered, and they were eager to dump their troubles and sadness and go home. One could not control it. My father was furious with them, but his hands were tied: they were refugees, he needed them, and they knew it.

One night there was particularly loud fighting and shouting across the way. My father's orders to stop evaporated into thin air as Josef and Janosch rolled drunkenly on the ground in the courtyard. They had knives, and there was blood all over the place. Father, Georg, Dieter, even the General ran over and threw cold water on the two madmen with their red eyes and the foam hanging from their mouths like bloodhounds. Finally they lurched off in different directions.

The next morning Josef dragged himself across the courtyard, up the stairs, and into the kitchen, where he fell on the tiles, fainting from loss of blood. Over and above the many cuts in his face he had almost lost two fingers. My mother let out a cry when she tripped over his body.

And then, on a later day, I was back playing contentedly with the puppies in the courtyard, putting doll clothes on them and tucking them into the doll carriage. Their mother, Mirza, anxiously followed my every move.

A door dropped into its lock. Click. A pigeon had been pecking about in the sand for seeds and looked up as the rest of the flock flew up to the tower. The air was still except for the pounding of Tafelmeier's hammer. Pluto, in the shadow of his doghouse, perked up his ears.

A door dropped into its lock. Click. The pigeons cooed. One fluttered in a wide arc and landed quite near me; then four more lifted off and sailed across to the seeds. Peck, scratch. Mirza whimpered. She missed her puppies, which were asleep in the doll carriage. I circled in front of the house. When I stopped, Mirza stood still. When I resumed, Mirza followed. Excess water dripped from the geranium boxes in the windows.

A door dropped into its lock. Click. I lifted my head. Squinting, dazzled by the evening sun, I saw something in the form of a cross gliding down the steps from the door of the house where the Slavs lived.

That is Josef, I thought. His trousers were tucked into his heavy boots. From a distance his face appeared dirty, or was that several days of stubble?

It was late afternoon, shortly before dinner, and everyone was in their rooms. The darkening air hung exhaustedly across the courtyard as the day relaxed, but here and there one still heard some rattling, scolding, milking buckets clanking.

My mother came hurtling out of the house and down the stairs into the courtyard. A threatening note, a haste, a question mark in my voice, had frightened her as I ran in and cried: Mummy, Mummy, come quickly! Quickly.

We gaped as Josef came tottering across the courtyard toward us, holding Svelva in his arms. Was it she? Her head hung down, her hair covering her face, on her breast a red stain. What? Was that blood? One of her stockings was rolled down to her ankle, the other was draped along the ground, caught on her toe. Her arm escaped Josef's grip and swung lifelessly at her side. What? Horrible, horrible, whispered my mother incredulously, moving toward Josef in a kind of trance.

No one said anything. Josef just stood there. Svelva's body seemed heavy. He looked up to the sky without moving his head, a thin white sickle of moon below his iris.

Slowly he sank to his knees, would not let go of her. Svelva sank with him to the gravel. He bent over her face, bent to her ear, as if he were whispering to her, his body racked with spasms. Between sobs he blurted out incomprehensibilities.

The news raced across the courtyard like wildfire, attracting a circle of ravenous gawkers. My father too came running, pushed the people aside, and stopped in front of the tableau. For a moment he stood frozen.

What? For God's sake. Quickly. He had understood immediately. Someone, go to the telephone. Call for help! Josef… Fritz touched his shoulder.

Josef had buried his face in Svelva's wet, red breast, saw nothing, felt nothing.

My mother wanted to wrench me away and took my hand, but I disentangled myself. I wanted to be with the growing throng, share the belief and disbelief on their faces, the whispered questions, the remarks of the farm people, my friends, join Resi König and the baby on her arm, merge with the assembled multitude.

My mother wanted to protect me, but I had been the first to see the catastrophe, instinctively sensed the horror. My voice had already proclaimed terror; I had understood before I could know.

At some point an ambulance came thundering across the bridge, followed by a convoy of American cars. Every eye tore itself away from Josef and Svelva toward the gate. Who is coming? What is going on? Their eyes mirrored sensationalism and horror. For a moment they exchanged the one impression for the other, broadened their perspective, devoured the spectacle of the Jeeps, then the Americans who had left their cars and hastened toward them.

My father gestured at the scene that the crowd enclosed. A tragedy, frightful. The throng made way, allowing the authorities a path into the inner ring where Josef was kneeling, where Svelva was lying. His face was vividly encrusted with Svelva's blood. Lenerl nudged me and pulled a disgusted face.

Without hesitating, Josef let go of Svelva and stood up, turning his gaze to the ground by remote control. The American GI took him by the arm, drawing him out of the stigmatizing circle, leading him past the shocked faces, the knowing grimaces, on into the waiting Jeep.

Mrs. Tafelmeier vented, spitting after him: Filthy trash, I done seen it comin' right away, she said.

Approving nods. The onlookers' heads swiveled together, following every step, all the way to the Jeep. They stared at the legs, which were still visible. A merciful darkness had taken his face and body to its breast behind the canvas cover.

A worker came running across the courtyard, screaming and waving, urging my father to come with him. Several Americans followed across the courtyard to the ill-fated house, others remaining behind with Svelva and her blood-drenched blouse. My mother had brought a cloth and covered her with it. I looked at the cloth, bent quite closely over it. Was Svelva still breathing? The cloth lay motionless, as if on a bed, covering what rested beneath.

Over in the workers' house they found Janosch, Svelva's father. His body was hanging from the second-floor banister, his feet almost touching the floor next to an upended stool. Janosch too was dead.

Now the crowd could not decide. The misfortune covered by the cloth was already old news. The fresh horror—not yet verified, merely announced—slipped out through the open door, written on a horrified face alarmed by a scream.

Most of them pressed their way across the courtyard to the house, where my father now stood in the doorway to block the view.

Get off to the side, he called with a peremptory gesture.

A woman had slipped by my father with little Miriam on her arm, handing her over to my mother. Adi and the child stood off to the side, a few meters away from the stream of people, away from the Jeep where Josef sat. Miriam's little body was racked with sobs. She was dirty and looked forlorn, full of fear. She did not know what had happened. Brownish streams ran down her red cheeks and snot hung from her nose. My mother's expression reflected swooning horror. She took her white lace handkerchief from her bodice and cleaned the child's face.

Where is Mama? Miriam thought. A little breeze blew through the red bow that sat in splendor atop her hair like a propeller. Her heart pounded. Her thoughts ran away with her. She looked at the finger, at the ring on the hand holding her. She saw the horse and brook in the ring of the strange woman. There she built a room for her little heart, around the hand, fleeing into a child illusion.

The crowd began to stir. They all looked toward the entrance to the Slavs' lodgings. Janosch's lifeless body was carried from the house, through the door, down the steps. They laid it next to Svelva, uncovered, the beard framing the bluish face, red veins crossing the temples like rivulets and running off into the gray hair. A fly, unhindered, made its way through a bloody gash in the throat.

The gapers could not gape their fill of this horrifying incomprehensibility, a Slavic misfortune from which they dissociated themselves. The foreigners! The riffraff. They had seen it coming, heard the screaming, known from the tone exactly what would happen. No need to understand them, the wholly Other. What good could ever come out of the Balkans anyway? These were barbarians. You could recognize those shameless sluggards right off. Opinions had hardened long before they came to the farm. Nothing but trouble, and now a murder, too, two murders. Sumthin' like that warn'ta been possible under Hitler.

A blanket was laid over Janosch.

Never would we really know what happened, or how.

The father killed the daughter in shame at her disgraceful liaison, then hanged himself?

Or: Josef murdered Svelva, then the father hanged himself out of grief.

Or: Svelva tried to kill her father, but Josef took the knife and murdered her in the heat of their argument. Then ... what?

Later, when all the formalities were dealt with, Svelva's and Janosch's bodies laid into an ambulance, after everything said had been said, after the things to be cried out had been cried out, after the night air had swallowed it all, after the people had gone away shaking their heads, the house across the way remained unlit, my mother still stood with the little girl on her arm in the courtyard.

What to do? Miriam played with the malachites at her throat, twisted the necklace stone by stone through her little hand.

What a sweet child you are. Here, take this apple.

A black GI approached my mother. She pried the silent child away from herself with a deep sigh and handed her to him.

That poor, poor little Miriam, said my mother, holding me quite close to her warmth. A hint of moon shone behind the trees. From afar came the barking of dogs. Through the open door of the stables a ray of light stole across the court-yard and dissolved in the far shadows. Everything seemed unreal, as if in a play, where eventually the curtain falls on what was reality just a short while ago, bringing people back to their seats, to the person next to them, to the space, the light, the door, finally to the street outside.

Mummy, if I promised to keep a secret until I die, can I tell you anyway, since you're my mother?

She bent over to me. Naturally you can. What is it, then?

After everything that had happened on this day I had no room left for Justa's secret. Mummy, I said, Justa told me she is never going home again. She is moving in with the black American, Jim, who is just as black as the one Miriam is with. She says that you and Papa can't forbid her anything anymore and she is going to have a new baby. And Jim promised her lots of money.

A door slammed shut, killed the light across the yard. The moon chose to hide behind a cloud. My mother and I listened into the night's emptiness.

The death of the dead I could not grasp. But the death of parting stood with us, an old friend now, familiar.

Oh, that poor wretch—my mother to herself. Come along now.

She took my small hand and we went up the stairs inside, into the room, to the table, where I could forget the day, and my heart was lighter.

A Long Walk

WE ARE EXHAUSTED FROM OUR LONG WALK, Ludwig and I. We cross the bridge to the carp ponds; then, leaving them behind, we follow the meandering paths to the reservoir and back through a tongue of dark evergreens along the moor.

The best thing now would be a hearty Bavarian meal, Ludwig says. Just let me look into the ruins once more, I beg. Just for a minute, come on.

We step through the arched entrance to the stables. The stone troughs where the horses drank still stand in their place, burned into the devoured stall with the weight of tons. The blacksmith's iron hook next to the door—that is where Anita hung up her saddle. The pillars too are still standing, supports for the lost arch. The afternoon shines down from above, oblique through the window holes. There stood the door into the corridor, a gaping mouth.

The spent blue of the Blue Room and the Green next to it. The blackened remains of a roof truss. The attic. Phosphorized beams. A doorknob, touched a thousand times. Hopes behind doors. Muffled quarreling. Thoughts in these rooms. Explosions bursting outside through open windows. Extreme tenderness from lovers, and everything my extended family hated.

Staring at the cement floor, I see the dried blood from slaughtering day, the meat hook, the wooden hammer, the crusty leather apron; I hear the sloshing of the rubber boots, see the rats goggling from the air raid hole, the pearls of sweat secreted by the cracked wall, the blackest black of the tenderly laid-out pelts; rooster feather branches hum in the wind; peals of laughter roll across red lips; Olga's Rossiya moya rodina, the sickly sweet odor of her sweat; my father's cane, its metal tip drawing a blue line to the house in the nameless snow; the iron rail the railway pushes through the fields, the sharp tone of the station whistle; a dead sheep stares through the milk glass of its eyes, its apple-red tongue wedged in its jaw; the noose of the hanged man dangles in the elegant curve of the staircase; vibration in the ink-blue air, when low-flying planes buzz the city; red bugs collect on red clothes; through the old glass a child's hand forms a room for sympathy; the forest full of pillars, the green canopy a fairy roof; the saw saws into thick ice, glass cubes of startled water; the carp standing still in the sea-grass garden; the creak of the steps beneath Umer's boots; Justa sobbing; junk piled up in the attic, to be forgotten by coming generations; Aunt Julia's soft skin, the corners of her mouth turned down slightly—did she not believe in her resurrection? Root brushes scour the floors.

Over there at the door I see a fox that has lost its way, standing panting on the step.

We duck under the arch, out into the courtyard, find our car, and drive out the gate. The film runs backward. First the tree-lined avenue, then the fields, the orderly housing developments on both sides of the road, and...

Meanwhile, it has become late afternoon. To our left, against the milk-cold sky, the Alps are arrayed like a rose quartz necklace. The motor hums and carries us with luxurious ease from my childhood back into the present. I am still not completely here in the car, still lingering at the moss-covered stone bridge, still looking through the window into the ruined nook, still seeing the onion tower that sits atop the chapel like a cap.

Through this journey Ludwig and I are allies. I have linked him to my earliest memories, to the very distant past, long before we went missing in the togetherness of the complex marital thicket. The sharing of earliest childhood, the times that have imprinted themselves on the flesh of one's muscles, tattooed one's soul: these are the strongest bonds. They always accompany you, like music for a film. Parallel to the ego runs yesterday.

In my memory there exists a black-and-white group photo of the farm children on the gravel under the linden tree, with me hidden somewhere among them. In the foreground is a scooter. No one is laughing. It could almost be a glimpse from the Third World, where people know nothing of cameras and stare mistrustfully at the photographer. The childish horde is an amiable chaos in checkered shades of gray, a study in bygone fashions: the hairstyles, the bare or covered legs, without shoes or with wooden sandals—a vanished historical instant.

It was on this farm, in this place, that my father was happiest in the end. He was no businessman, did not believe in the German Economic Miracle. He lost himself in gloomy predictions, as if he wanted to prepare everyone for some inevitability, which indeed finally arrived when multiple sclerosis came to nest in his body. He was his own dark prophet. In the background of his thoroughly clear head swarmed thoughts that created an emotional chaos. Figures from Faust, Mephisto, the witches. These he repressed, since otherwise he would have had to cry. Then he would have given himself away, right? He would have been declared crazy. Sometimes he stood in front of the mirror in the vestibule— beneath its glass danced gray flecks of moisture, corroding, growing—and stared at himself for a long time, as if he wanted to play it safe, ensure he was still there. When he heard someone, he quickly moved along.

In my parents' first fabulously blue car, which they bought in the fifties, my mother chauffeured my father through the countryside. This way he could at least stare into the fields he could no longer walk, contemplate from the shelter of the car the people he no longer wished to know.

When I was ten we moved away from the estate. My father had pains in his legs. Often he walked with difficulty, propped on his cane, until he reached the next place he could sit down and fall into his gloomy thoughts. The walking stick he had previously used for teaching, pointing, educating, giving orders was now there only to lean on. Still the same cane, it had aged with Father, playing its reliable role like a living friend. In the house it was my mother's arm my father

leaned on. His gaze, once so blue, so strict, pointing so directly into the distance, grew narrow, mostly looking downward, grew limited, shortened.

My mother got to know a new Fritz: the third, one she would never even have bad-dreamed. A seriously ill Fritz. First he was the familiar Fritzl, then Fritz, then Oh, Fritzl. My mother became his mother: patient, kind, always in a good mood. A slowed-down form of herself, she kept pace with her patient.

Ludwig had never known my father, but he fell in love with my mother before he dared love me. She would have been the one, we often jested.

I close my eyes. Ludwig's hand lies on my knee, warm and firm, stealing away only to shift gears. Oh, my father. He hated all touching. When he grew ill he withdrew even more from everything physical, like a snail that creeps back into its house at the slightest touch. He had built so thick a wall around himself that even knocking on it became senseless.

The gesture, Ludwig's hand—already the door is opening to my parents' apartment in Munich, where my father, frozen in his illness, always sat in the chair by the window. Without my mother he did not move. A raging paralysis held him in its grip. His wife was motion. She moved him.

Come, Fritz, we're going to take a few steps, she said encouragingly, and took his arm.

I can't right now. "Come on, it will do you good," he mimicked her. Do you have any idea...

Then he hung heavily on her arm and slowly placed one numb foot before the other, through the rooms, the corridor, and back to the chair. His legs no longer obeyed. It was as if he were walking on slippery ice, as if he had wheels beneath his feet.

THE BARITONE

For practical reasons I had the key to my parents' apartment, and one afternoon when my mother had gone shopping I decided to surprise my father with a visit.

I opened the door and cautioned my two-year-old son, Oliver, to be quiet. We walked on tiptoe. From the living room droned loud opera. A baritone was singing. Oliver's small hand in mine, we snuck along the hallway. The door was ajar.

At the open window stood my father, on uncertain feet, propping himself up on the arms of his chair and looking out into the trees. With one hand he made an inviting gesture to the imaginary public beneath on the pavement, and as he did so he moved his lips in synch with the song on the radio. It seemed as if he wanted the people going by on the street below to take him for the gifted singer.

Perhaps someone looked up to him, or waved, or wondered, and perhaps that was what amused him. But the scene was not funny, not for me. It reminded me of a Charlie Chaplin film in which the actor, about to starve, turns his shoelaces with his fork like spaghetti. It was not even tragicomic. It had something very intimate, a forbidden intimacy, like catching someone in the act of a forbidden kiss.

As my father noticed me, he pulled himself together, mumbled something in embarrassment, fell back into his chair, into his immobility, and said angrily: Turn off the radio! I can't reach the button.

There he sat once again in his chair and let the moment glide off into insignificance. But for me it became a keystone in the mosaic of his character. Perhaps it had been Fritzl standing there for a moment, the Fritzl only my mother still knew, the Fritzl she loved so much, the funny one who let himself go and told naughty jokes, who had a good sense of humor, even indulged in nonsense now and then, did magic tricks, loved to bewitch others, laughed heartily, got into the spirit of things. This man I scarcely knew. By the time I came to know my parents, that Fritz had already stolen away. Had his loveless childhood grabbed him by the tie and pulled tight? Was he ashamed of being himself? In any case, the dutiful iron German citizen had stepped into the place of Fritz's self. It was a safe disguise.

The word "love" is so hackneyed, so kitschified, that one scarcely uses it. In the German language one does not tell one's child "I love you." One would sooner say "I like you," as if one had to dilute it.

If you had let them, Father, you would have been loved by as many people as you needed. By your children, too.

BELLS

Having reached the village, we look for an inn. Church bells are ringing. The precise beats remind one that time is slipping away. Not in the American sense that time is money; rather that life is fleeting, that one is always approaching the end. Often Mr. Death stands with his sickle, playing the cuckoo in the clock.

We find the inn and a cozy wooden bench. A saucy waitress with a Baroque bottom and rotund arms hurries past us, three steins in each hand, balancing them deftly without spilling a drop. Under her apron bulges her money pouch, as if she were close to giving birth. She recommends pork roast with sauerkraut and dumplings. The stein of wheat beer, the plump waitress, the mountain of food in all its heartiness remind us of where we come from, from this stretch of land on the world map. On the radio someone is playing the zither.

We have to show all of this to our American grandchildren. The pleasant aroma of the roast. The waitress's balancing act. The estate, which now belongs to the general gesture of the past, the scent of our ancestors. The Alps too, naturally. And the precise theater of the church bells.

Father, look! Here are your great-grandchildren.

I told my brother, Uli, about my visit to Goldachhof, how all the stories came back into my memory quite clearly, one locked into another, like gears; how I remembered scents; how faces, gestures, characters popped up before me. Aunt Julia, bending backward, crooking her leg to check the seam of her stocking; my mother arching her eyebrows; my father raging, whip in hand—it all came back effortlessly. That there were no people running around the farm, that everything was quite still, made it easier to remember the past. Characters could be placed as if on a stage. The woman in the window, the soufleuse, only her head visible, with some sort of hairdo. Also the winter day, the unlabeled weather.

I pushed my weight against the wall, broke through the mortar, through the structure, and entered my father's house. I felt the heat of intimacy. The yarn ball of history, the tidily rolled-up thoughts spooled out into events. The memory reel runs outside space and time: one feels ageless, sees with the eyes of a child, yet feels as one does today. When I had told it, lived through it, my childhood stretched out before and behind me like a strand of pearls on the neck of time.

Acknowledgments

What I had in mind at first was to write these stories down for my family. I had always urged my mother to write about this period of her life, but when I found the letters, suddenly I was the one carrying the ball. I had had conversations with my brother, Uli, and his friend Dieter about Goldachhof, the times after the war; but when I began to write, I felt as if I were lying on a psychiatrist's couch. One door opened another.

Many people helped to inject order into the chaos of memory's onslaught. Their advice, criticism, and encouragement were all pixels in the process of writing and rewriting:

Rita Dove, with her wise advice
John Casey, with his fruitful private writing lessons
Hans Magnus Enzensberger, with his kind letter
Christiane Landgrebe, with her early editing

Vera Graaf   Sheila Metzner
Claudia Steinberg   Camilla Carr
Barbara Epler   Ginky Spelman
Dennis Smith   Ingrid Roever
Sanda Weigl   John and Christina O'Boyle
Ottmar Engel   Fred Viebahn
Barbara Feinberg
Julian Connolly, the Russian source
Rados Protic, the Yugoslavian source

But without the following friends,
no book would have materialized at all:

Lianne Kolf, my agent: "Give me 250 pages—you can do it!"
Ingeborg Castell, with critically good advice
Ruth Greenstein, with her thorough editing
James Rickman, for his assistance with the manuscript
Eleanor Dwight, who introduced me to my publishers, Jeannette Watson
    Sanger and Helen Marx
Jonathan McVity, with his brilliant mind and translation

To my sons, Oliver, Daniel, and Fabian, who have created new
clans in our new homestead, America, far away from Goldachhof.